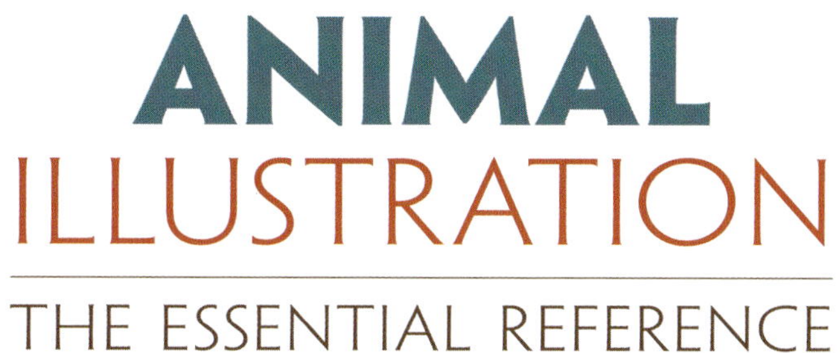

ANIMAL ILLUSTRATION

THE ESSENTIAL REFERENCE

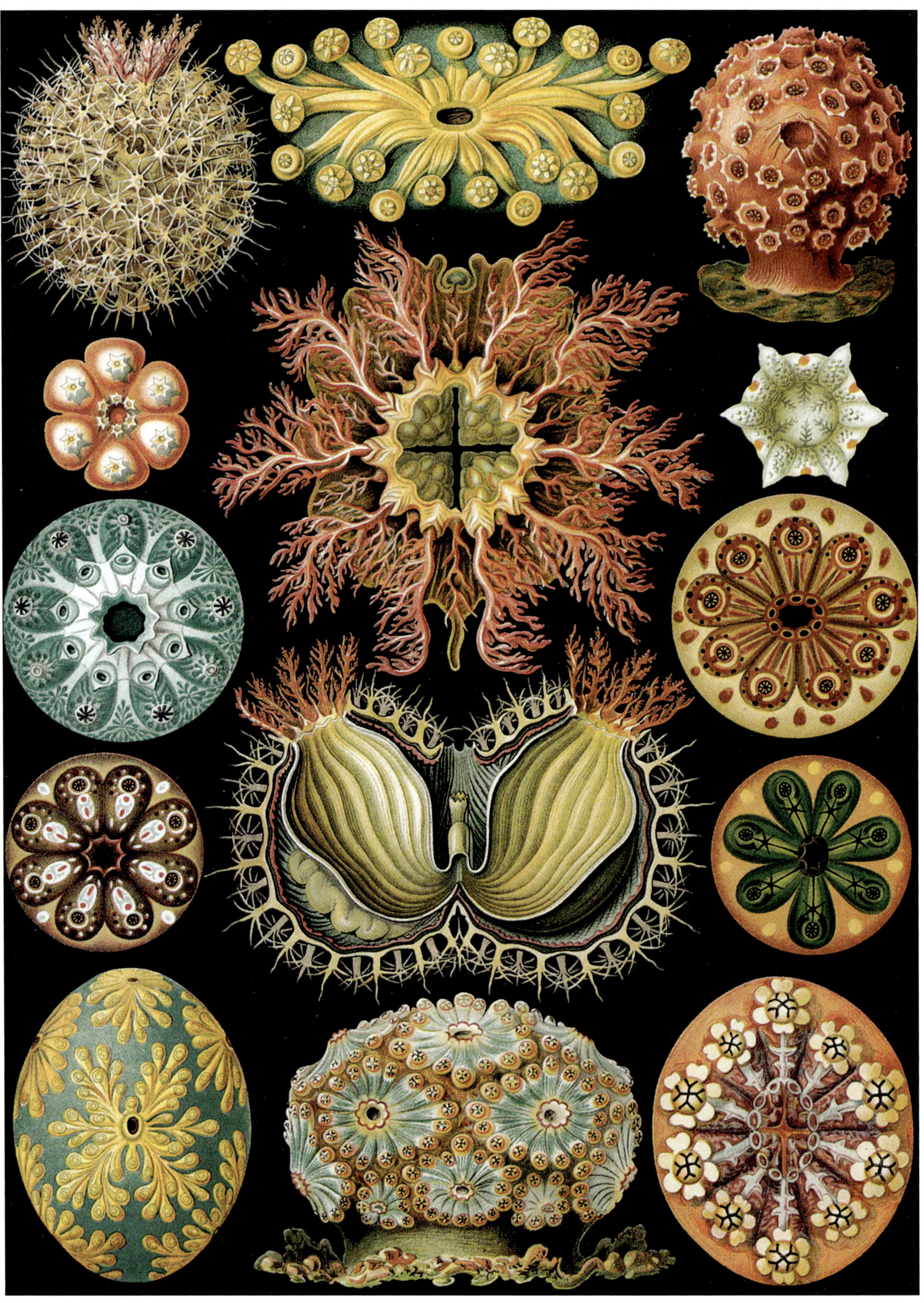

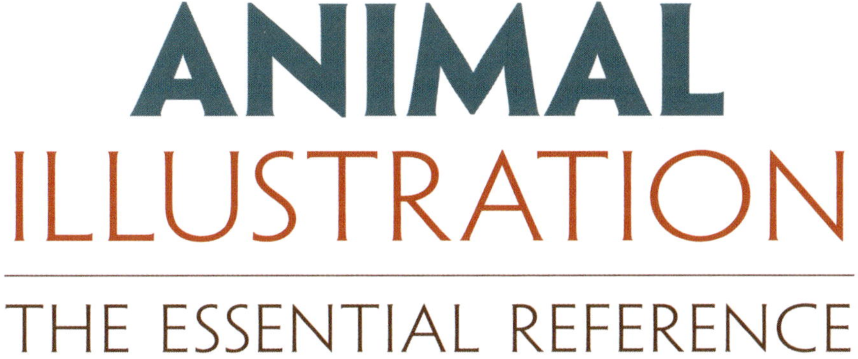

CAROL BELANGER GRAFTON

DOVER PUBLICATIONS, INC.
MINEOLA, NEW YORK

Frontispiece:
Various species of sea squirts
(a class of marine chordate animals)

Frontispiece and chapter opening images
(plates 1, 11, 29 and 93) are from
Art Forms in Nature by Ernst Haeckel.

Copyright

Bibliographical Note

Animal Illustration: The Essential Reference, first published by Dover Publications, Inc., in 2016, is a new compilation of images reprinted from authoritative sources.
For detailed source information see pages 135 and 136.

Library of Congress Cataloging-in-Publication Data

Names: Grafton, Carol Belanger, compiler.
Title: Animal illustration : the essential reference / Carol Belanger Grafton.
Description: Mineola, New York : Dover Publications, 2016.
Identifiers: LCCN 2016030285| ISBN 9780486799865 (paperback) | ISBN 0486799867 (paperback)
Subjects: LCSH: Animals in art—Pictorial works. | BISAC: ART / Subjects & Themes / Plants & Animals. | DESIGN / Graphic Arts / Illustration. | DESIGN / Reference.
Classification: LCC N7660 .G73 2016 | DDC 740/.432—dc23 LC record available at https://lccn.loc.gov/2016030285

Manufactured in the United States by RR Donnelley
79986701 2016
www.doverpublications.com

INTRODUCTION

Animals were the subjects of the first artists in prehistory. The creators of the first drawings on the walls of caves started a process which has evolved through enormous twists and turns, driven by the broad sweep of history; the evolution of culture; the vagaries of constantly changing fashions, styles, and tastes; the development of new mediums; and the application of new techniques and new technologies. The subject is so vast, the accumulated riches bequeathed to the world by animal artists so immense and so varied, it is truly inexhaustible. Every century has its media, from illuminated manuscripts in the medieval period, to book illustrations created in recent decades to illustrate contemporary works of fiction. The art of illustration, alive and well in the twenty-first century, continues to evolve and shows no sign of ever reaching an end point.

A brief survey can only touch on some of the high spots of this subject. A page from one of the greatest illuminated manuscripts of the late medieval period shows hunters in a clearing in the woods while their pack of hunting dogs celebrate a wild boar hunt with the Chateau de Vincennes in the background. From the late-seventeenth-century engravings by Merian, we have, side by side, creatures we can easily recognize and some which only ever existed in the minds and imaginations of their creators. Lizards and snakes on the pages of Albertus Seba's vast eighteenth-century works seem as coiled and ready for action now as they no doubt did then. Turning to the more patrician later eighteenth century, Buffon's mammals, however—even the lion—seem elegant and reserved, peaceful and thoughtful, like the time from which they came.

The nineteenth century brought new developments. Magnificent bird plates from Alexander Wilson and John James Audubon demonstrated that the young American republic was ready to contribute to the published studies and artistic records of the infinitely varied natural world. At about the same time in the early nineteenth century, new reference works from the Old World—such as Baron Cuvier's *The Animal Kingdom* early in the century and J. G. Heck's massive *Iconic Encyclopedia* published later on—brought to a much wider audience more detailed knowledge and better illustrations than had ever been available before. As the nineteenth century wore on, it brought with it an explosion in printing techniques and possibilities. Such new ventures as William Jardine's *Naturalist's Library*—forty elegant small volumes with the plates all printed in color—signaled that finely colored illustrations of the world's creatures were no longer going to be accessible only to the rich.

As publishing for a large new audience started to develop in the nineteenth century, the state of the art continued to be defined by the limited editions of folio volumes of magnificently printed and colored prints. The great works of Audubon, John Gould, Edward Lear, and many others were certainly produced as luxury items for the rich. The publication prices of these great color plate books of the eighteenth and nineteenth centuries may seem absurd now. A book that might have cost an original subscriber perhaps fifty British pounds two hundred years ago could bring hundreds of thousands of dollars at auction today; but at that time, that fifty pounds was more than a year's income for the vast majority of the population. It was difficult then, often the work of years, for an artist/entrepreneur to find fifty or a hundred wealthy people willing to commit that sum to the production of a magnificent book with hand-colored botanical or animal engravings, a book which we now consider a monument of that century's culture and accomplishments. Many such projects, only partially completed, were abandoned for lack of financing.

Illustration in a more popular sense also flourished as never before in the nineteenth century. Popular newspapers and magazines increasingly published books for huge new audiences, a reading public which had never existed before, who demanded pictures and more pictures, new ones every day, every week, and every month. From this massive activity, a small group of exceptional talents rose to the top. Supremely talented book illustrators, able to take on and bring a unique personal touch to any kind of project, became household names, such as Gustave Doré in France and the Detmold brothers in England. While a small number of artists were establishing the kind of reputation that would last forever, thousands of highly talented, though generally anonymous, artists were creating an unending flood of printed material—illustrations for ordinary and now largely forgotten fiction in largely forgotten magazines, illustrations for advertising and all sorts of now highly collectible printed ephemera.

To reinforce the idea that the depiction of animals, real or fanciful, color or black-and-white, in finely wrought engravings or in casual sketches, is all part of the same enterprise, throughout this book readers will find some examples from a few of the greatest artists in Western history: Leonardo and Dürer, Degas and Renoir, El Greco and Parmigianino. Complementing these are samples of the work from more talented artists who, like Doré and the Detmolds, turned their attention to illustrating works of literature and the imagination. Not to be excluded are several artists, such as the elusive French Art Nouveau and Art Deco artist E. A. Seguy, who used animal forms as the basis for highly personal graphic and design fantasies. It's a world with many corners and passages that always rewards exploration. Looking back at the past and forward to the future, we leave this story, by his generous permission, with a selection of illustrations by the contemporary dinosaur artist par excellence, James Gurney.

John Grafton
Princeton, NJ
June, 2016

CONTENTS

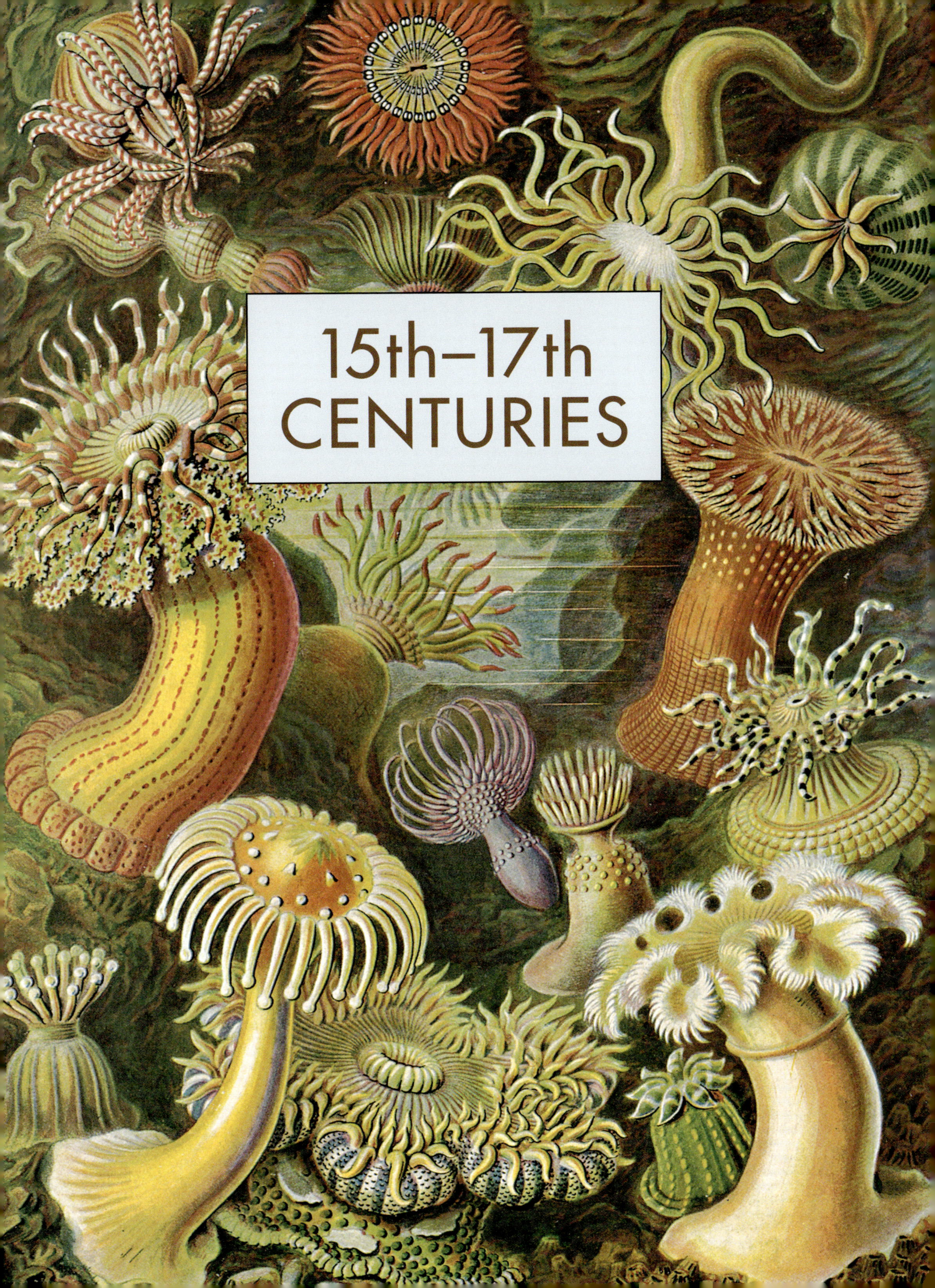

15th–17th CENTURIES

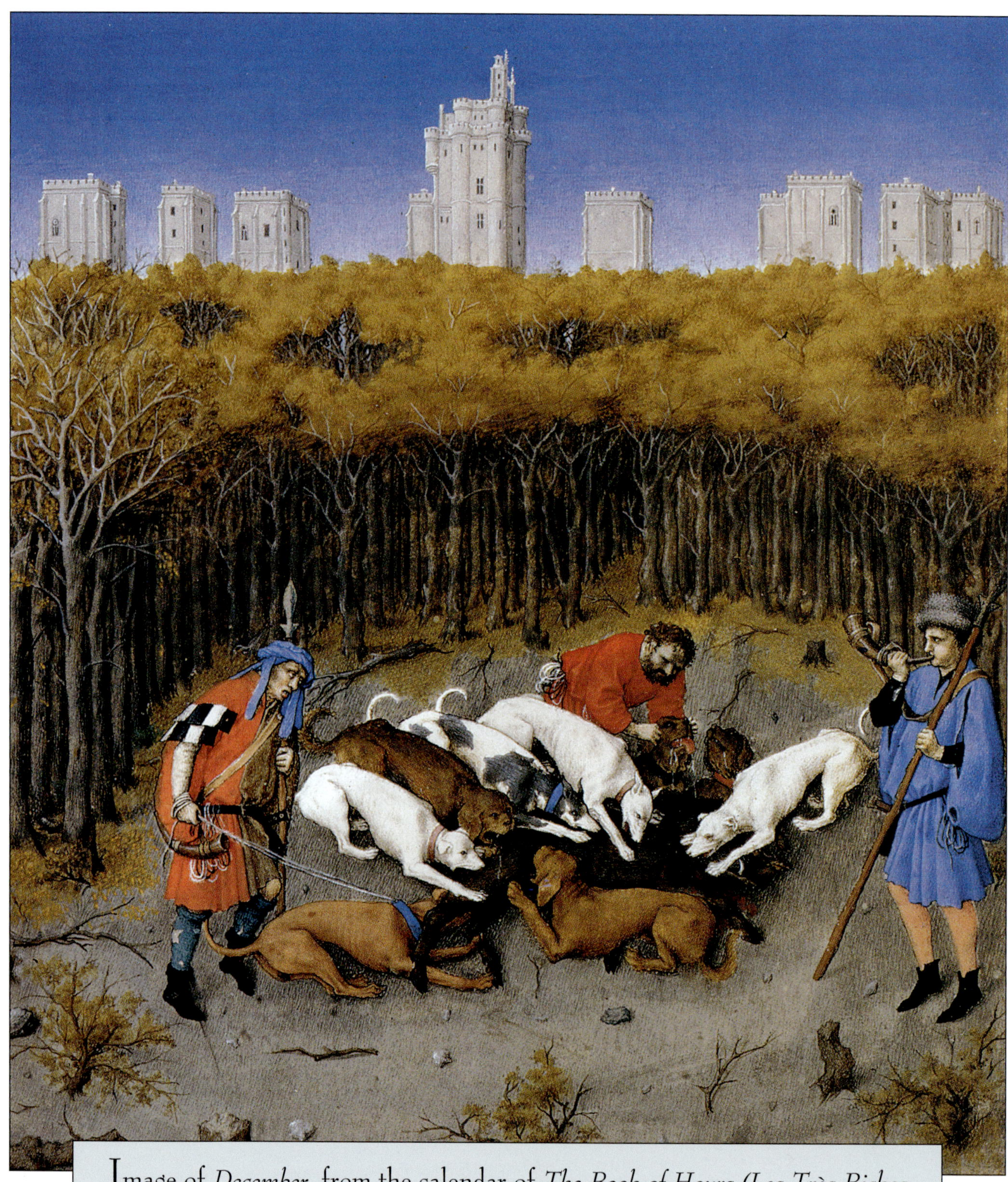

2 Image of *December*, from the calendar of *The Book of Hours (Les Très Riches Heures) of the Duke of Berry* by the Limbourg Brothers (France: c. 1400–16).

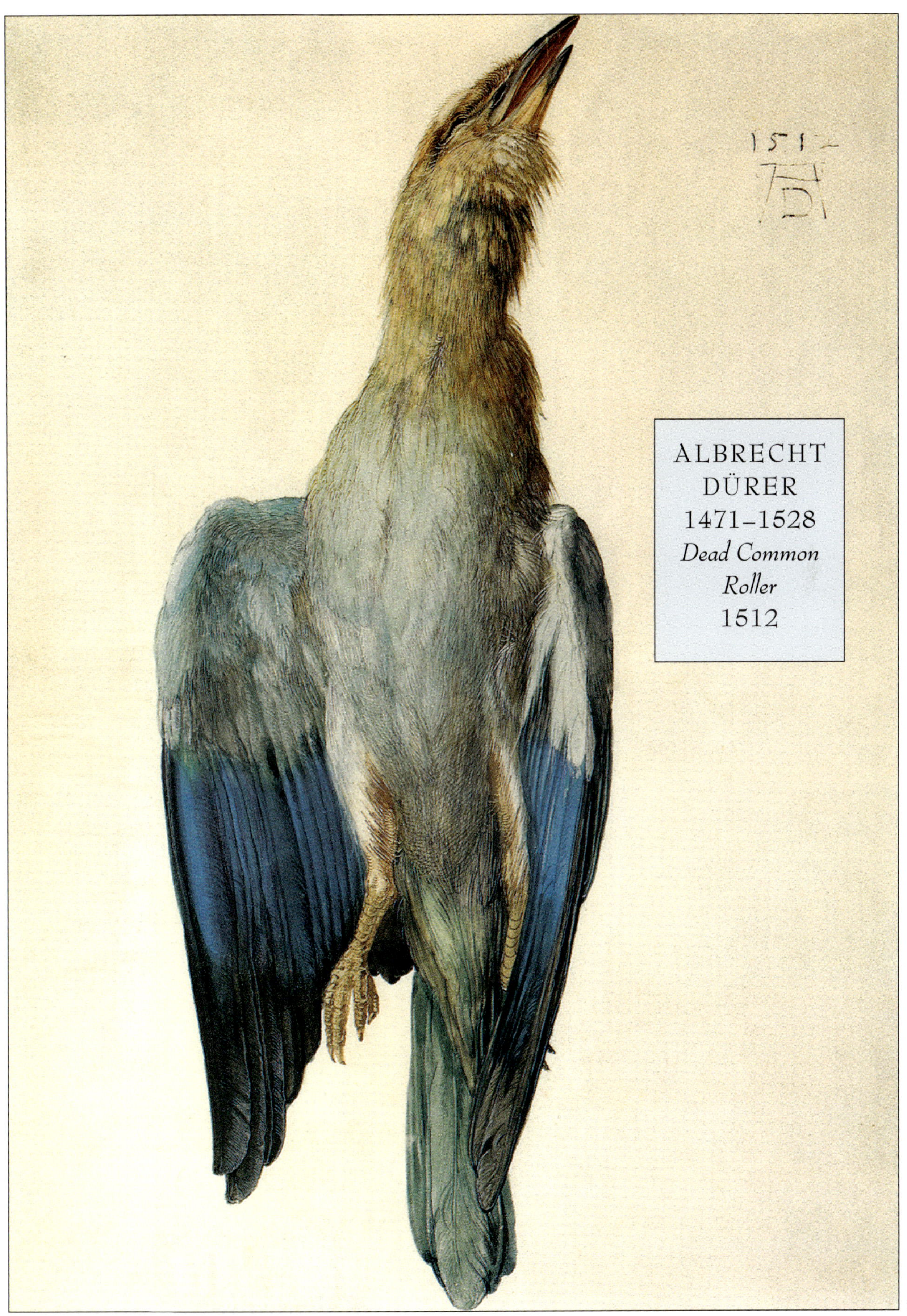

ALBRECHT
DÜRER
1471–1528
Dead Common
Roller
1512

3

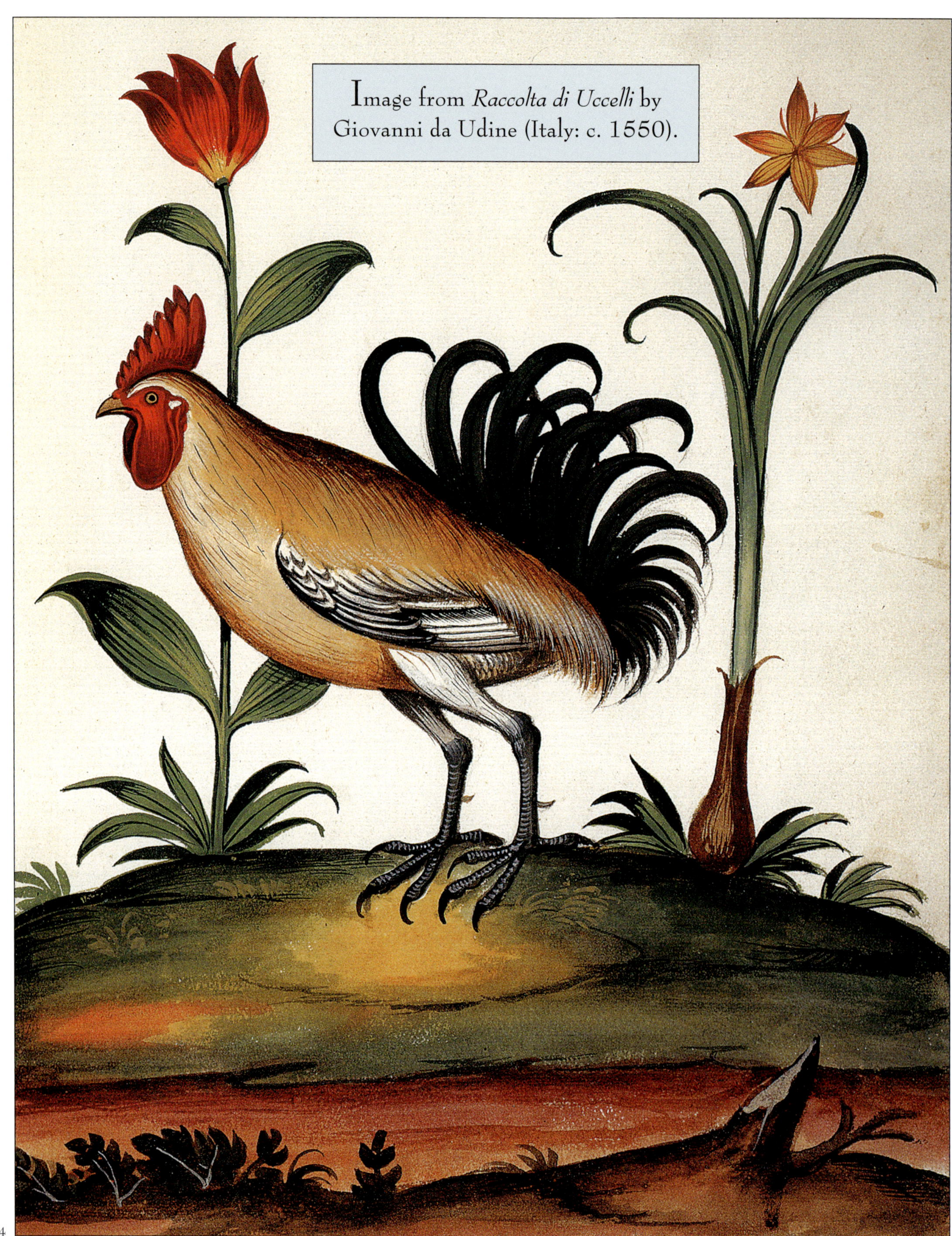

Image from *Raccolta di Uccelli* by Giovanni da Udine (Italy: c. 1550).

Albrecht Dürer (1471-1528) / *Rabbit,* 1502

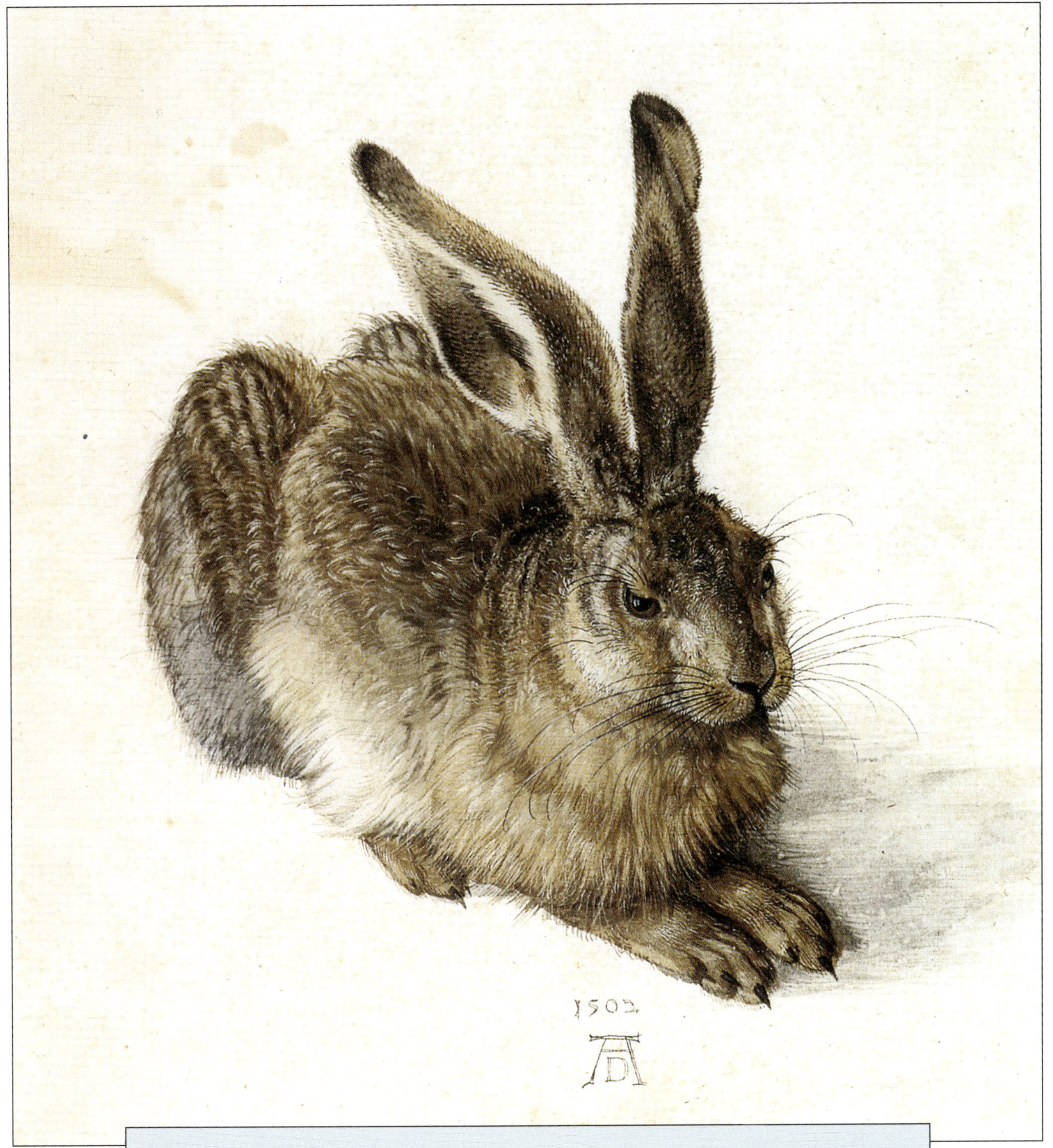

Images of classic animal drawings and prints, published by Dover as *Great Animal Drawings and Prints,* edited by Carol Belanger Grafton (Mineola, NY, 2006).

6

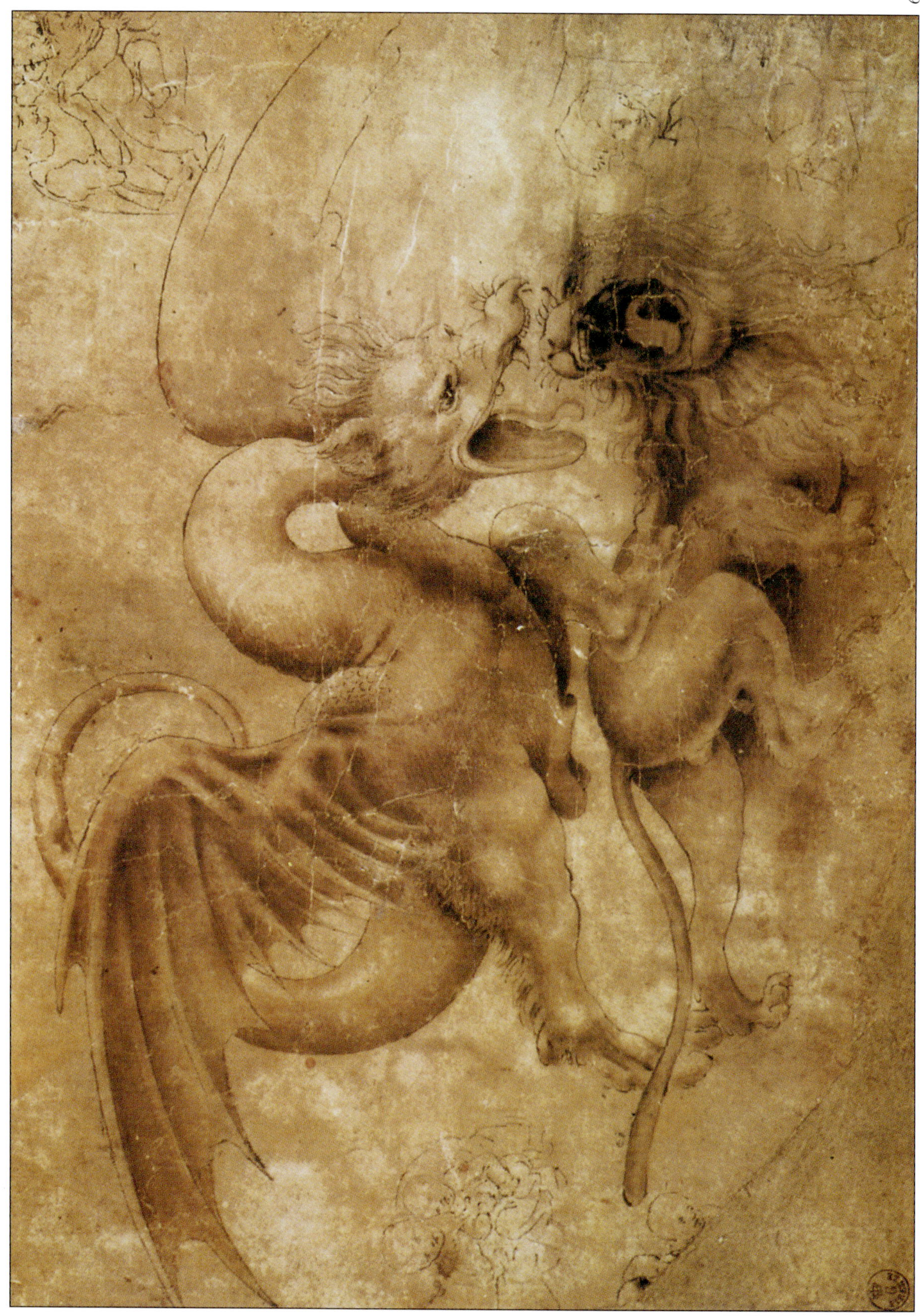

Leonardo da Vinci (1452–1519) / *Dragon Striking Down a Lion*

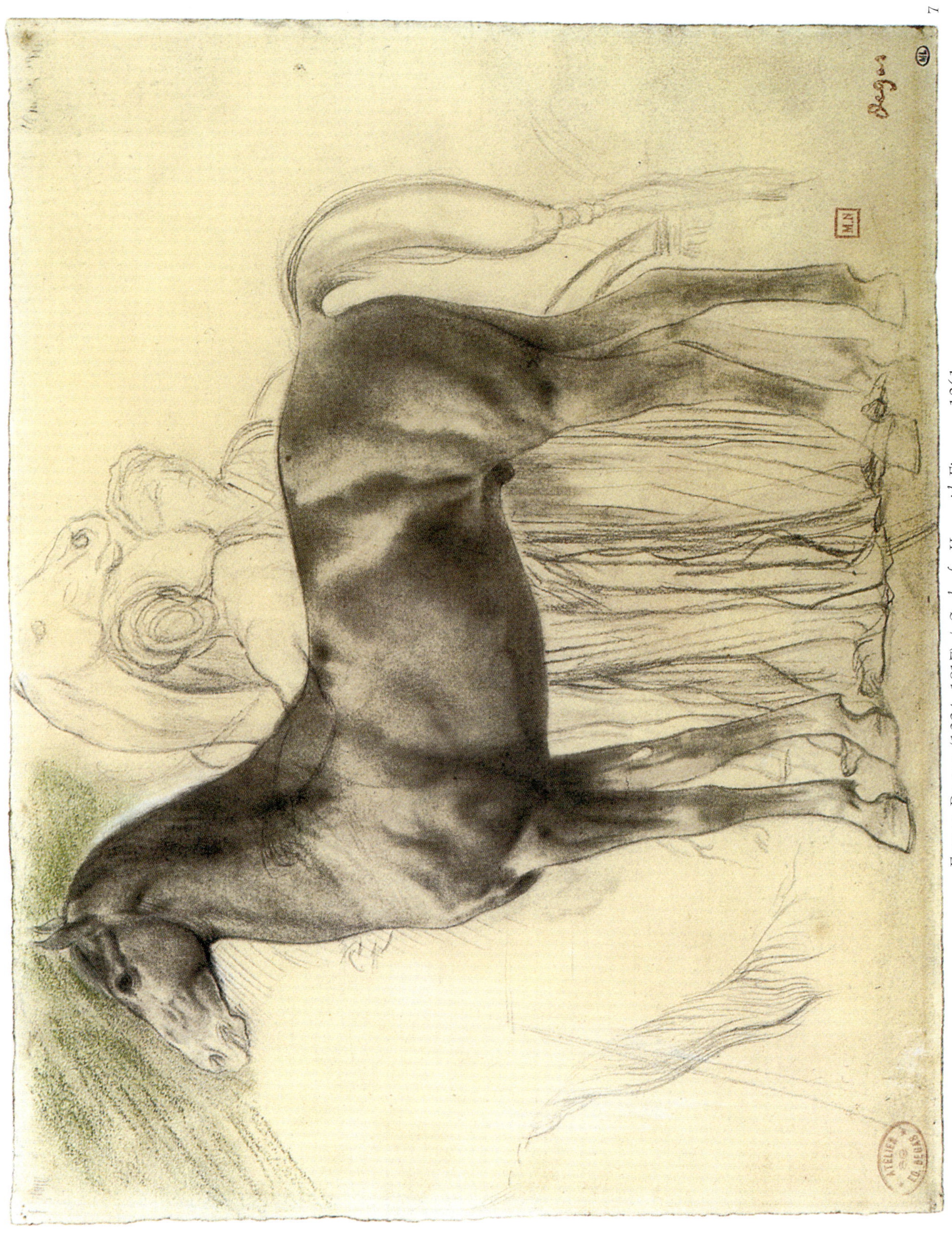

Edgar Degas (1834–1917) / *Study of a Horse with Figures*, c. 1861

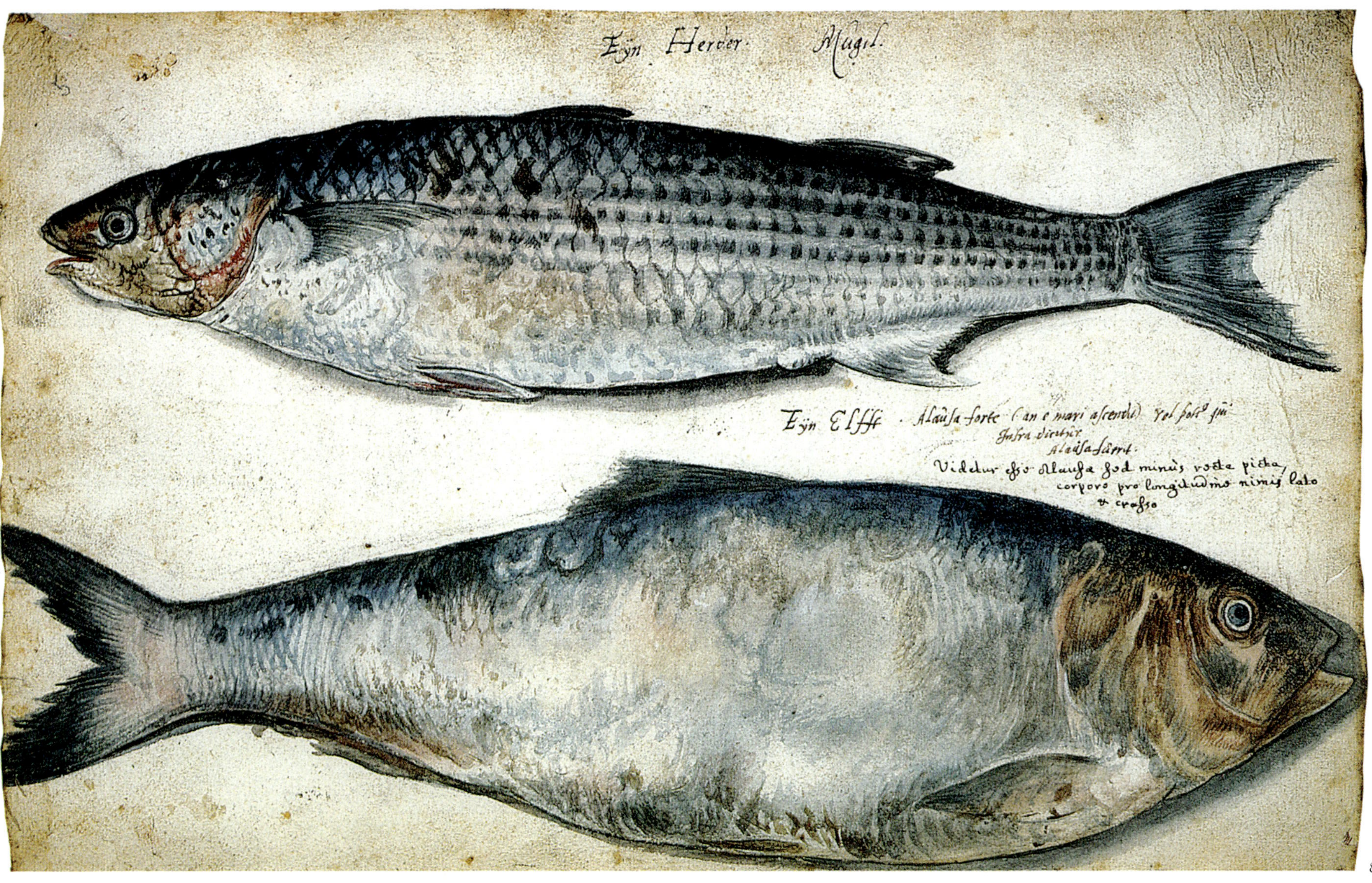

Image from *Historia piscium* by John Ray (Flamburgh, England, 1686).

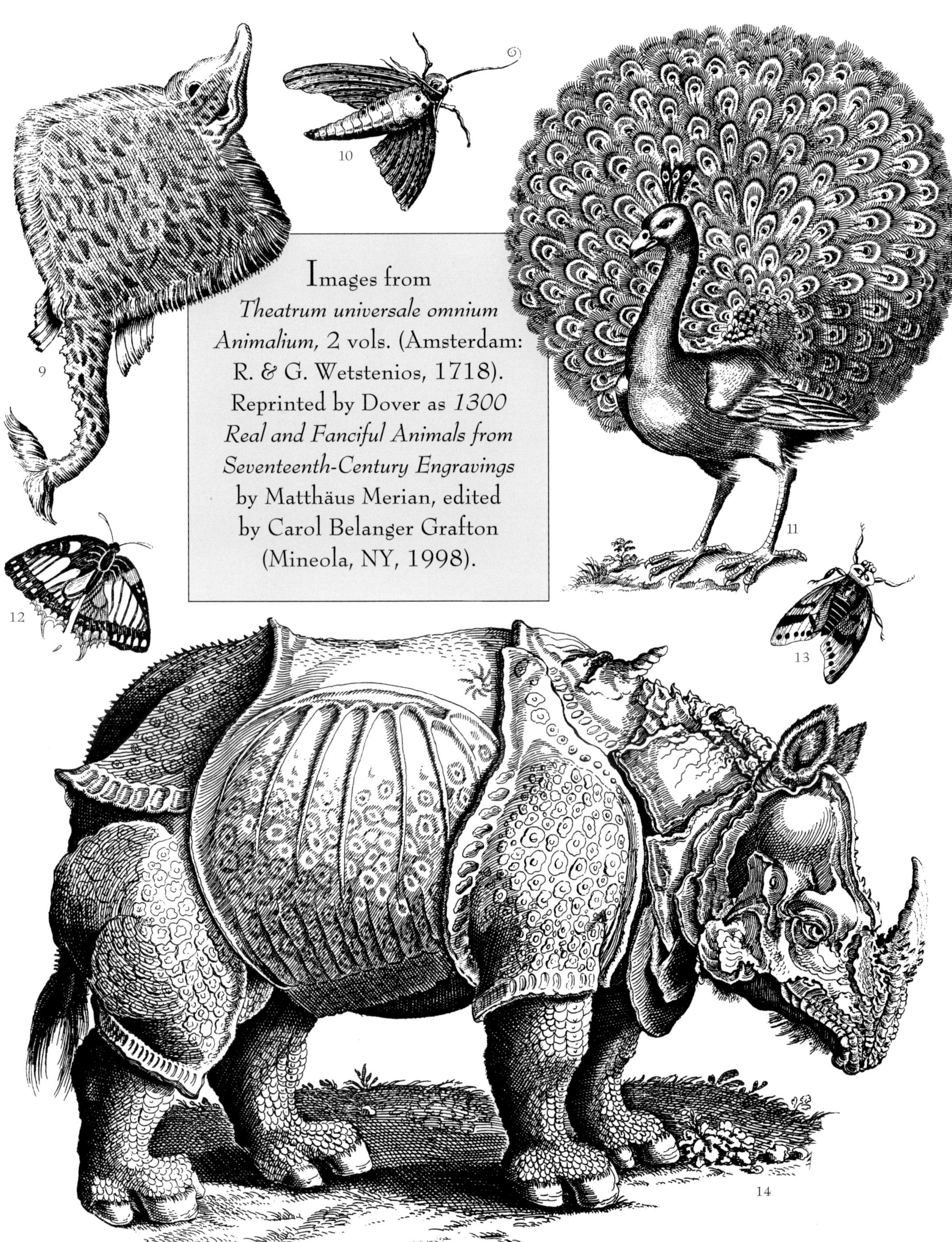

Images from *Theatrum universale omnium Animalium*, 2 vols. (Amsterdam: R. & G. Wetstenios, 1718). Reprinted by Dover as *1300 Real and Fanciful Animals from Seventeenth-Century Engravings* by Matthäus Merian, edited by Carol Belanger Grafton (Mineola, NY, 1998).

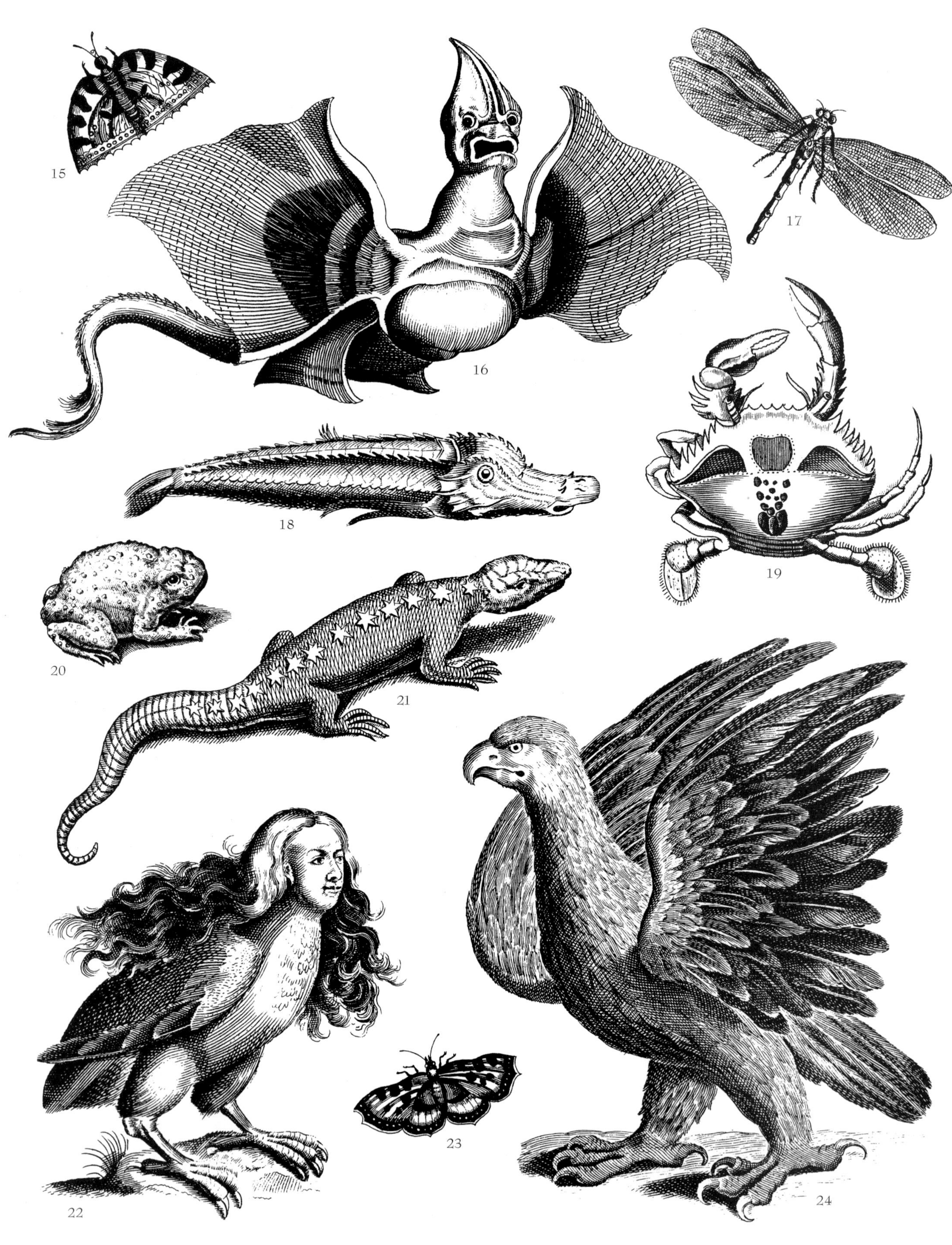
15
16
17
18
19
20
21
22
23
24

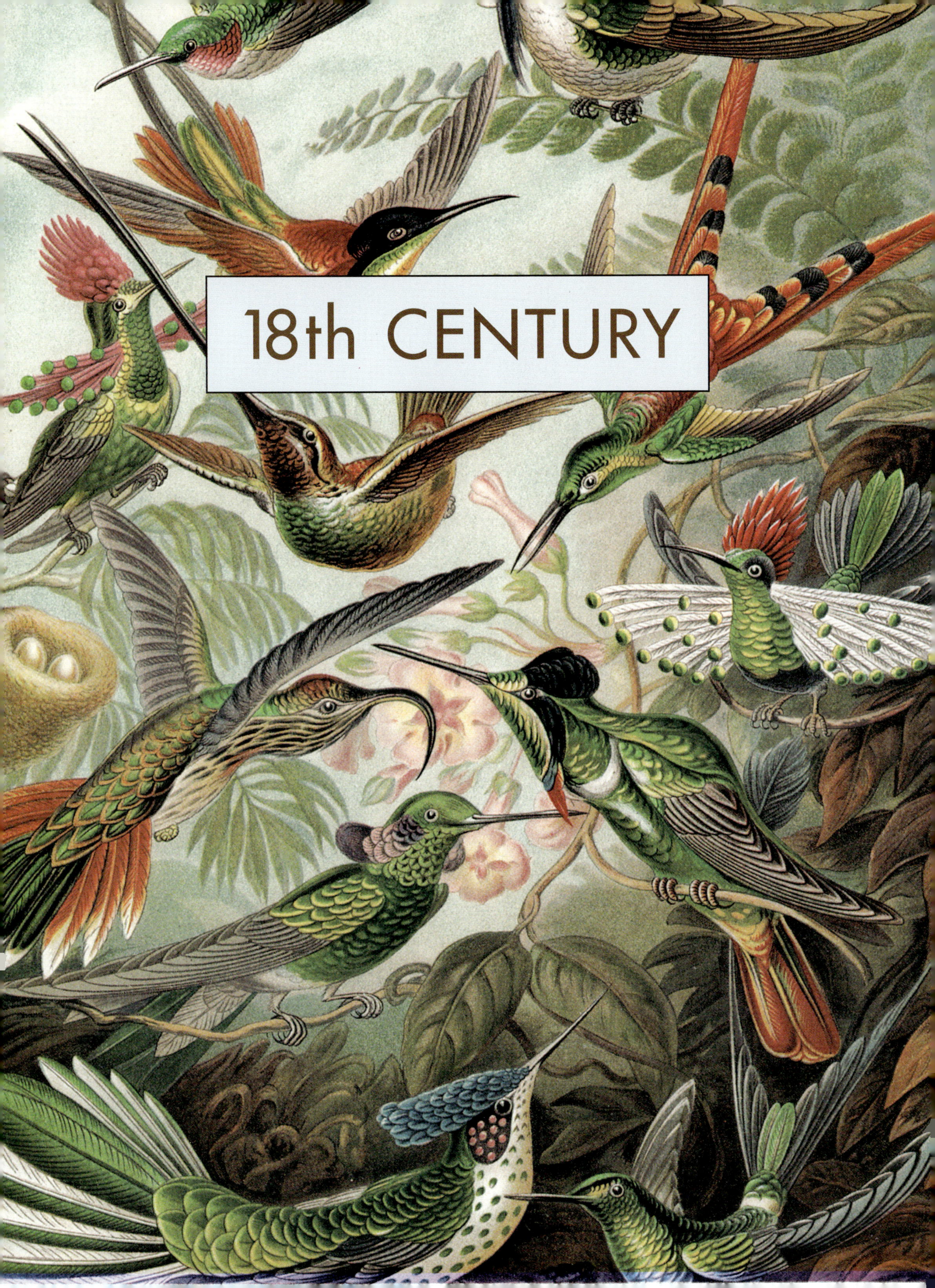

18th CENTURY

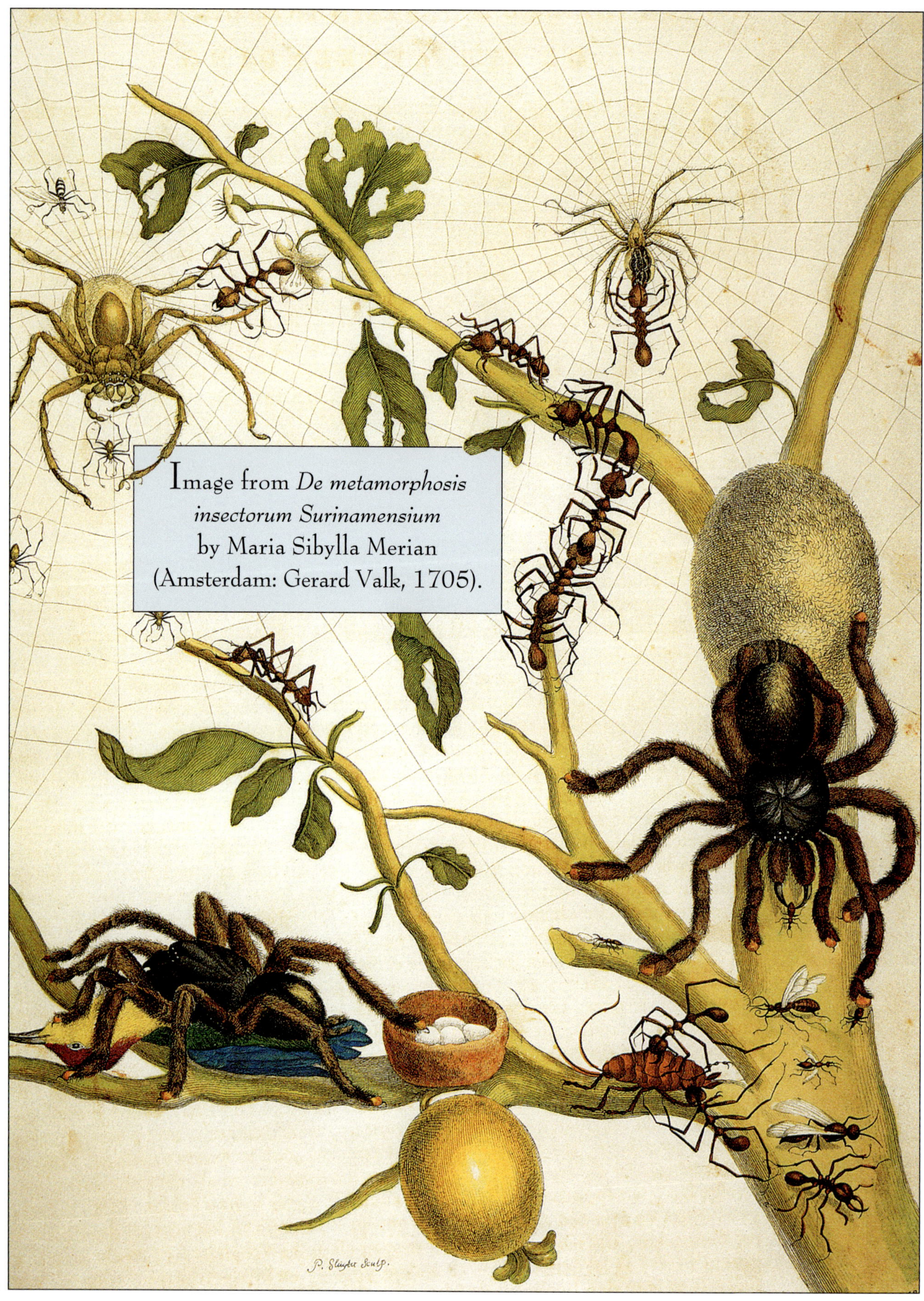

Image from *De metamorphosis insectorum Surinamensium* by Maria Sibylla Merian (Amsterdam: Gerard Valk, 1705).

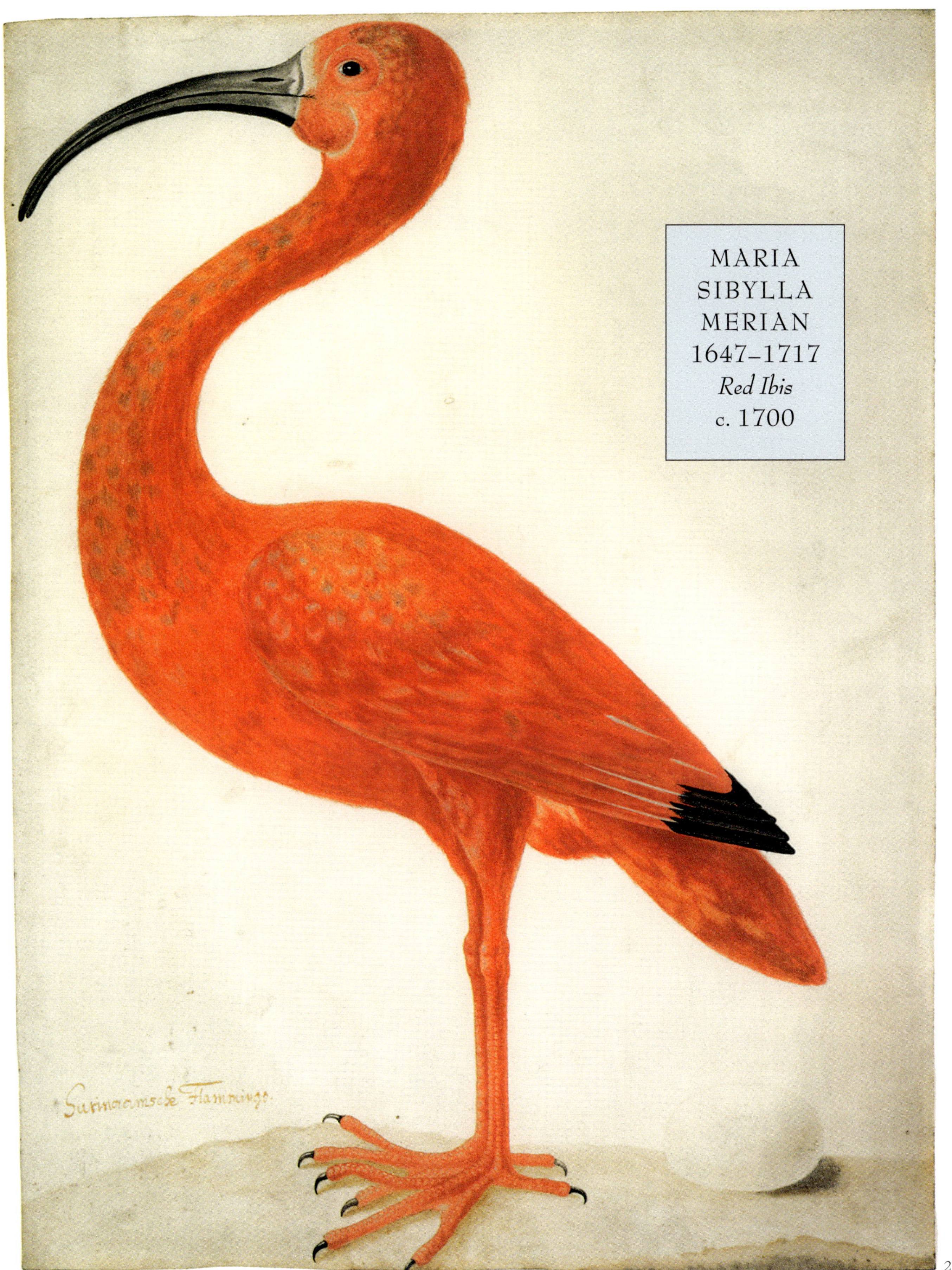

MARIA
SIBYLLA
MERIAN
1647–1717
Red Ibis
c. 1700

27

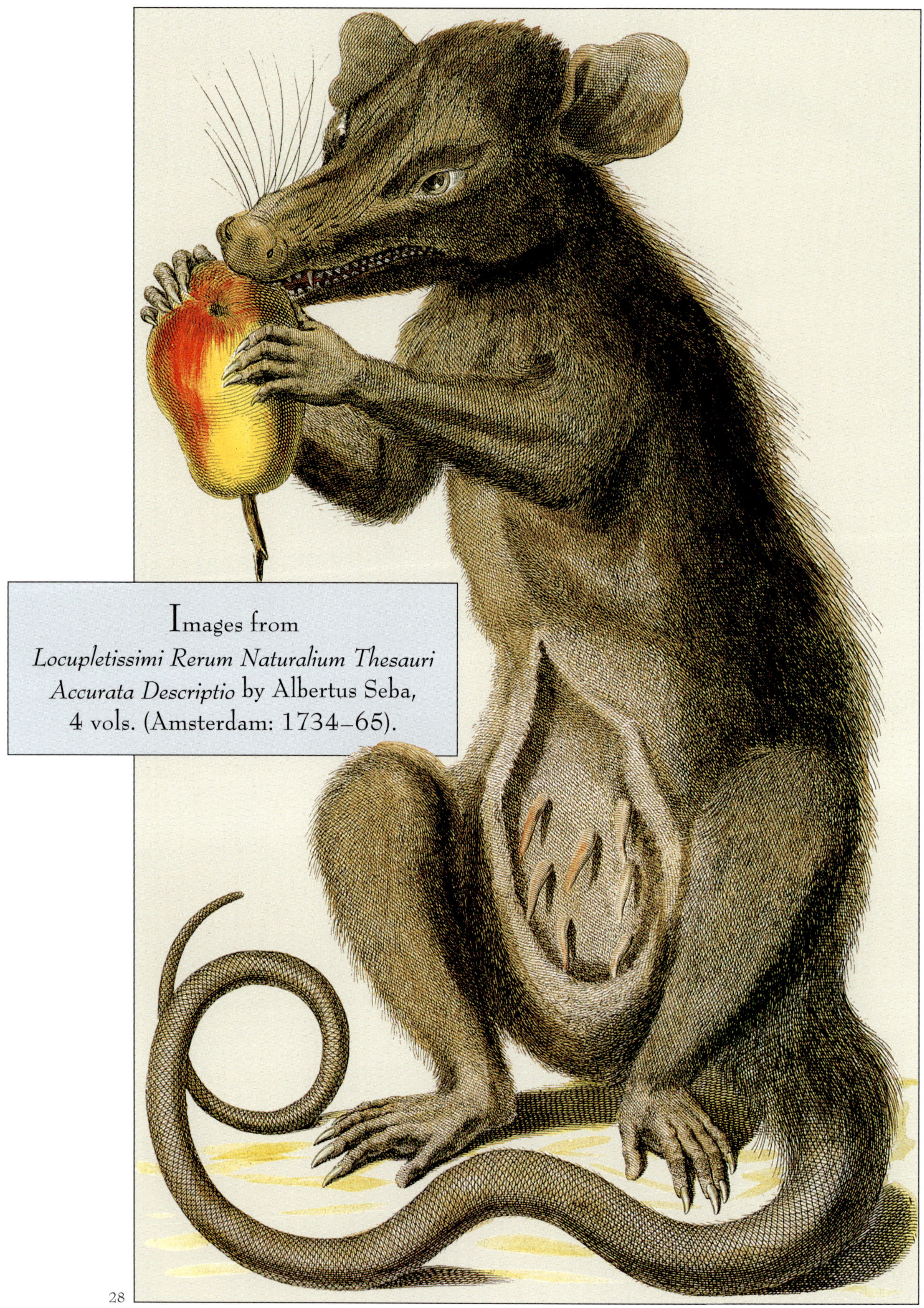

Images from
Locupletissimi Rerum Naturalium Thesauri Accurata Descriptio by Albertus Seba, 4 vols. (Amsterdam: 1734–65).

28

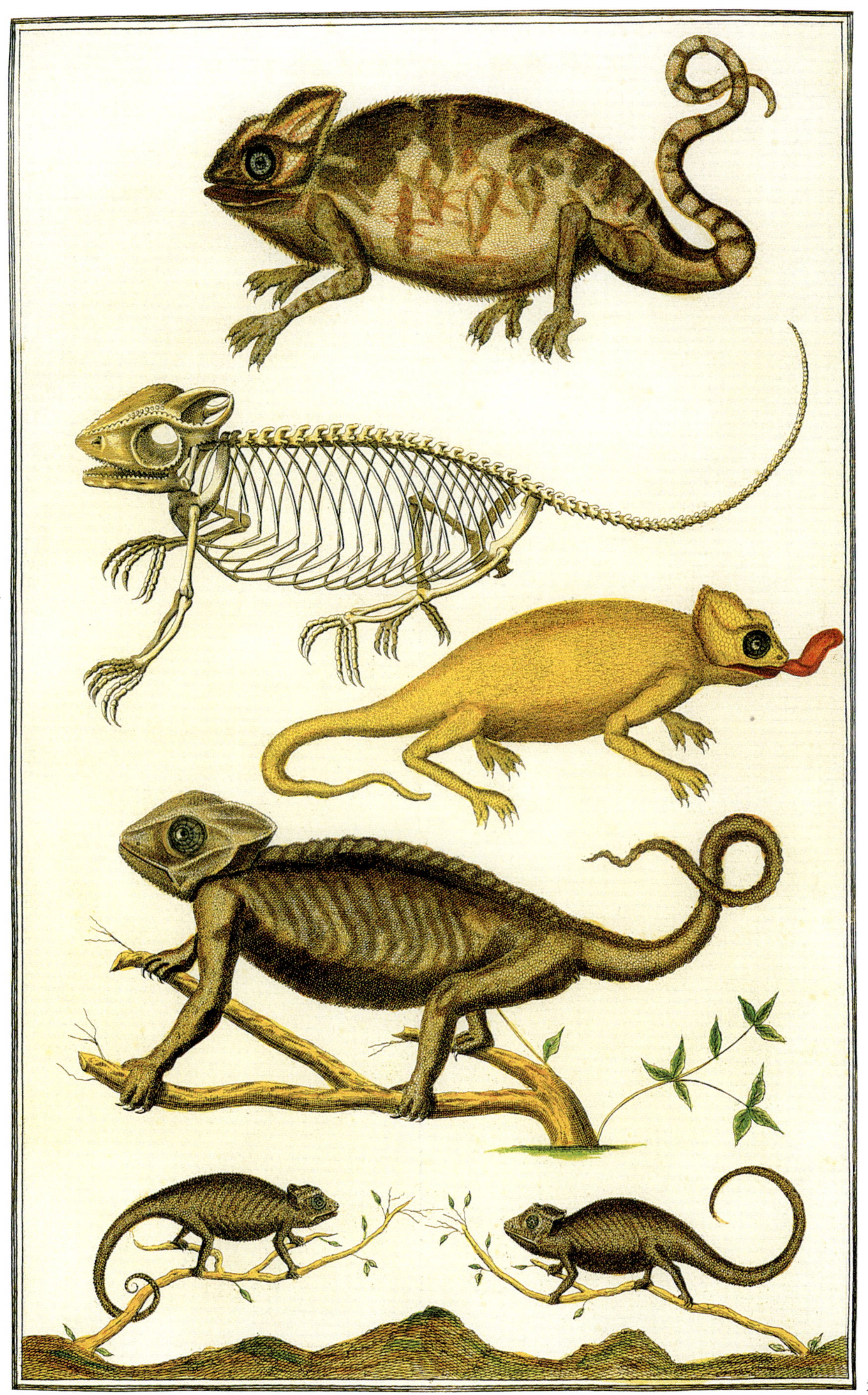

29

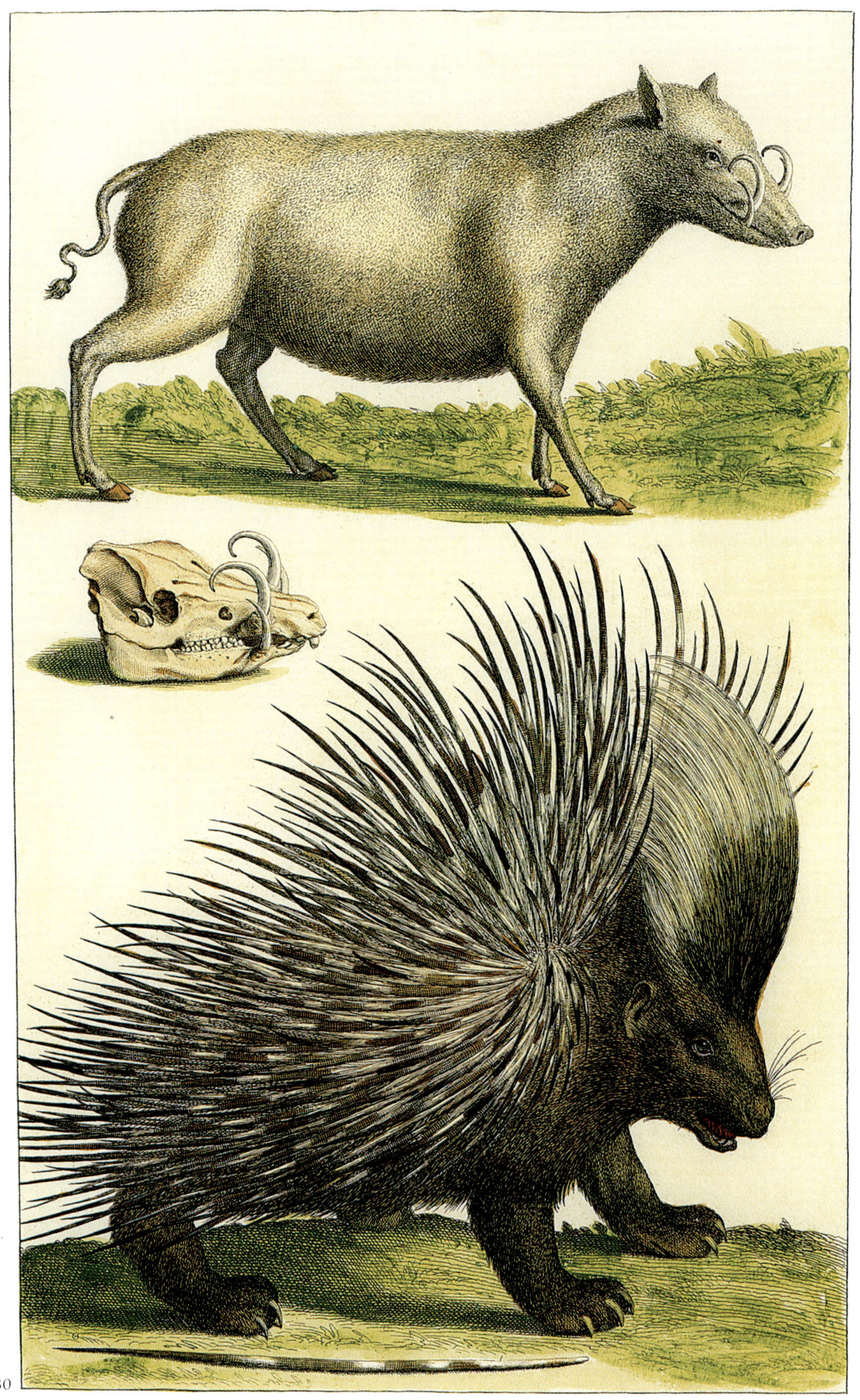

30

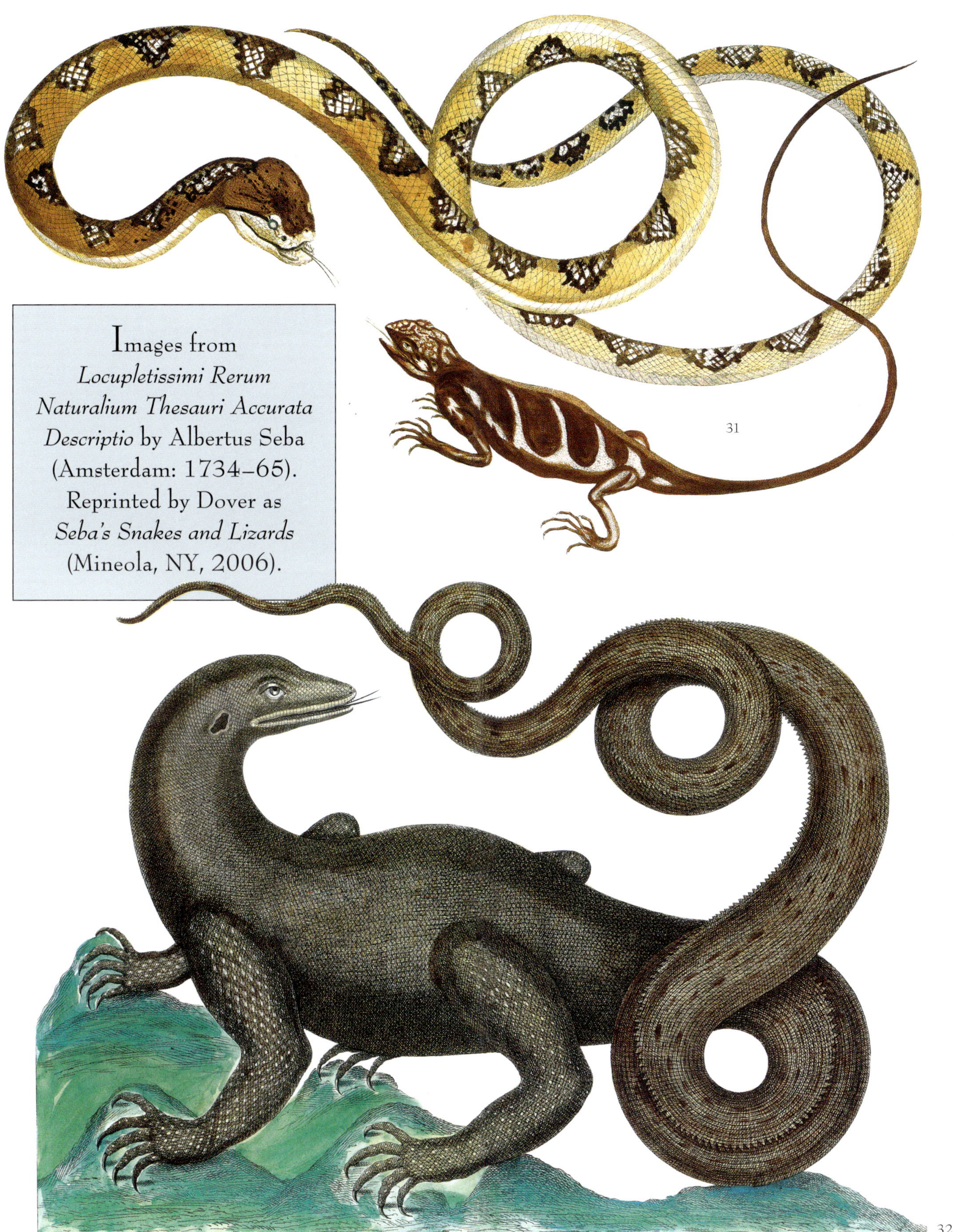

Images from *Locupletissimi Rerum Naturalium Thesauri Accurata Descriptio* by Albertus Seba (Amsterdam: 1734–65). Reprinted by Dover as *Seba's Snakes and Lizards* (Mineola, NY, 2006).

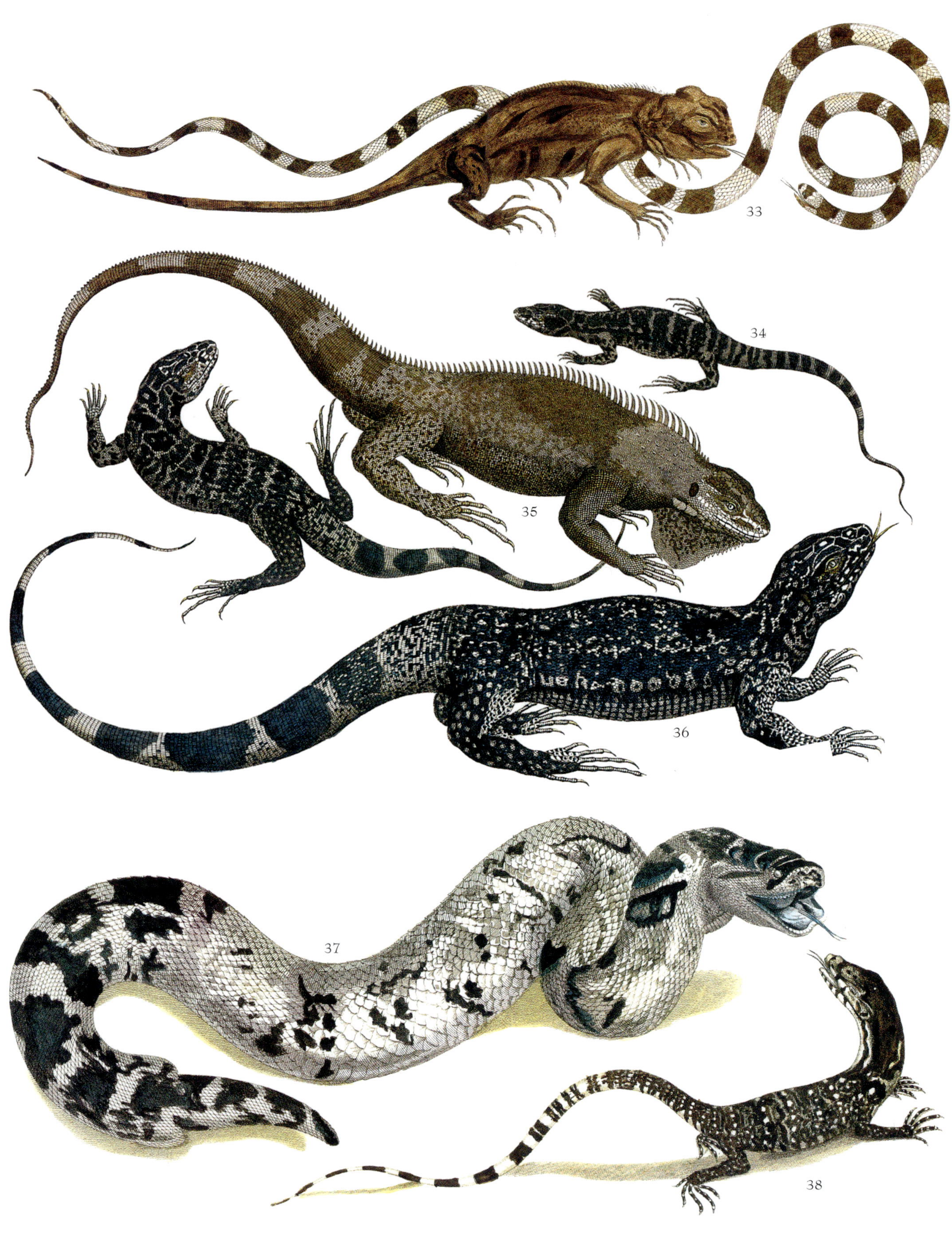
33
34
35
36
37
38

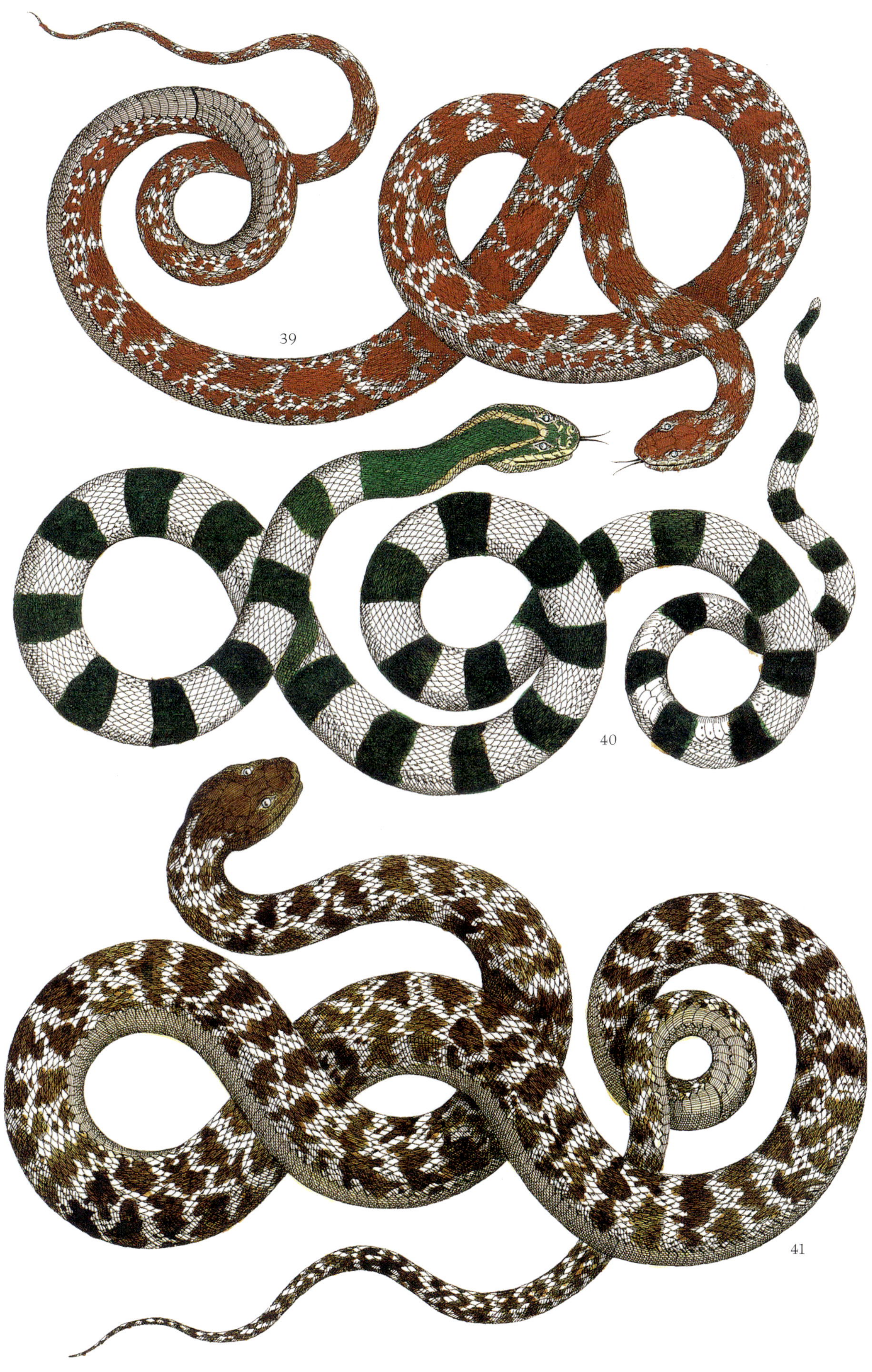
39
40
41

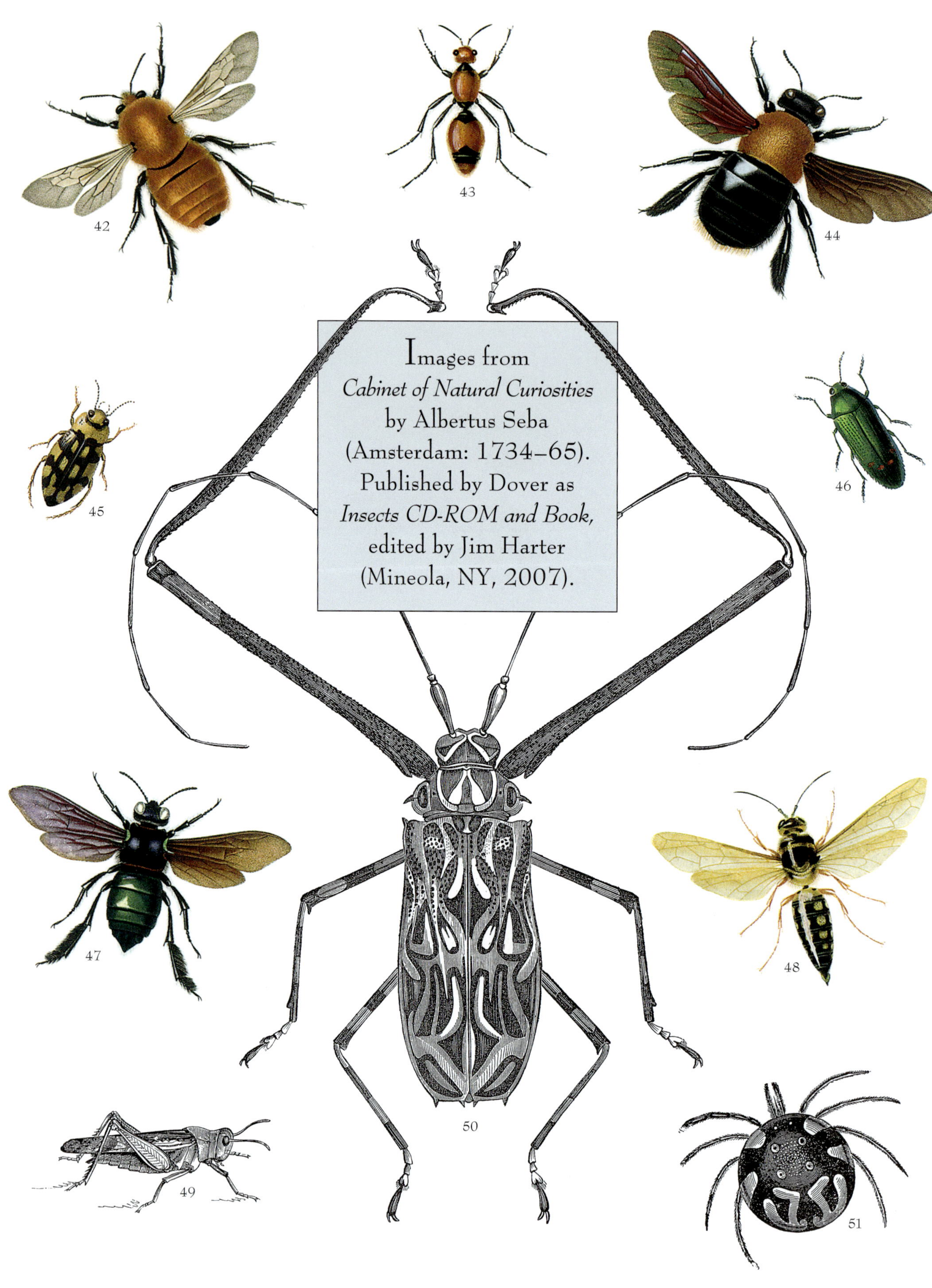

Images from
Cabinet of Natural Curiosities
by Albertus Seba
(Amsterdam: 1734–65).
Published by Dover as
Insects CD-ROM and Book,
edited by Jim Harter
(Mineola, NY, 2007).

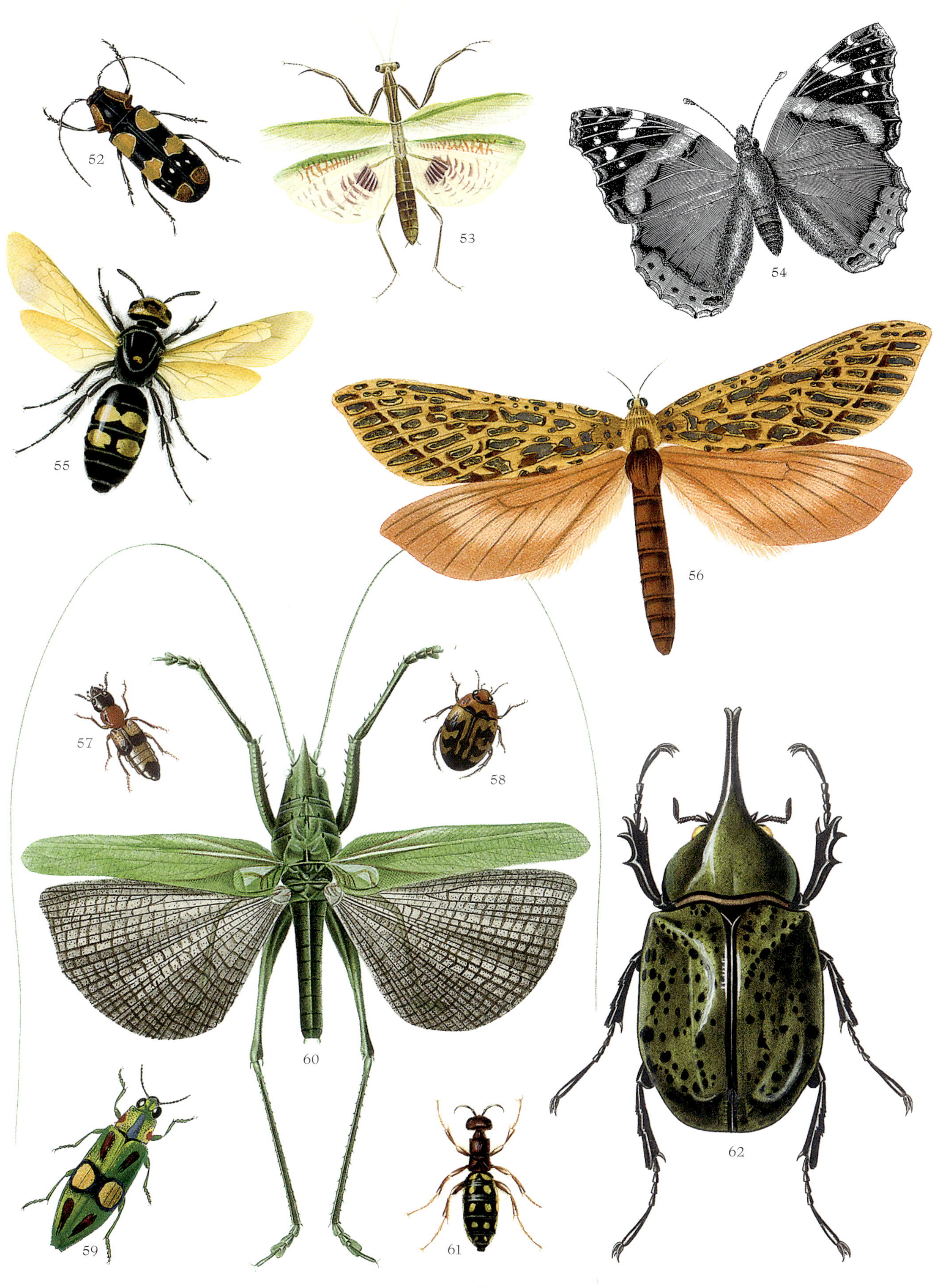
52
53
54
55
56
57
58
60
59
61
62

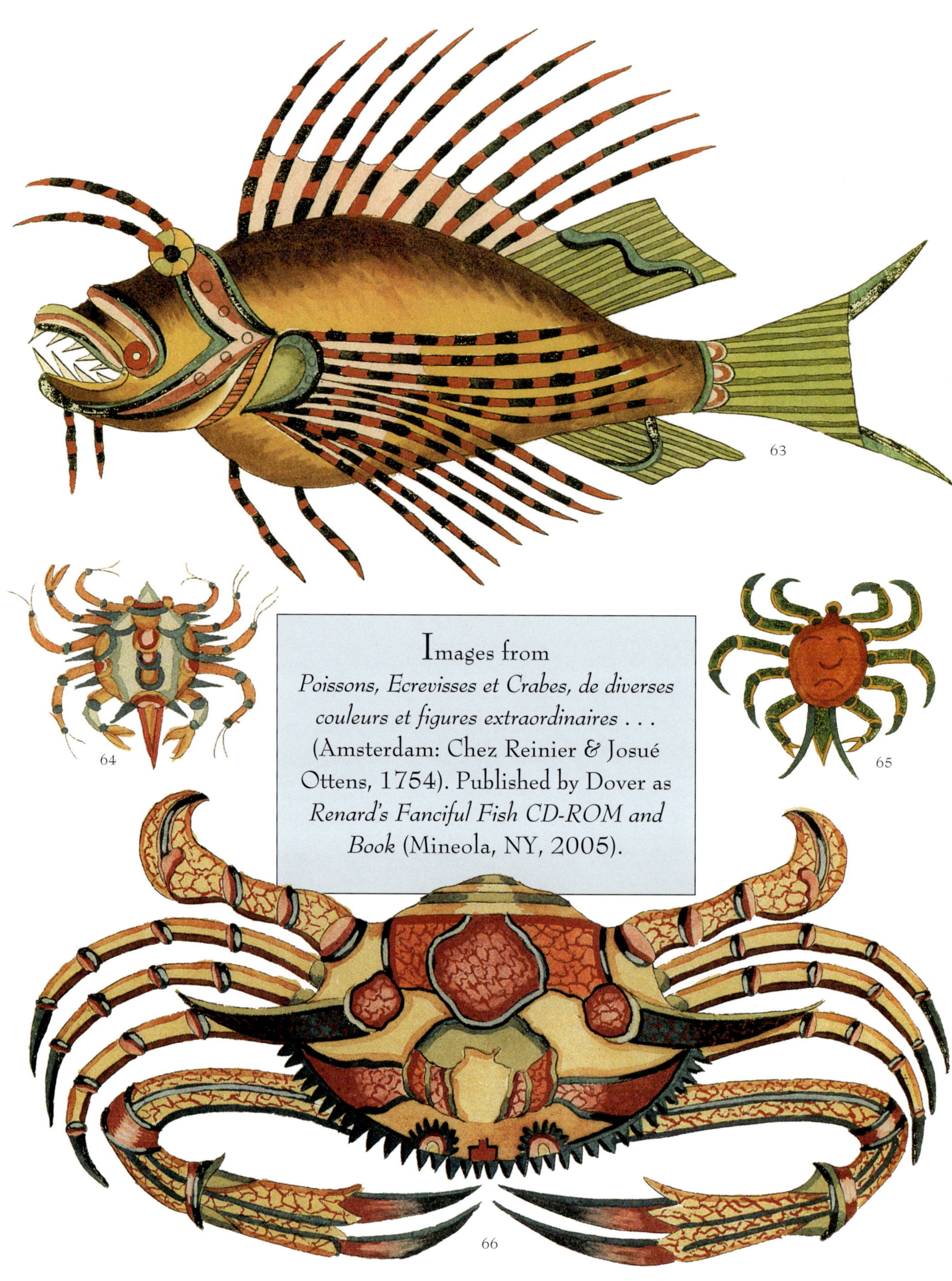

Images from
Poissons, Ecrevisses et Crabes, de diverses couleurs et figures extraordinaires . . . (Amsterdam: Chez Reinier & Josué Ottens, 1754). Published by Dover as *Renard's Fanciful Fish CD-ROM and Book* (Mineola, NY, 2005).

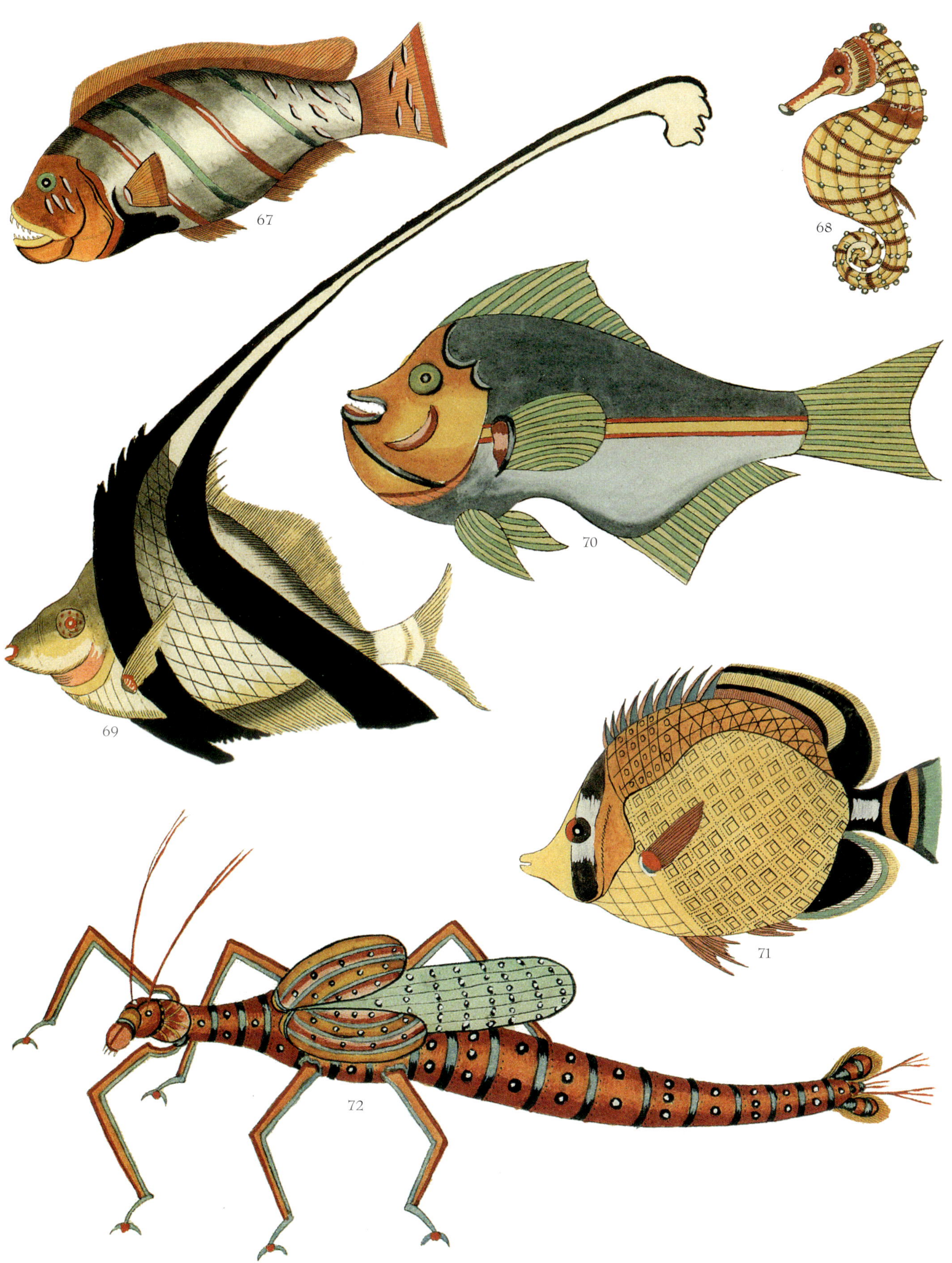
67
68
70
69
71
72

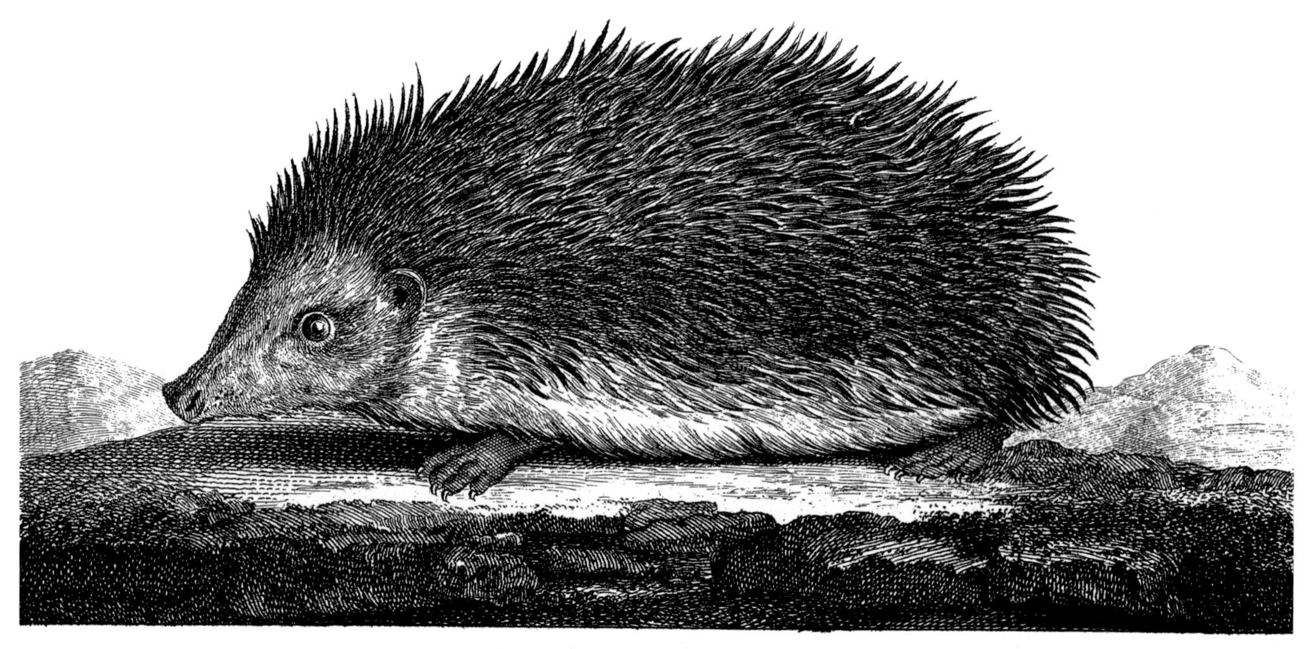

73

Images from *Histoire Naturelle, générale et particulière, avec la description du cabinet du roi* by Georges-Louis Leclerc, comte de Buffon (Amsterdam: J. H. Schneider, 1749–88). Published by Dover as *368 Animal Illustrations from Buffon's "Natural History"* (Mineola, NY, 1993).

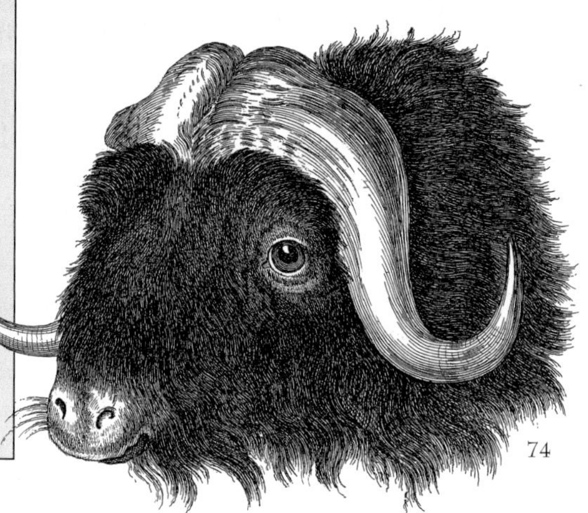

74

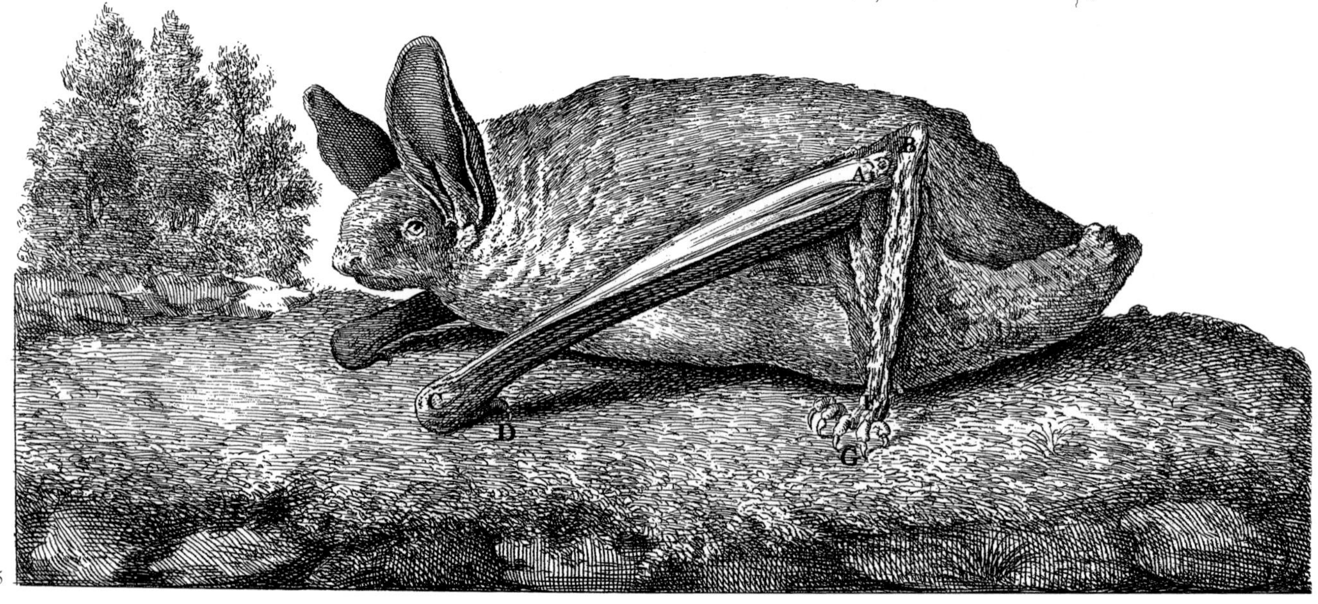

75

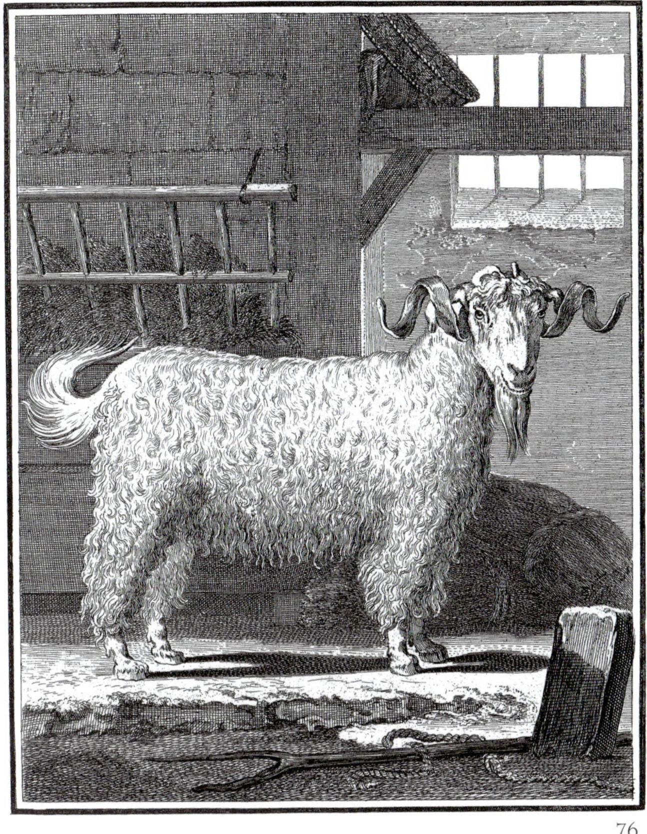

76

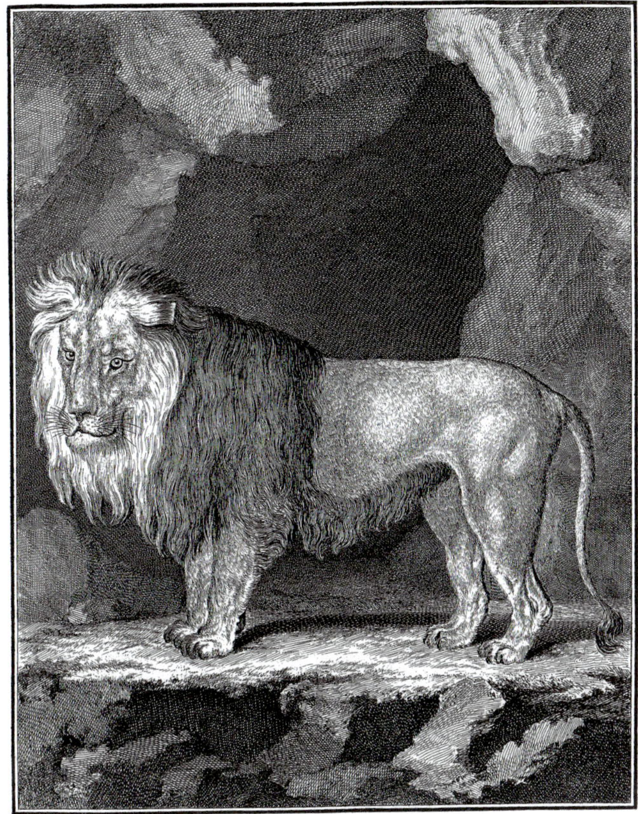

77

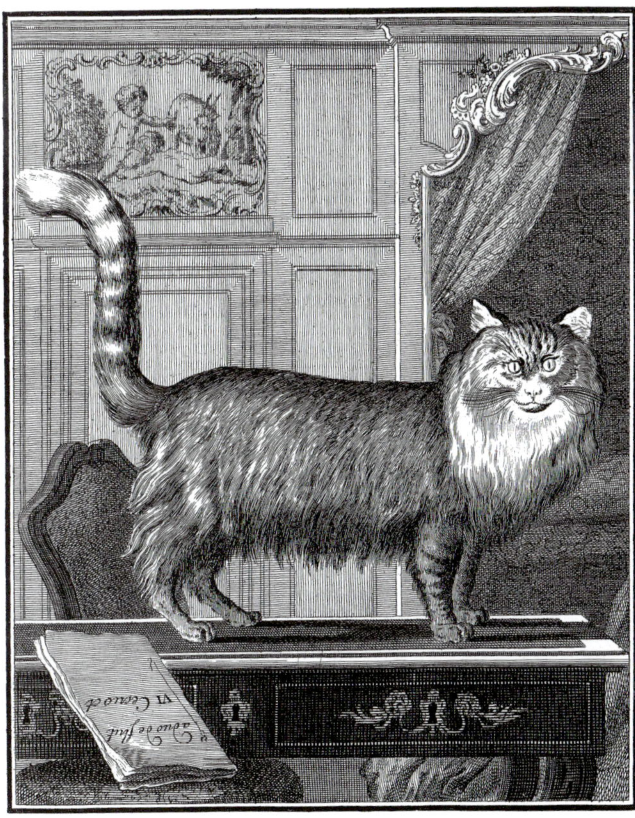

78

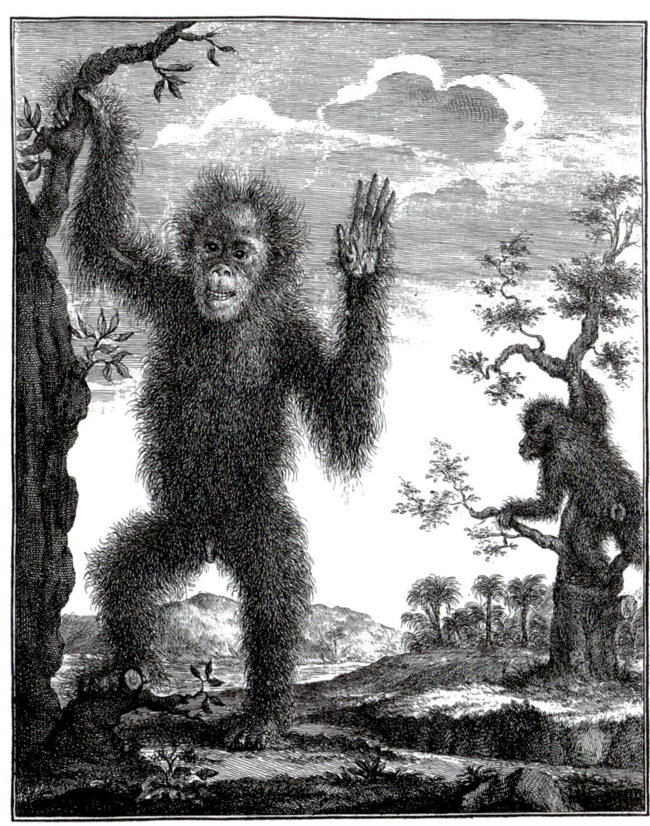

79

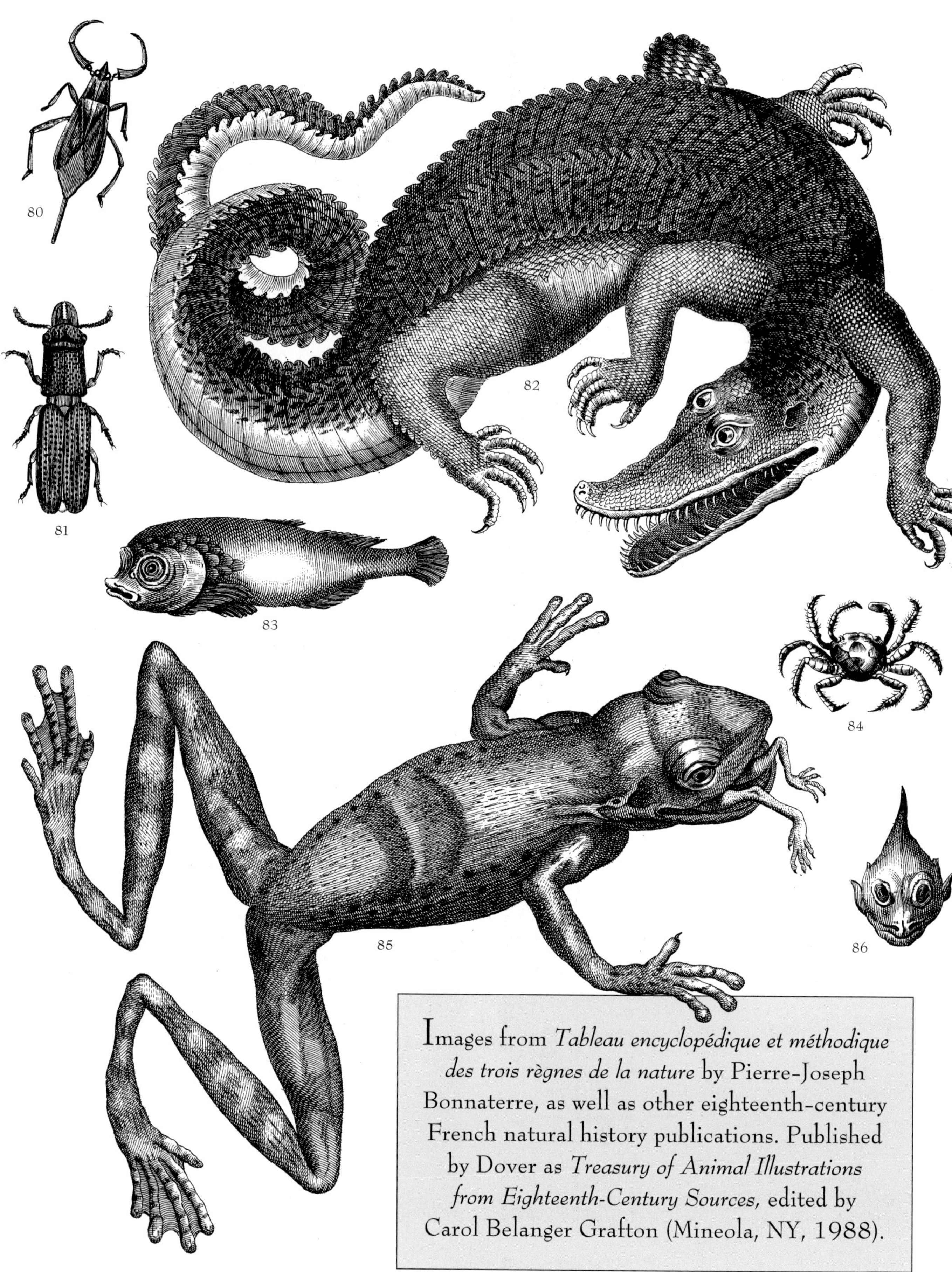

Images from *Tableau encyclopédique et méthodique des trois règnes de la nature* by Pierre-Joseph Bonnaterre, as well as other eighteenth-century French natural history publications. Published by Dover as *Treasury of Animal Illustrations from Eighteenth-Century Sources,* edited by Carol Belanger Grafton (Mineola, NY, 1988).

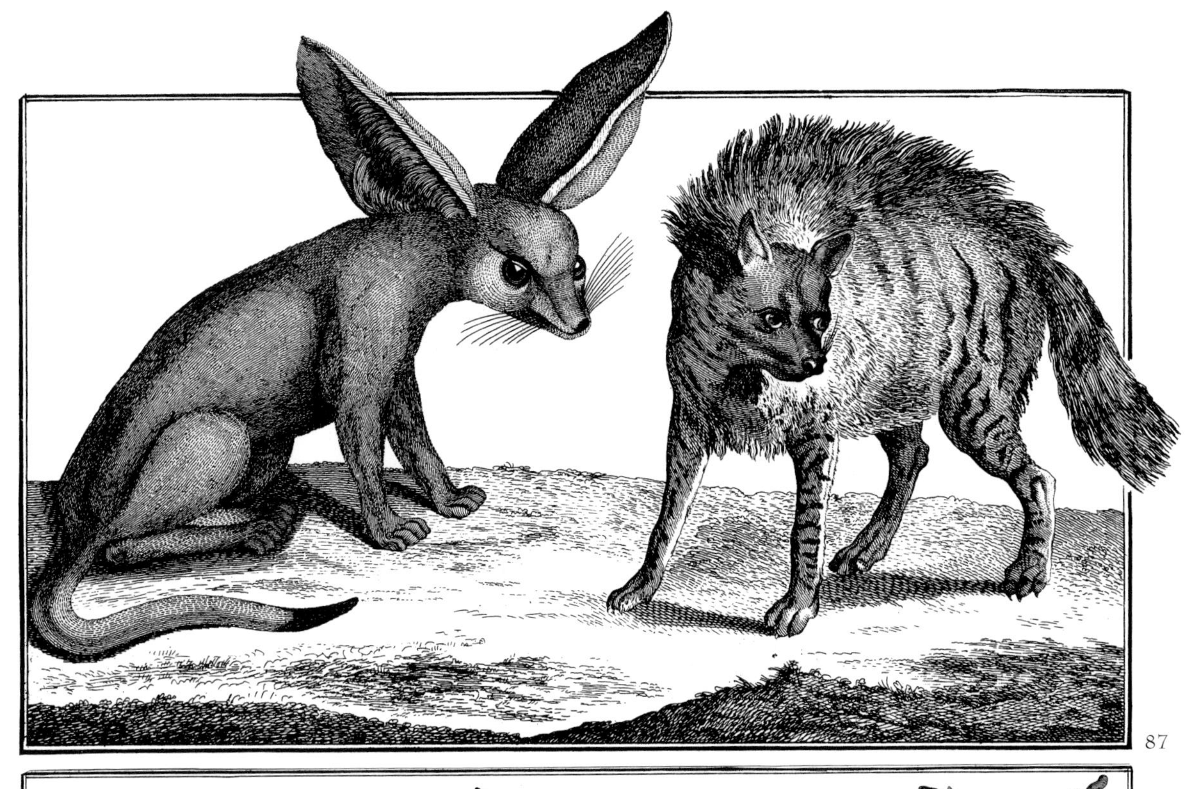

87

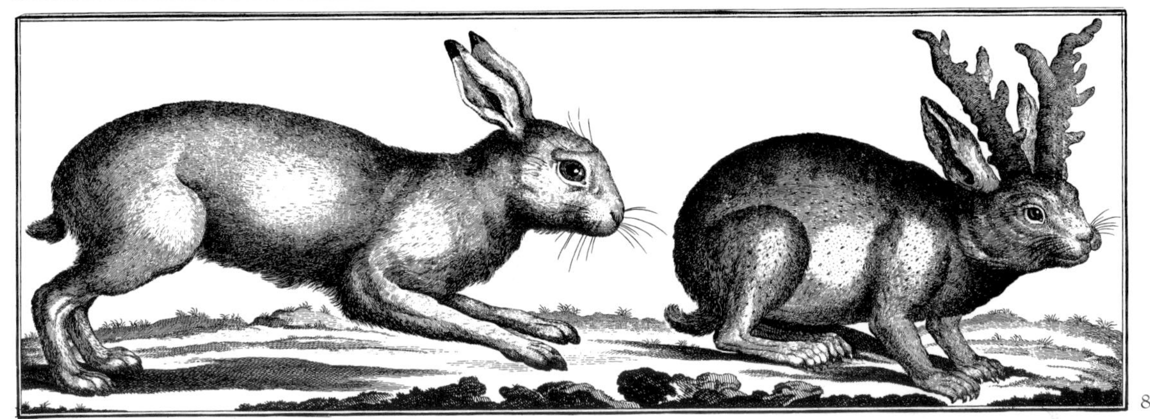

88

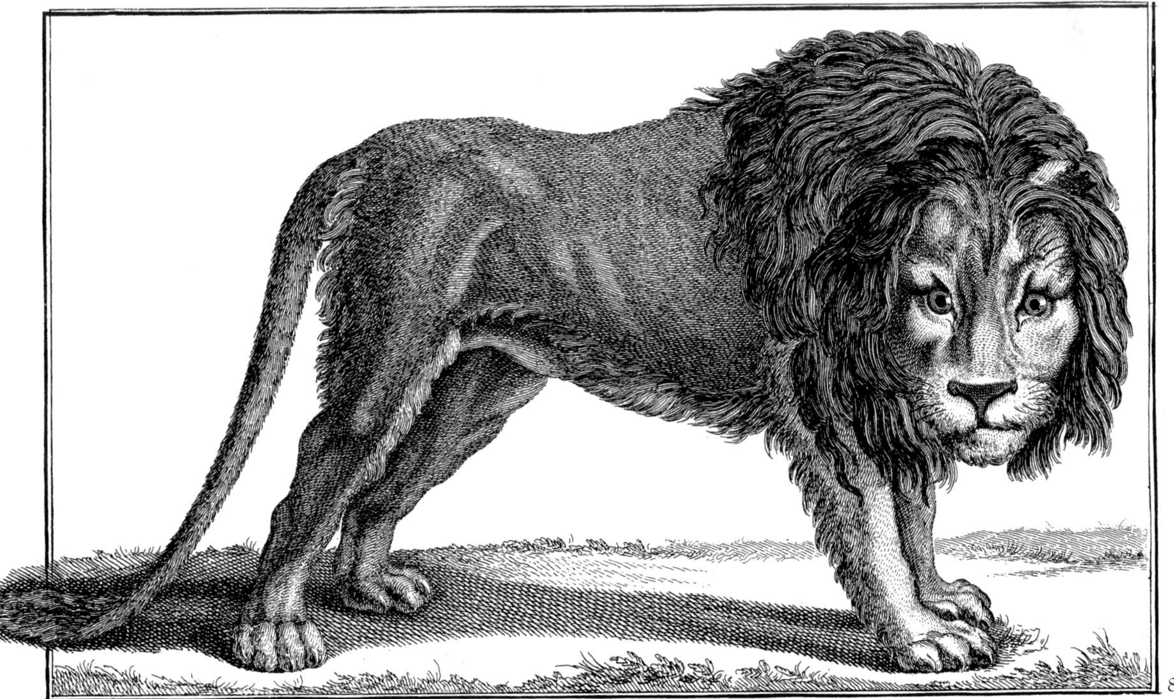

89

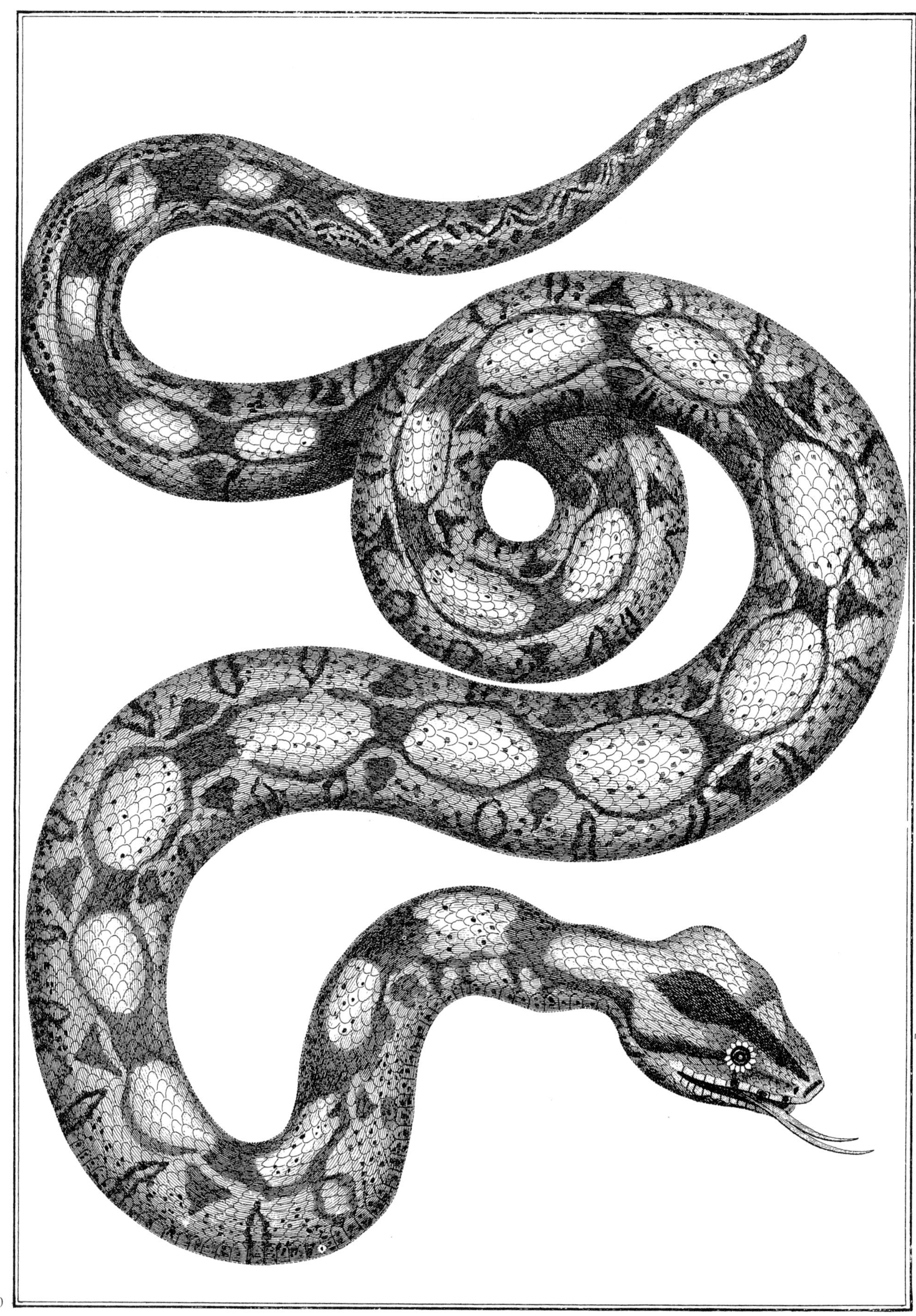

90

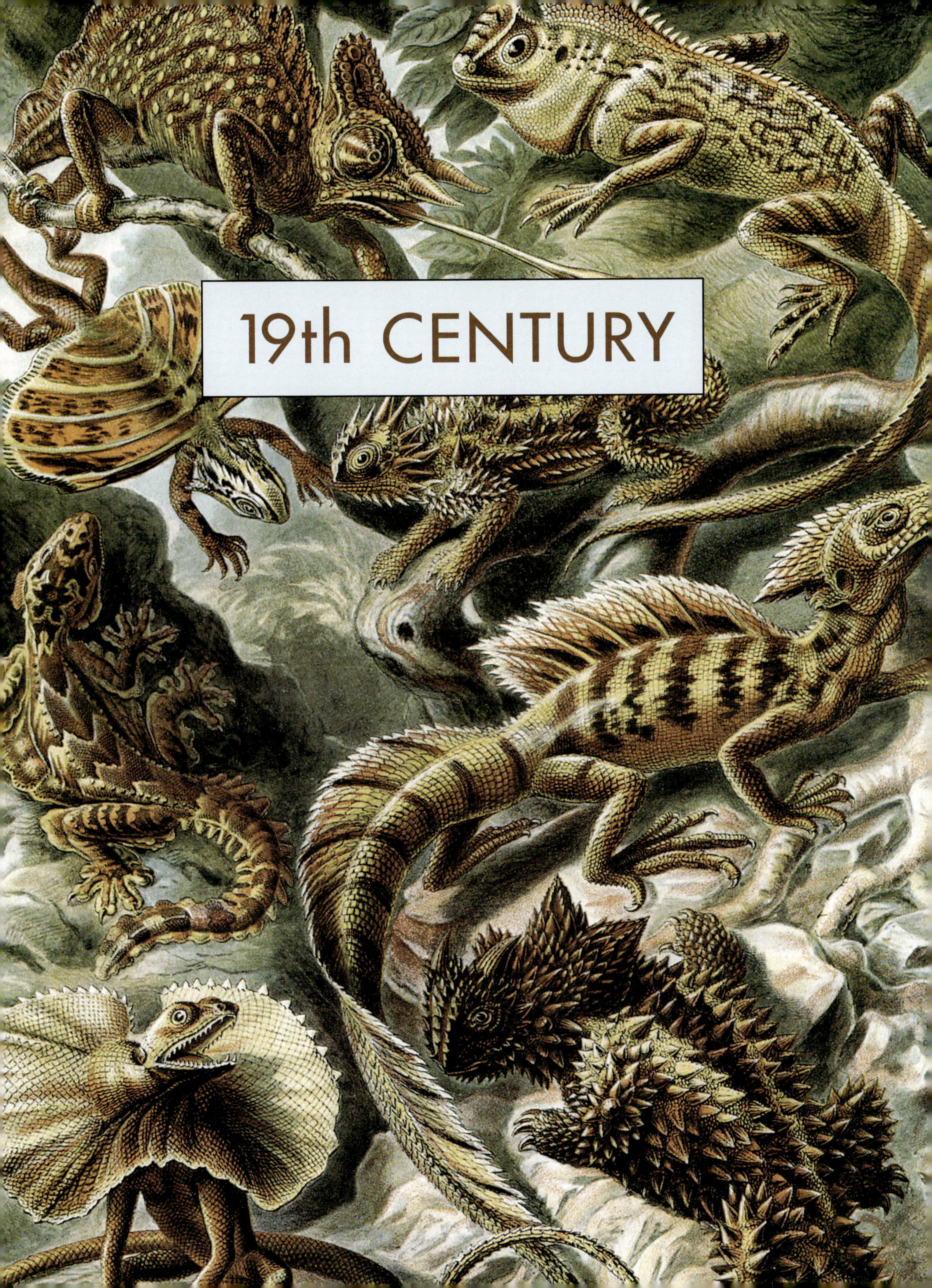

19th CENTURY

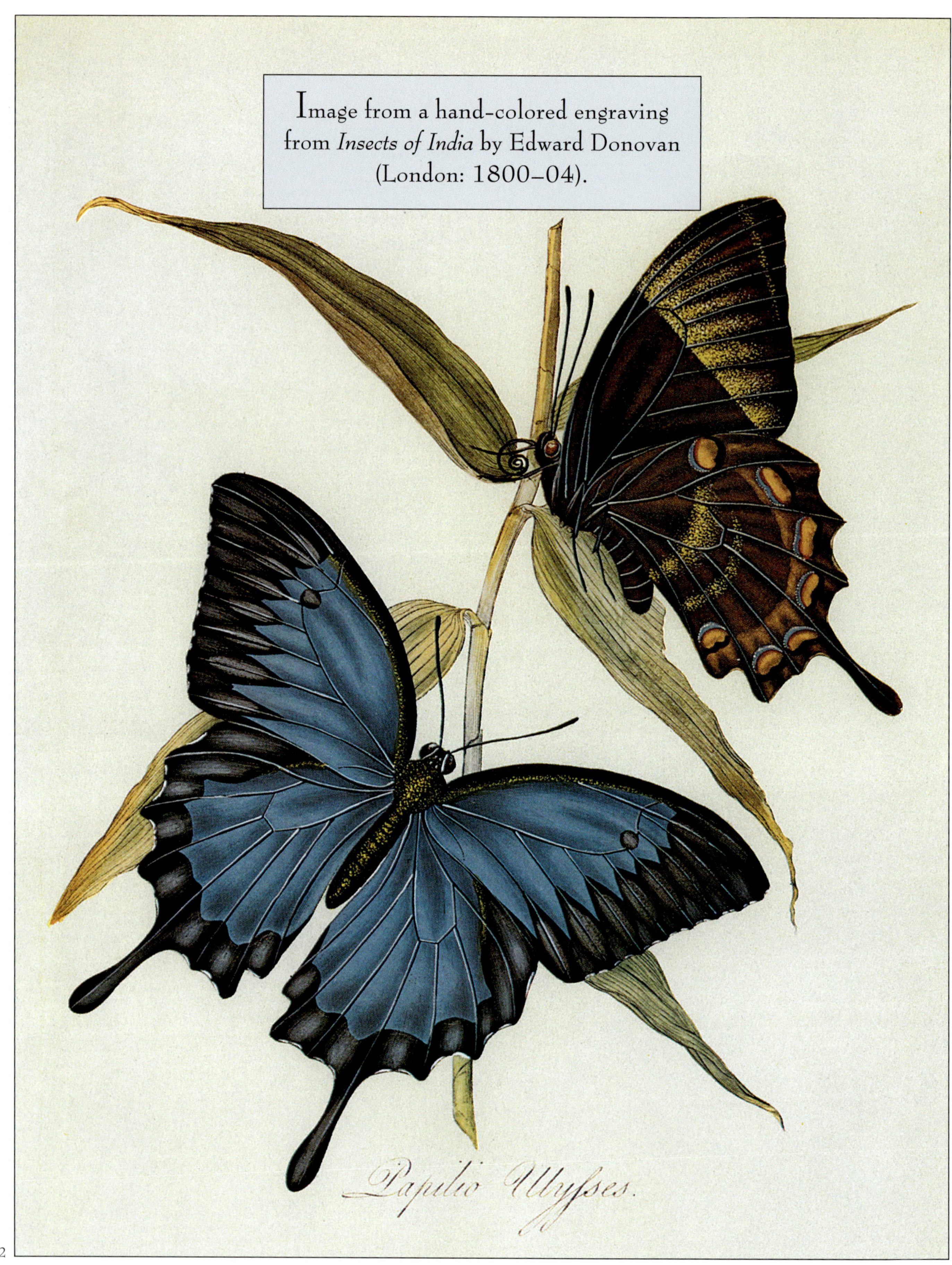

Image from a hand-colored engraving from *Insects of India* by Edward Donovan (London: 1800–04).

92

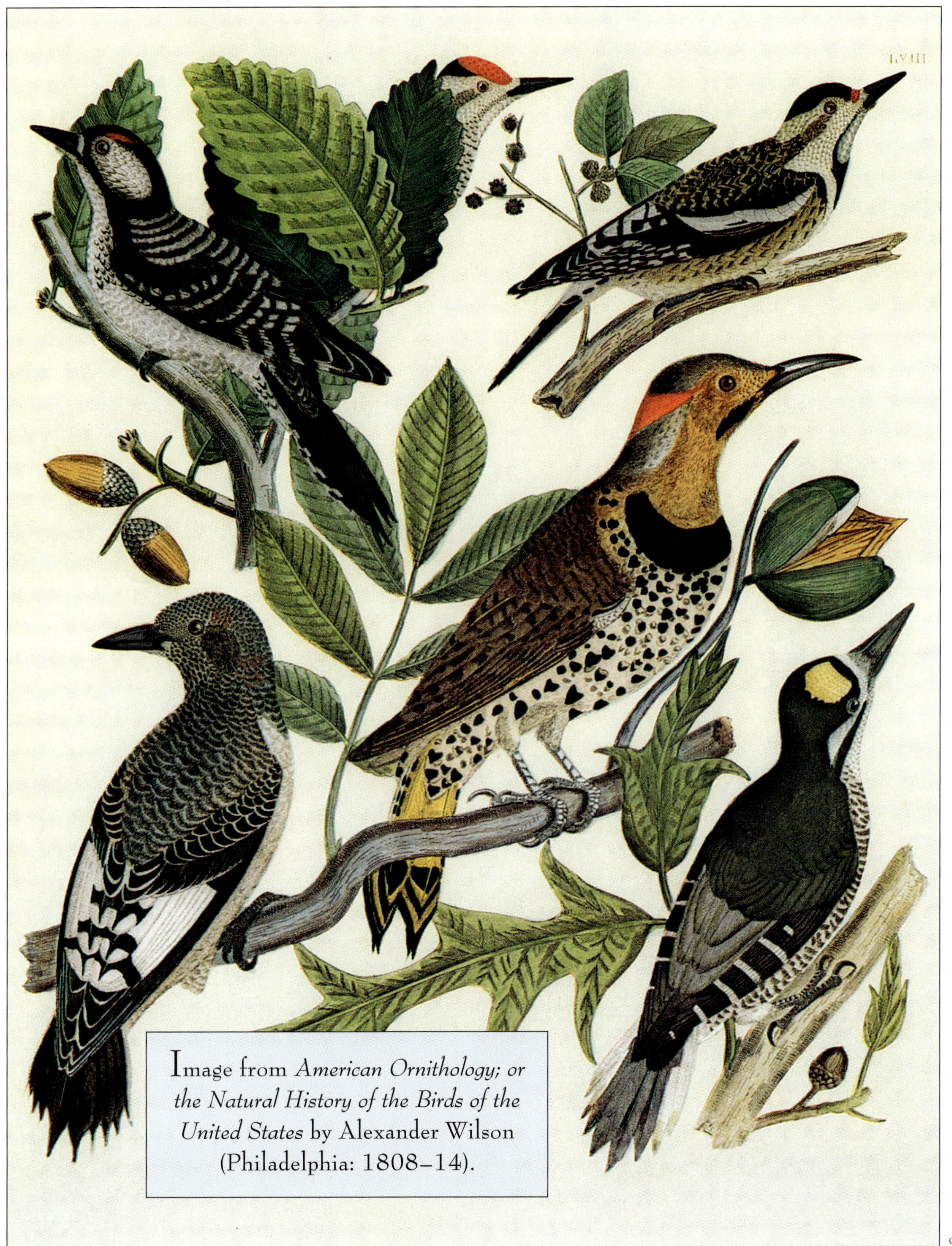

Image from *American Ornithology; or the Natural History of the Birds of the United States* by Alexander Wilson (Philadelphia: 1808–14).

93

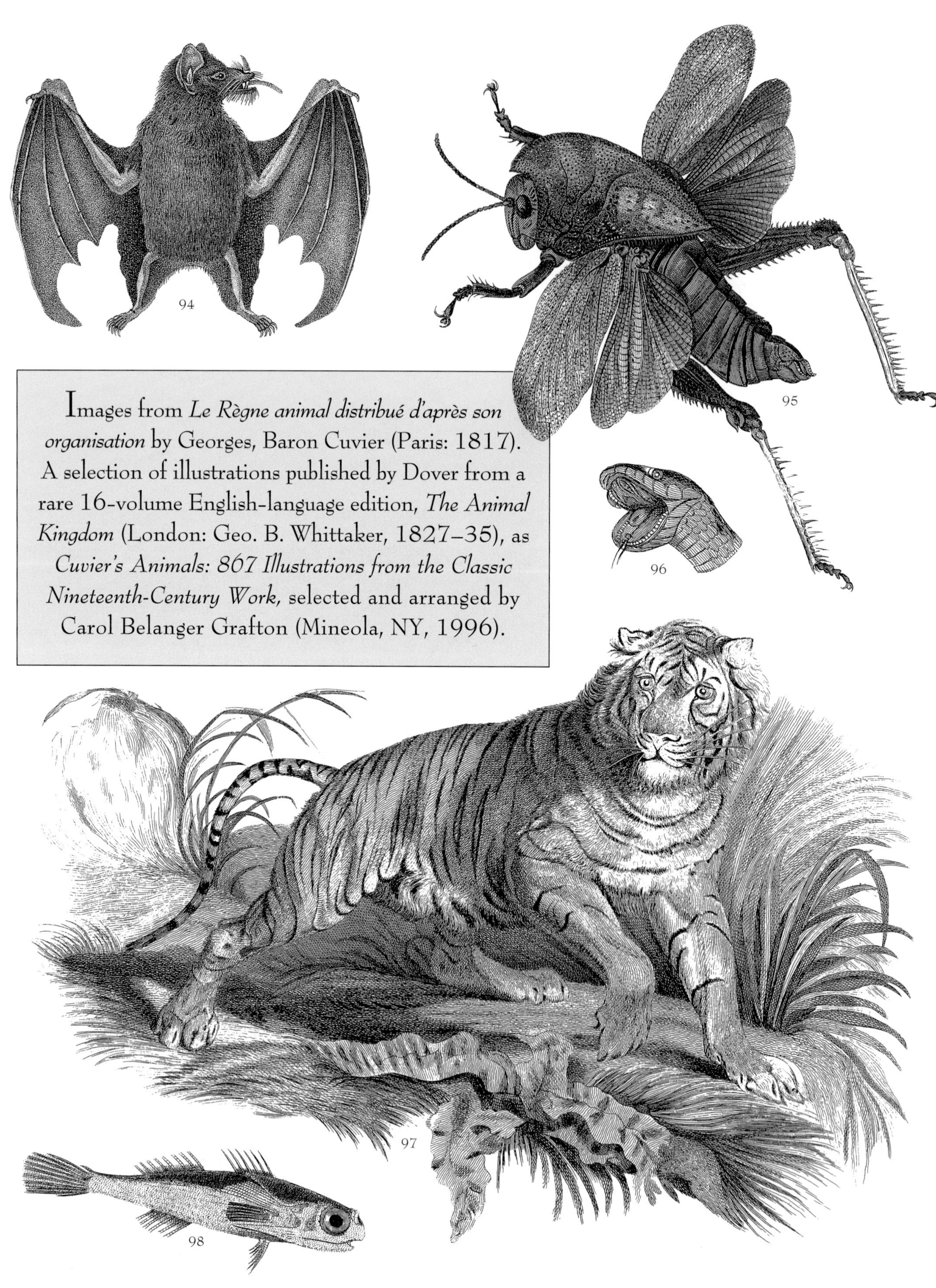

Images from *Le Règne animal distribué d'après son organisation* by Georges, Baron Cuvier (Paris: 1817). A selection of illustrations published by Dover from a rare 16-volume English-language edition, *The Animal Kingdom* (London: Geo. B. Whittaker, 1827–35), as *Cuvier's Animals: 867 Illustrations from the Classic Nineteenth-Century Work,* selected and arranged by Carol Belanger Grafton (Mineola, NY, 1996).

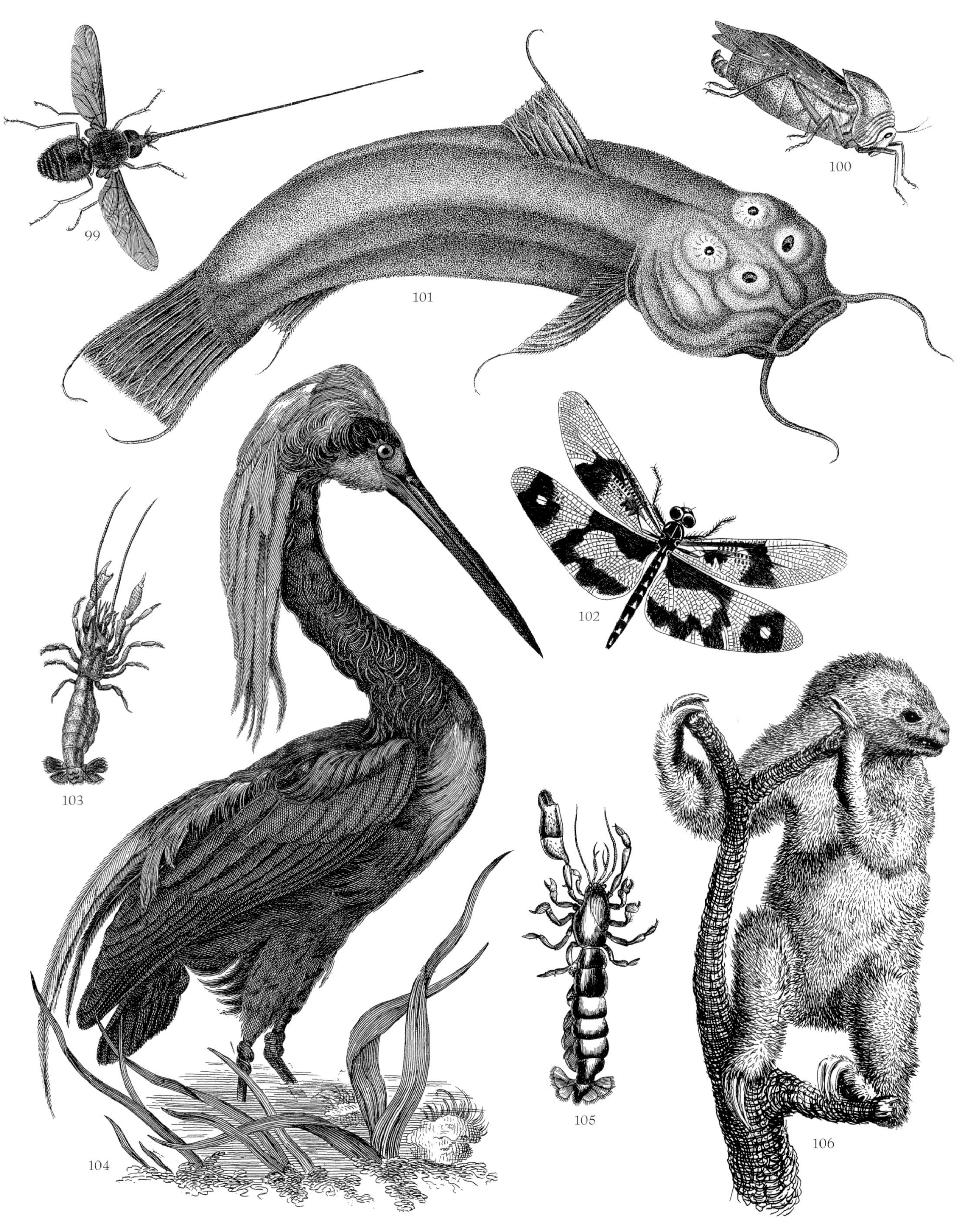
99
100
101
102
103
104
105
106

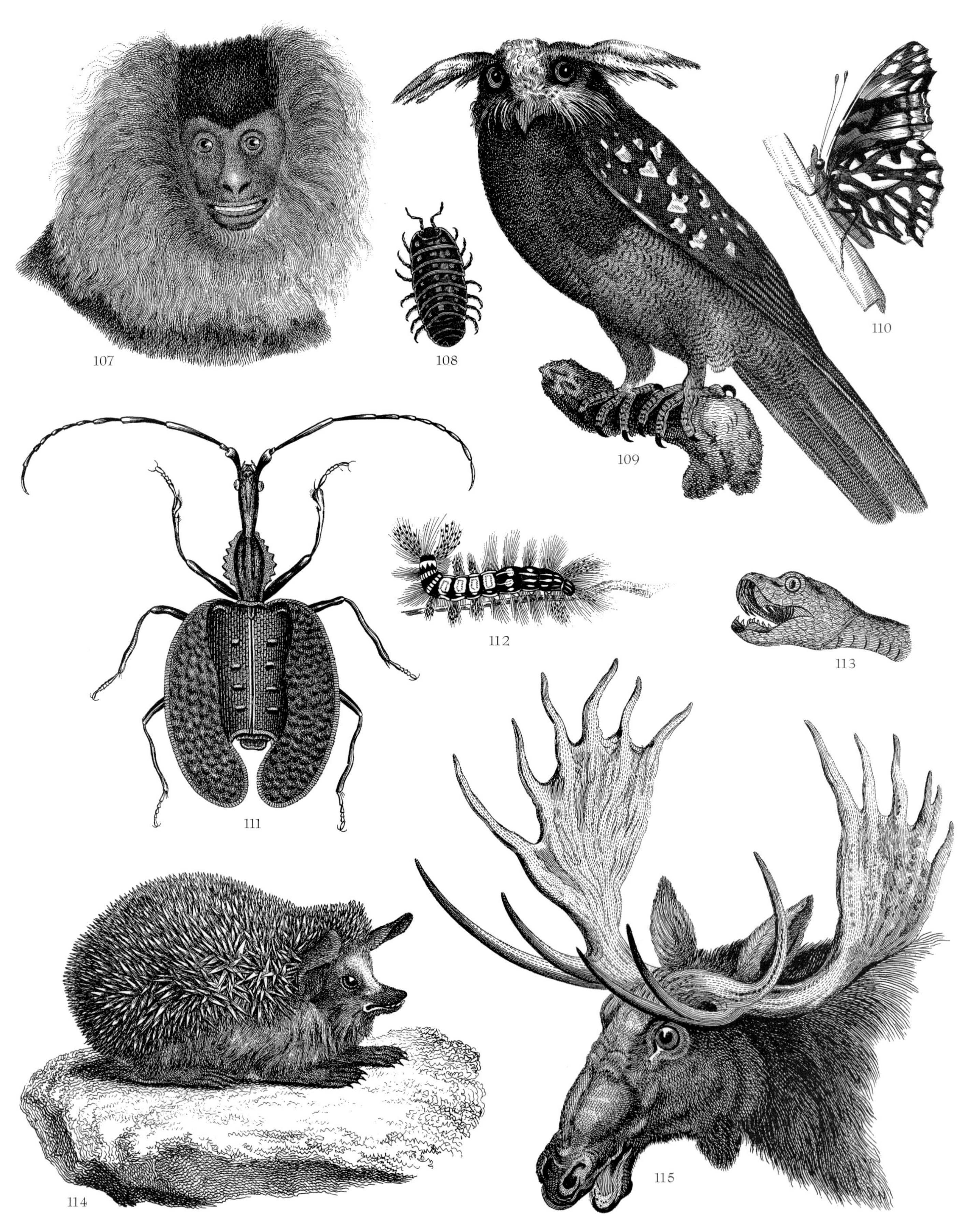
107
108
109
110
111
112
113
114
115

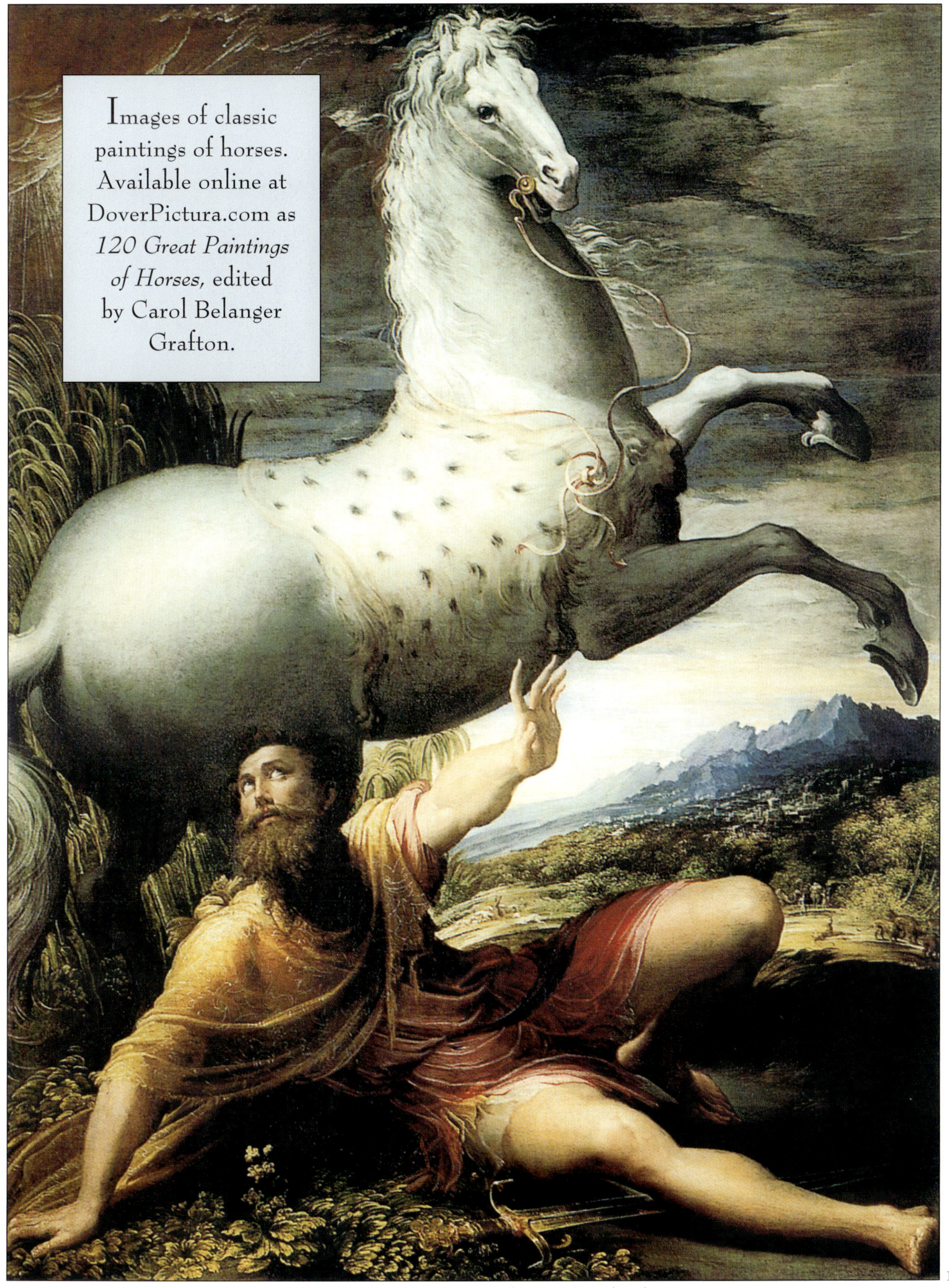

116

Parmigianino (1503–1540) / *The Conversion of Paul, c. 1530*

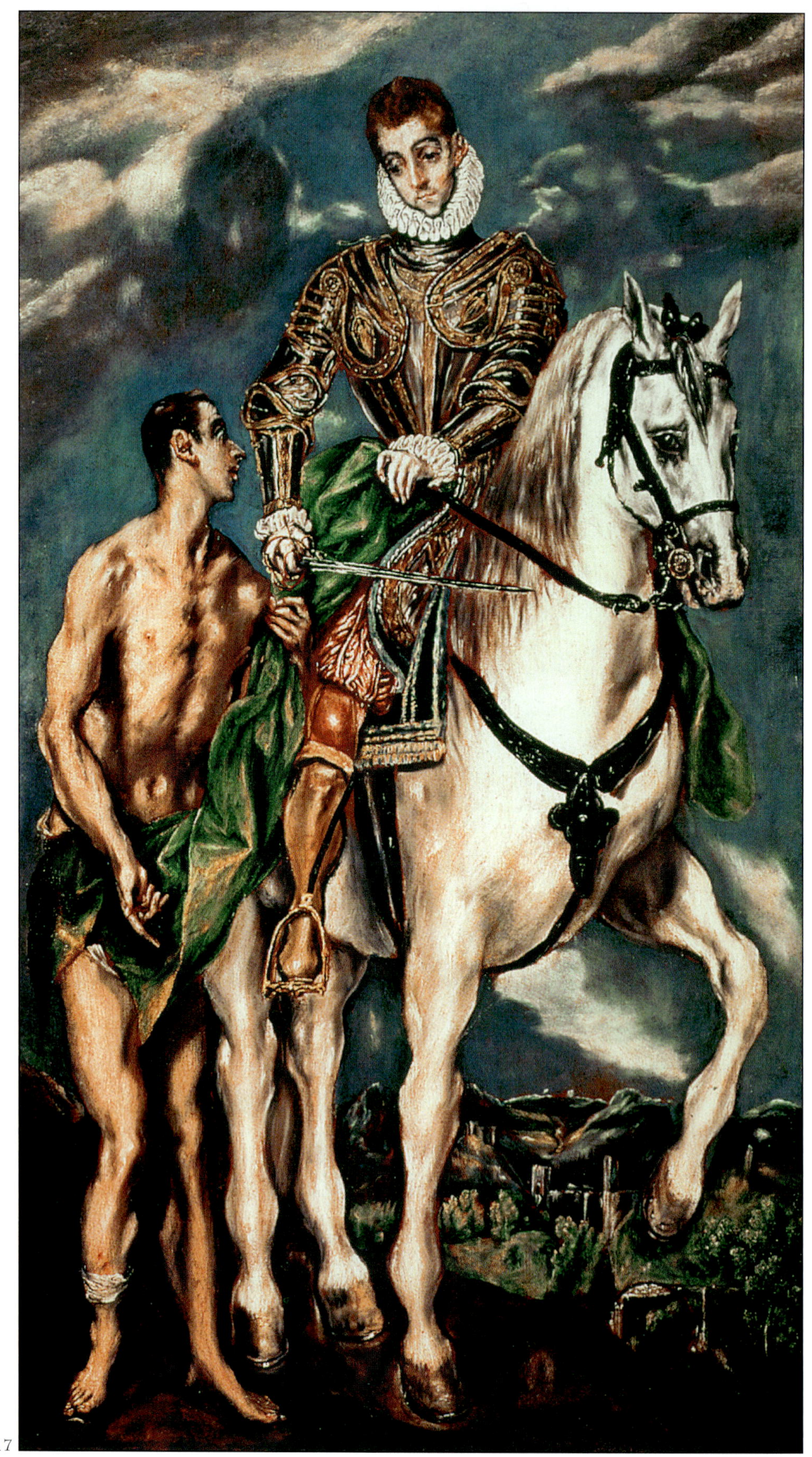

117

El Greco (1541–1614) / *St. Martin and the Beggar, 1597–99*

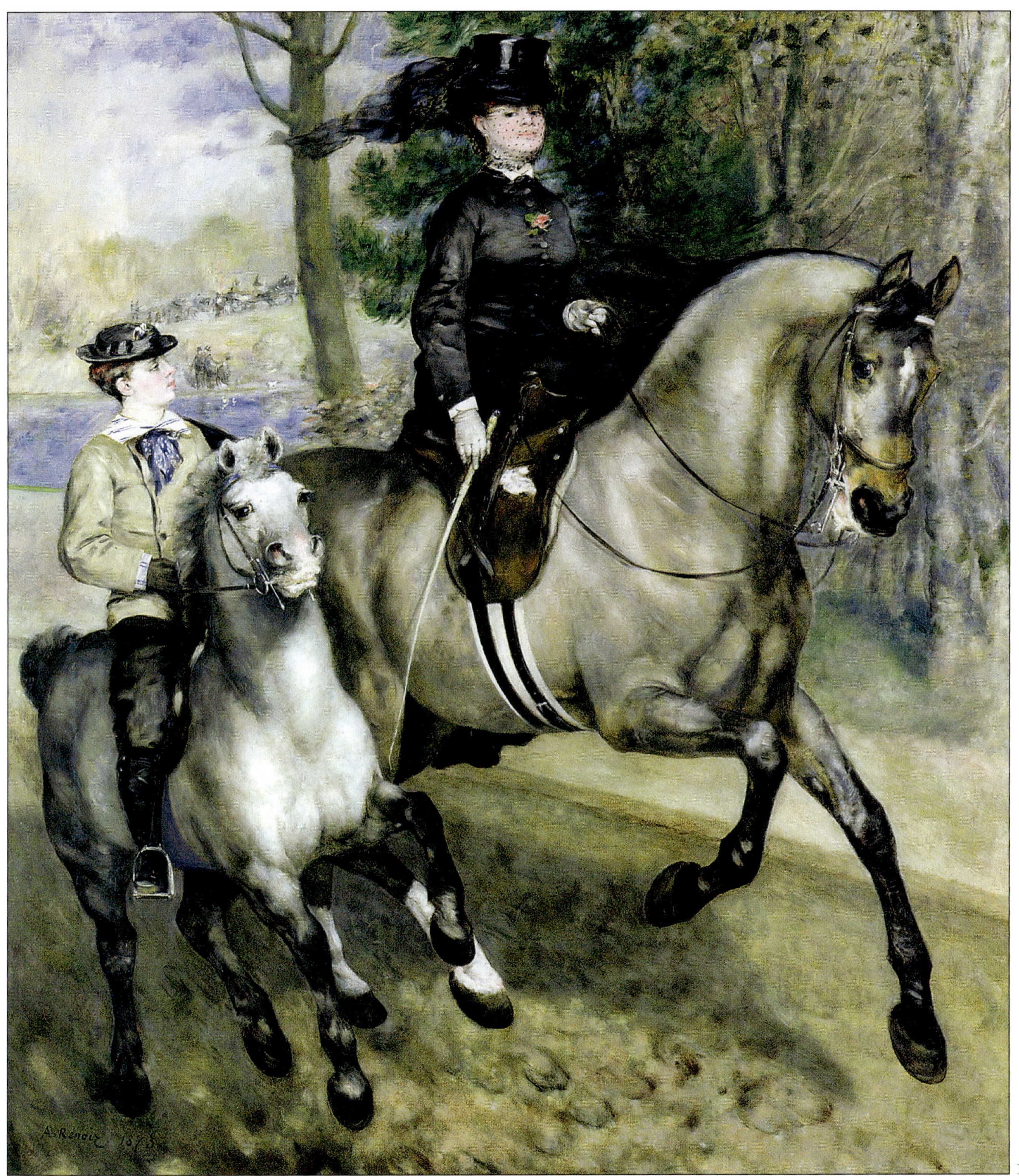

118

Pierre-Auguste Renoir (1841–1919) / *Horsewoman in the Bois de Boulogne, 1873*

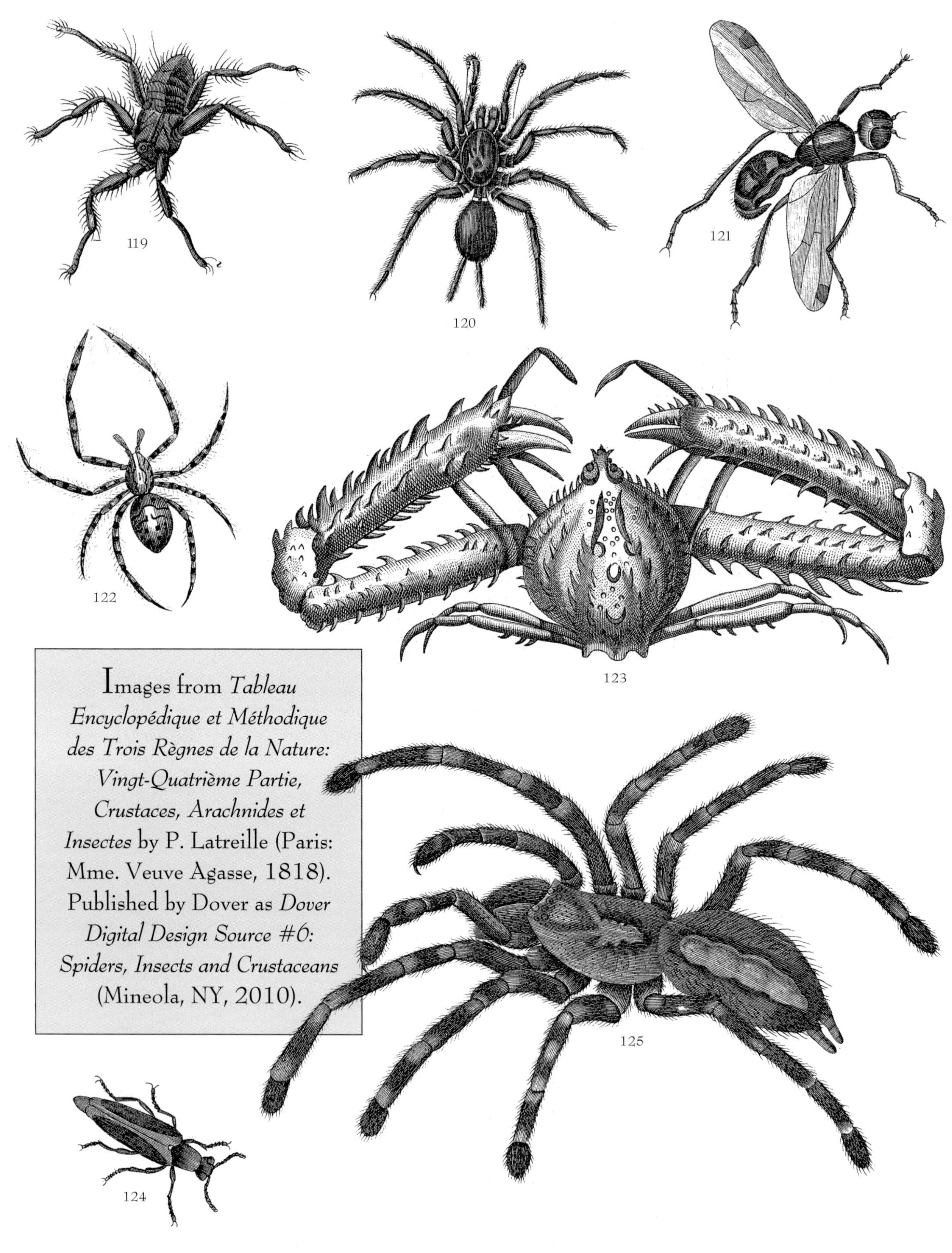

Images from *Tableau Encyclopédique et Méthodique des Trois Règnes de la Nature: Vingt-Quatrième Partie, Crustaces, Arachnides et Insectes* by P. Latreille (Paris: Mme. Veuve Agasse, 1818). Published by Dover as *Dover Digital Design Source #6: Spiders, Insects and Crustaceans* (Mineola, NY, 2010).

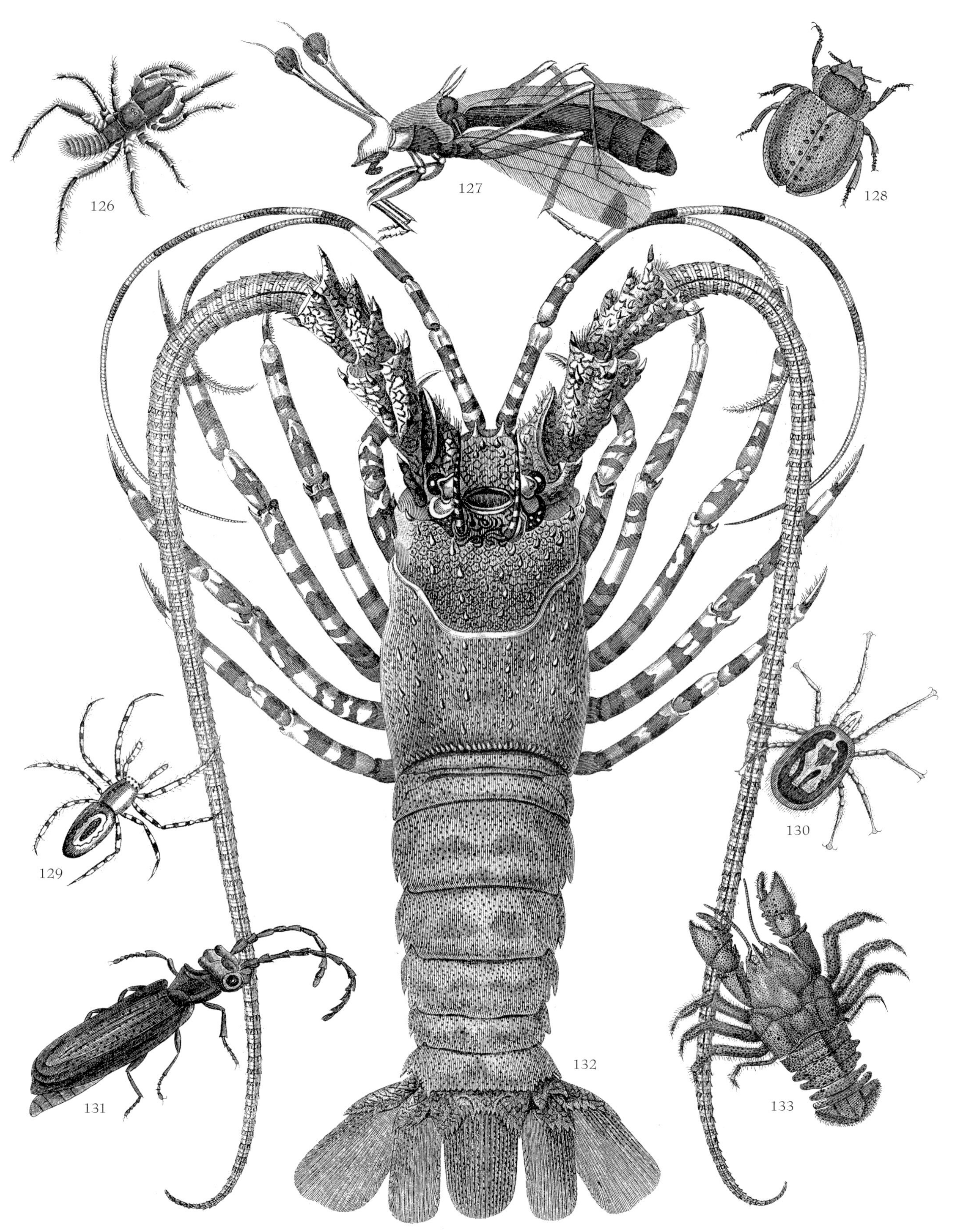
126
127
128
129
130
131
132
133

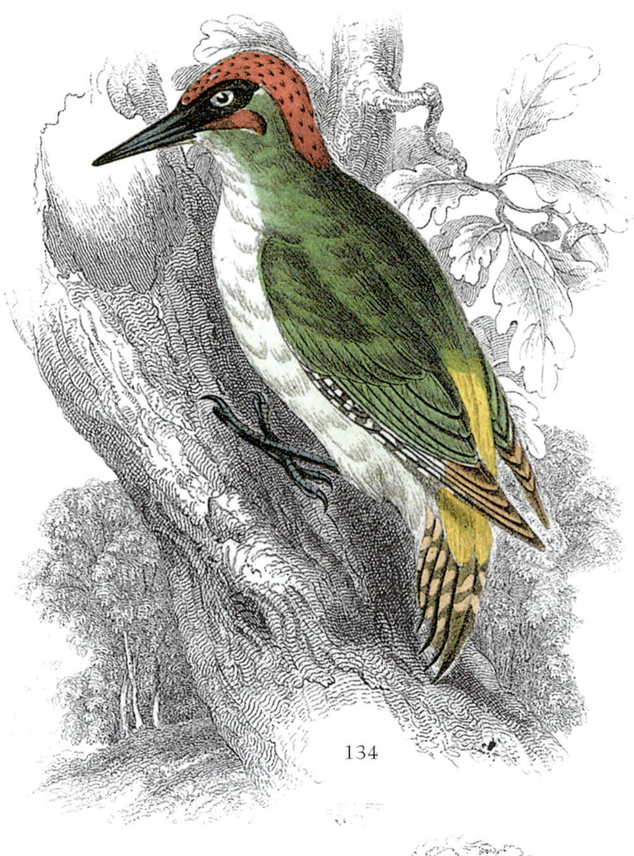

134

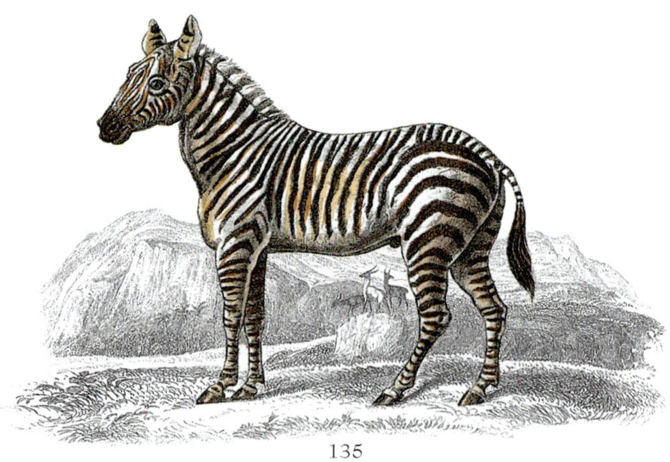

135

Images from Jardine's *"Naturalist's Library,"* 40 vols., by Sir William Jardine (Edinburgh: W. H. Lizars, 1833–45). A selection of illustrations published by Dover as *286 Full-Color Animal Illustrations from Jardine's "Naturalist's Library"* (Mineola, NY, 1999).

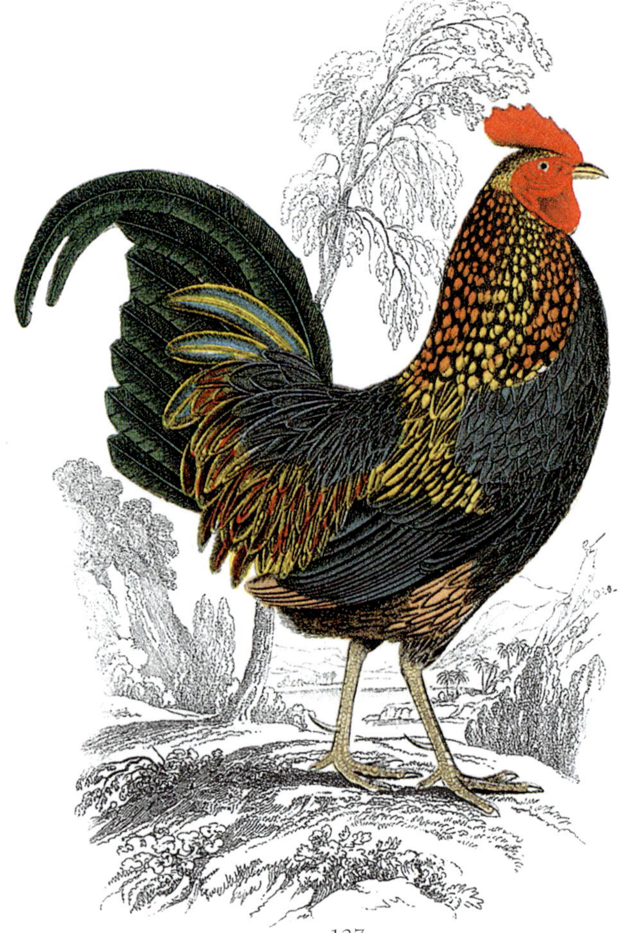

137

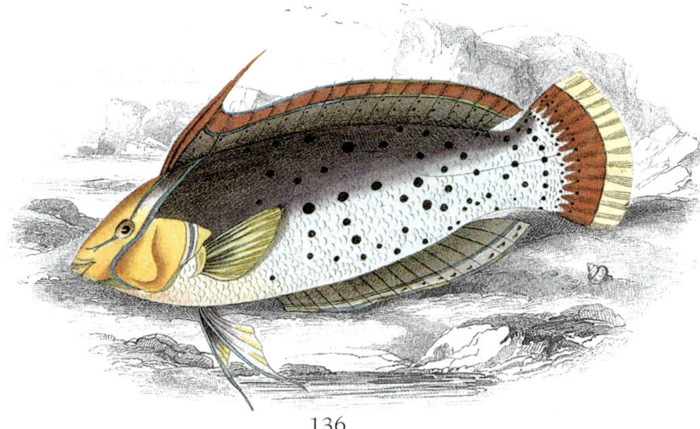

136

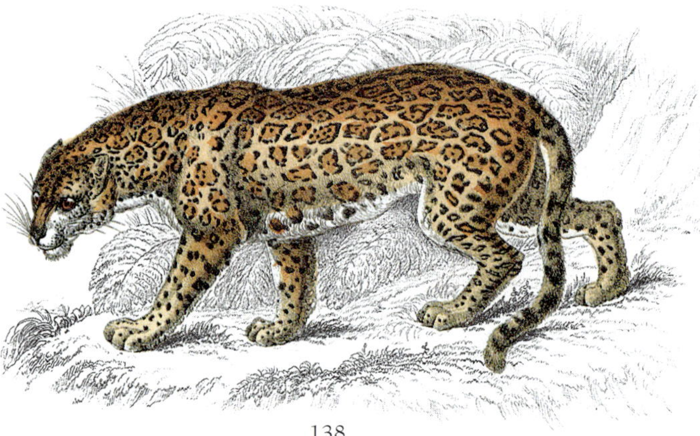

138

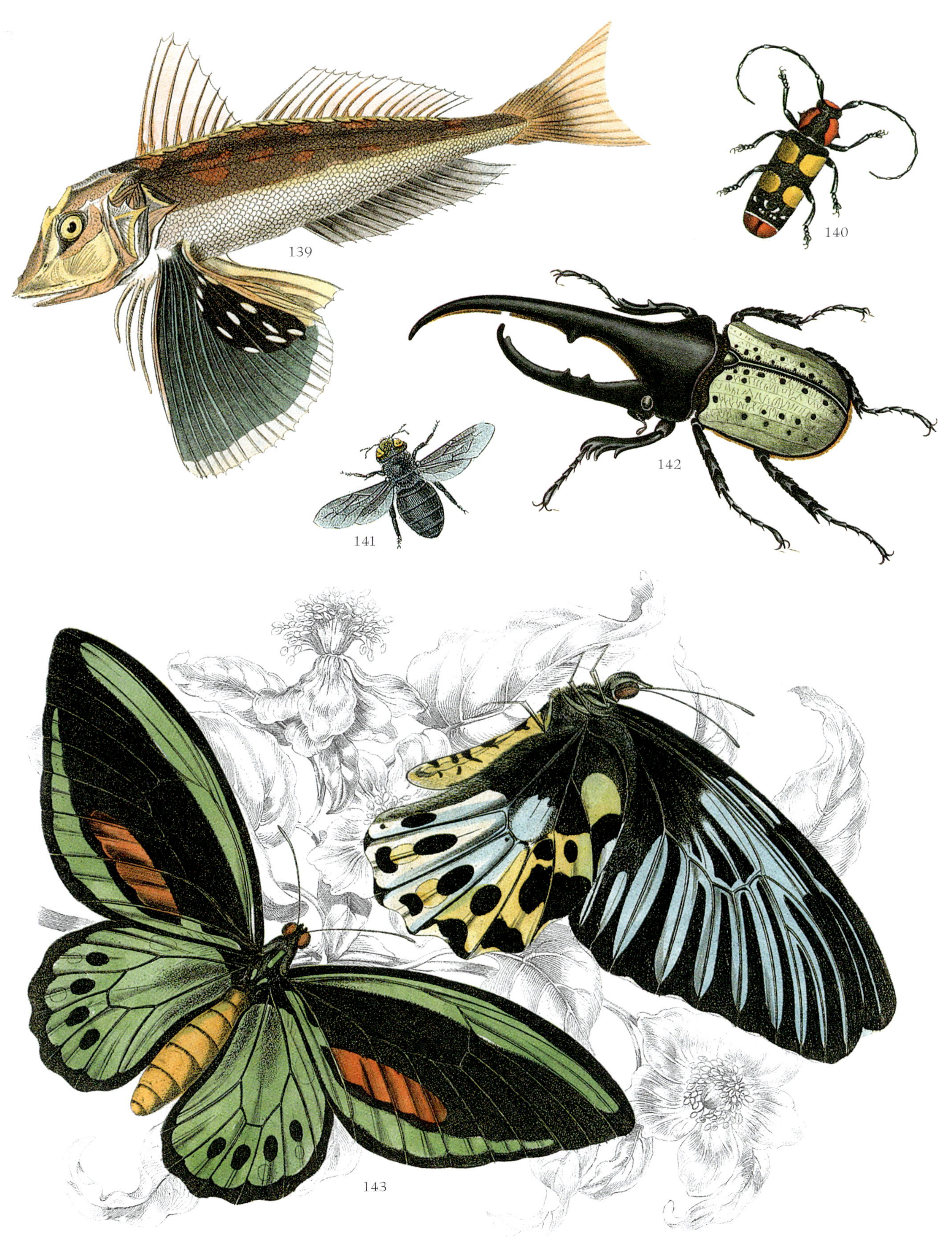
139
140
142
141
143

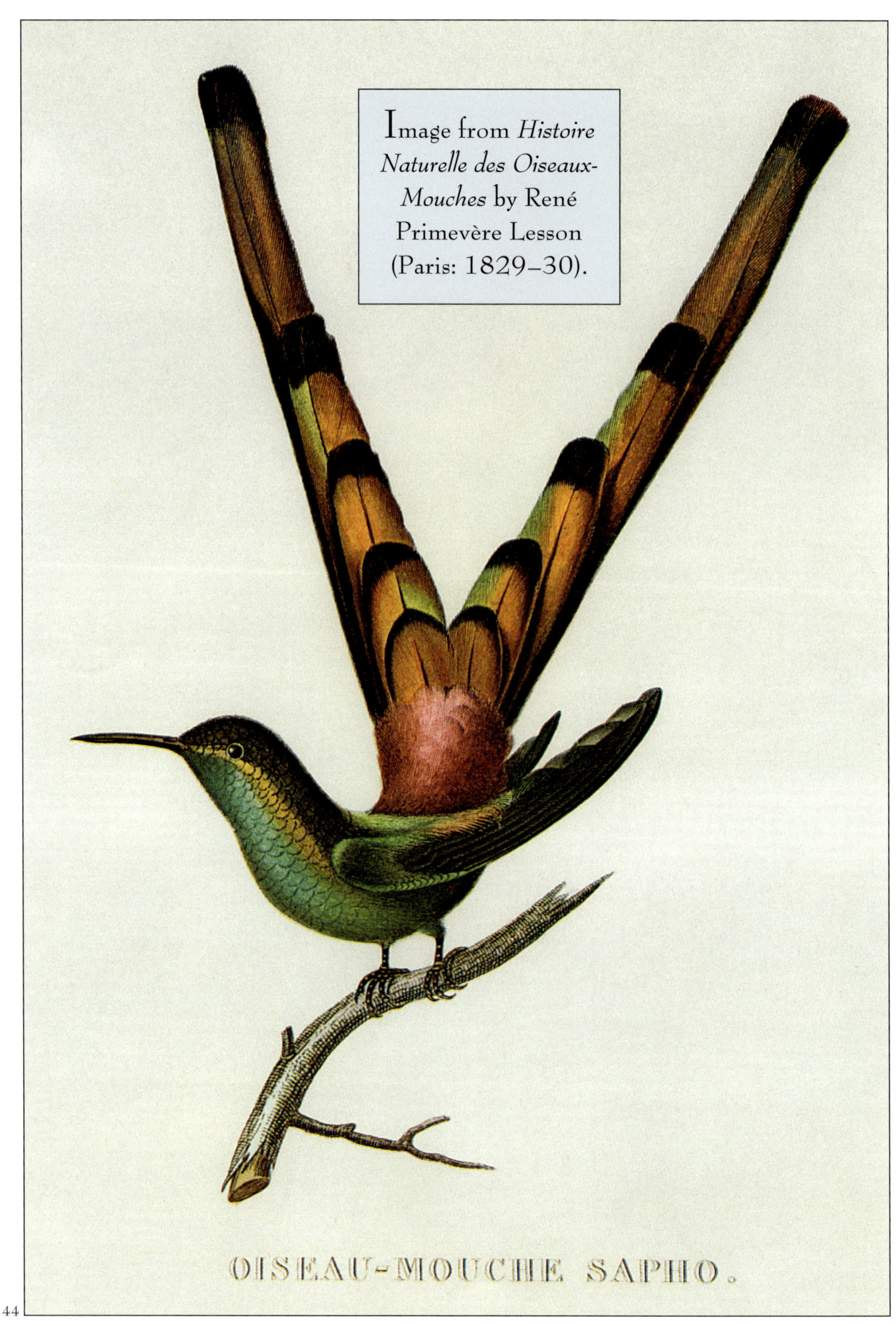
Image from *Histoire Naturelle des Oiseaux-Mouches* by René Primevère Lesson (Paris: 1829–30).
OISEAU-MOUCHE SAPHO.
144

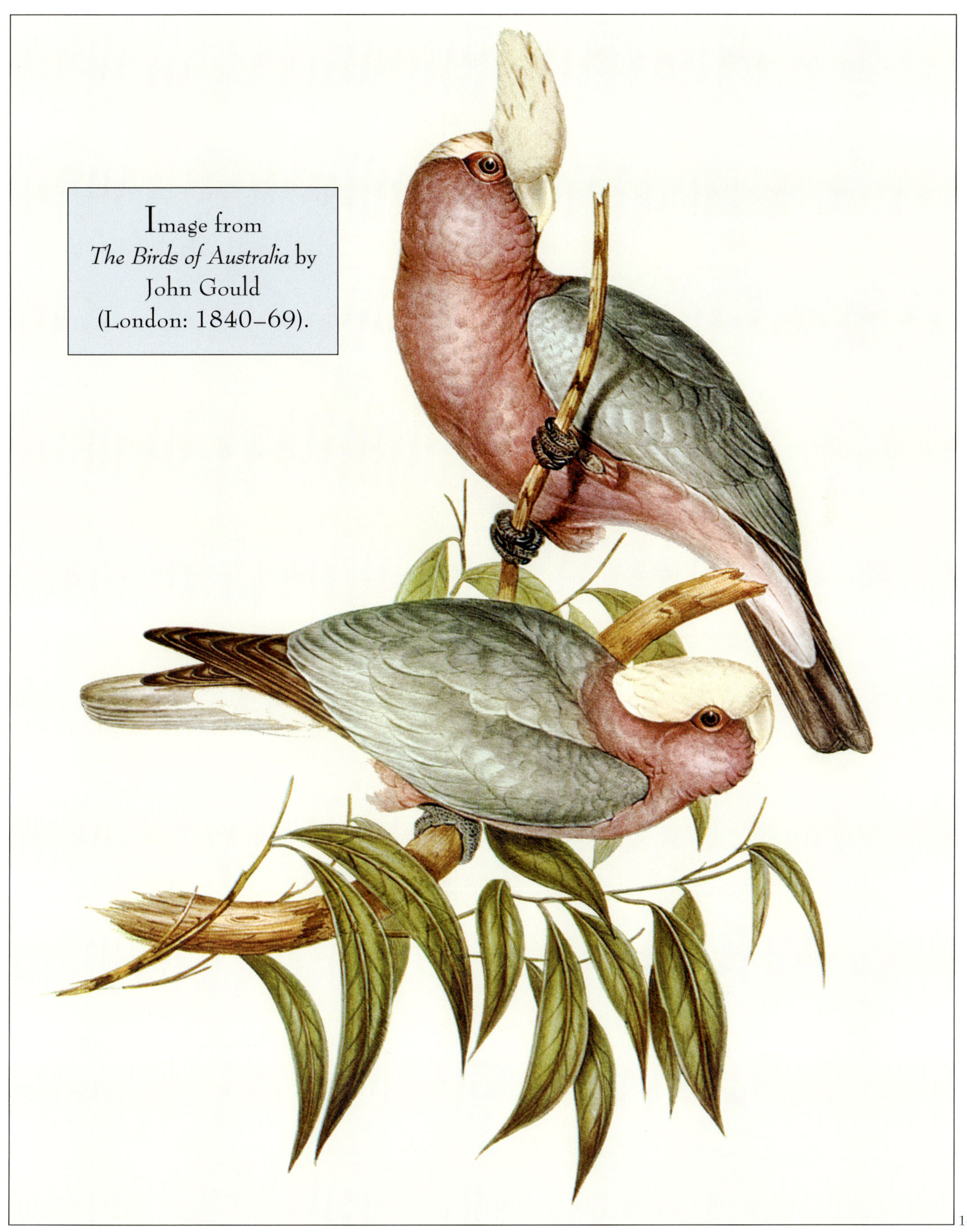

Image from
The Birds of Australia by
John Gould
(London: 1840–69).

145

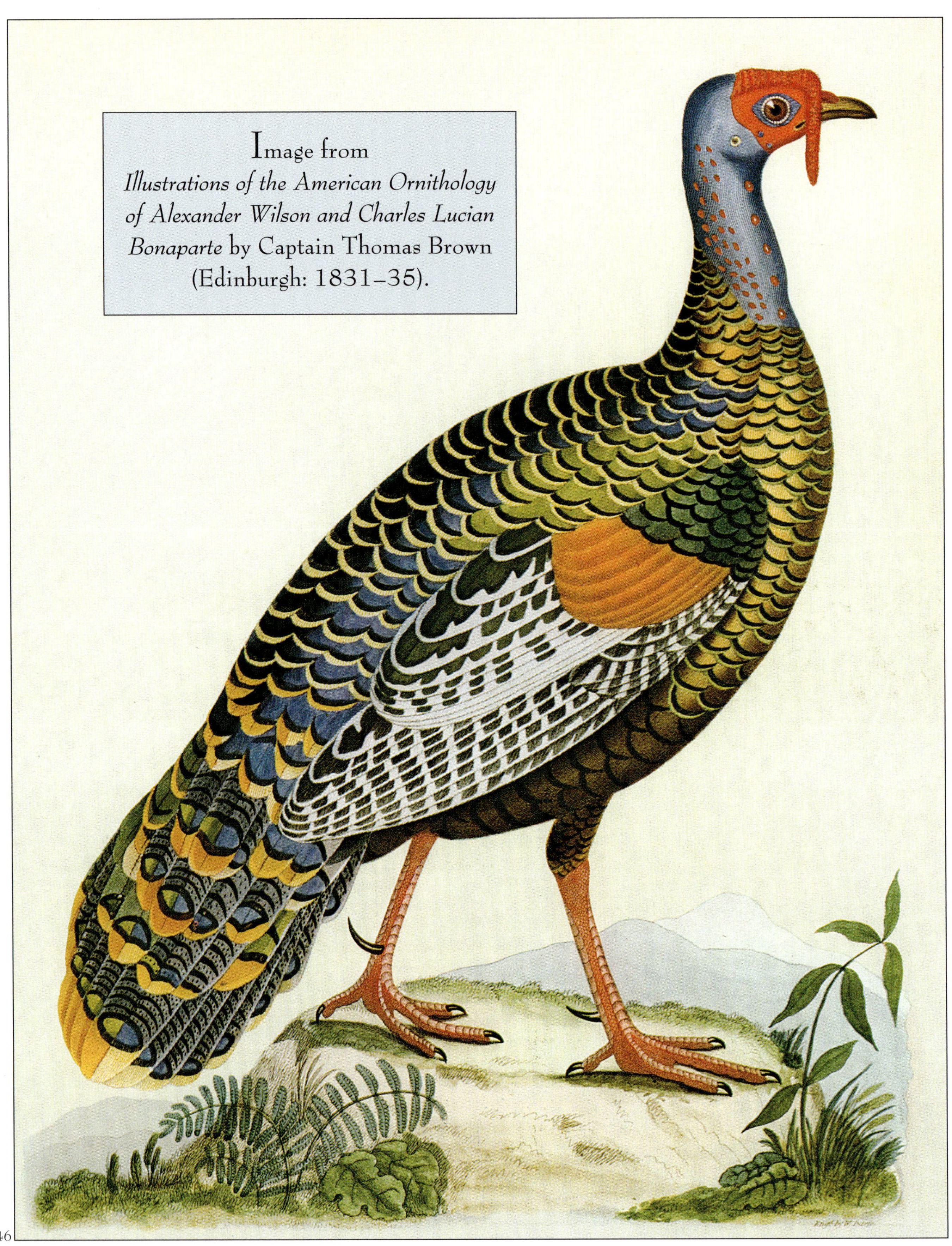

Image from
Illustrations of the American Ornithology of Alexander Wilson and Charles Lucian Bonaparte by Captain Thomas Brown (Edinburgh: 1831–35).

146

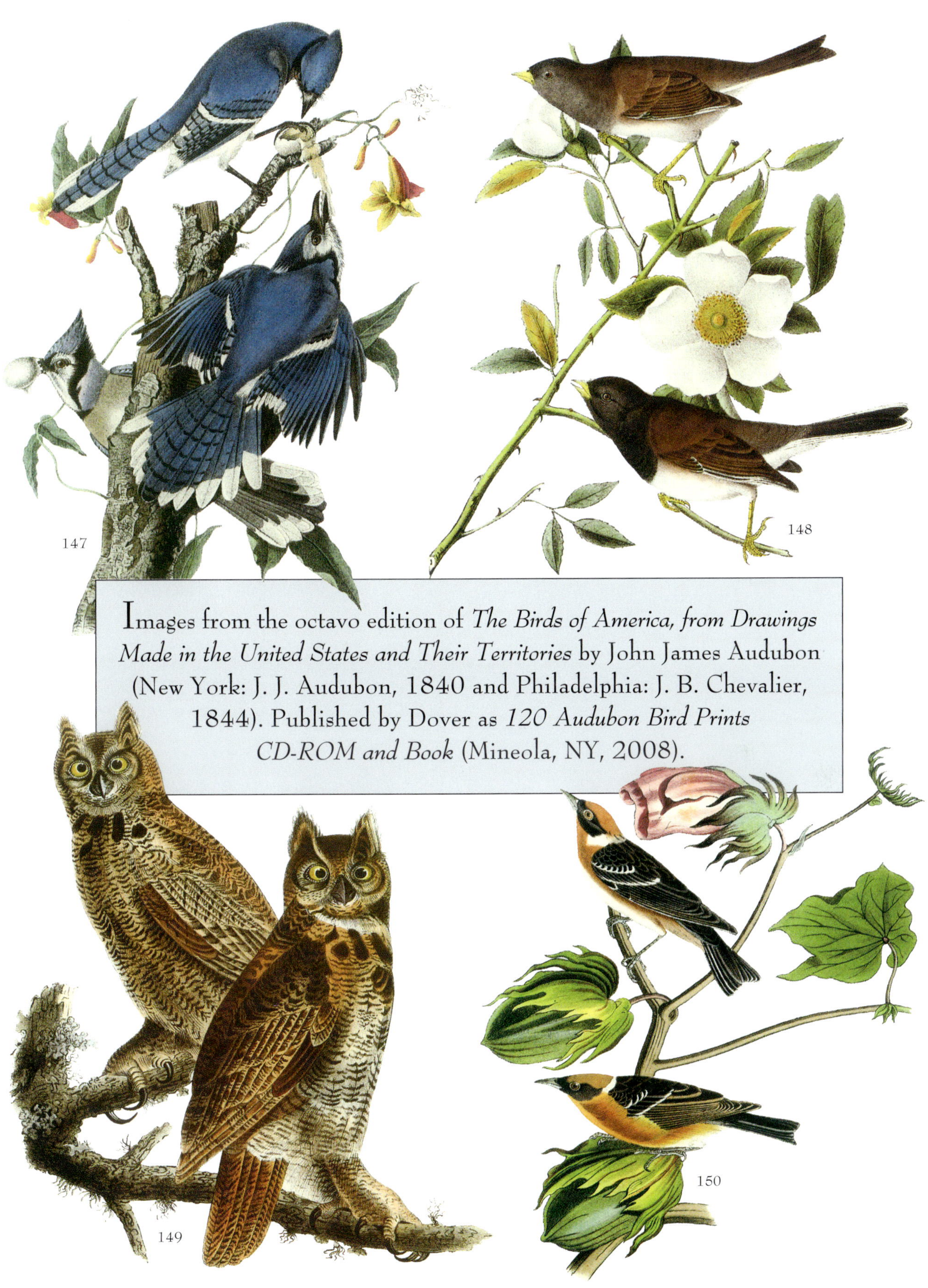

Images from the octavo edition of *The Birds of America, from Drawings Made in the United States and Their Territories* by John James Audubon (New York: J. J. Audubon, 1840 and Philadelphia: J. B. Chevalier, 1844). Published by Dover as *120 Audubon Bird Prints CD-ROM and Book* (Mineola, NY, 2008).

151

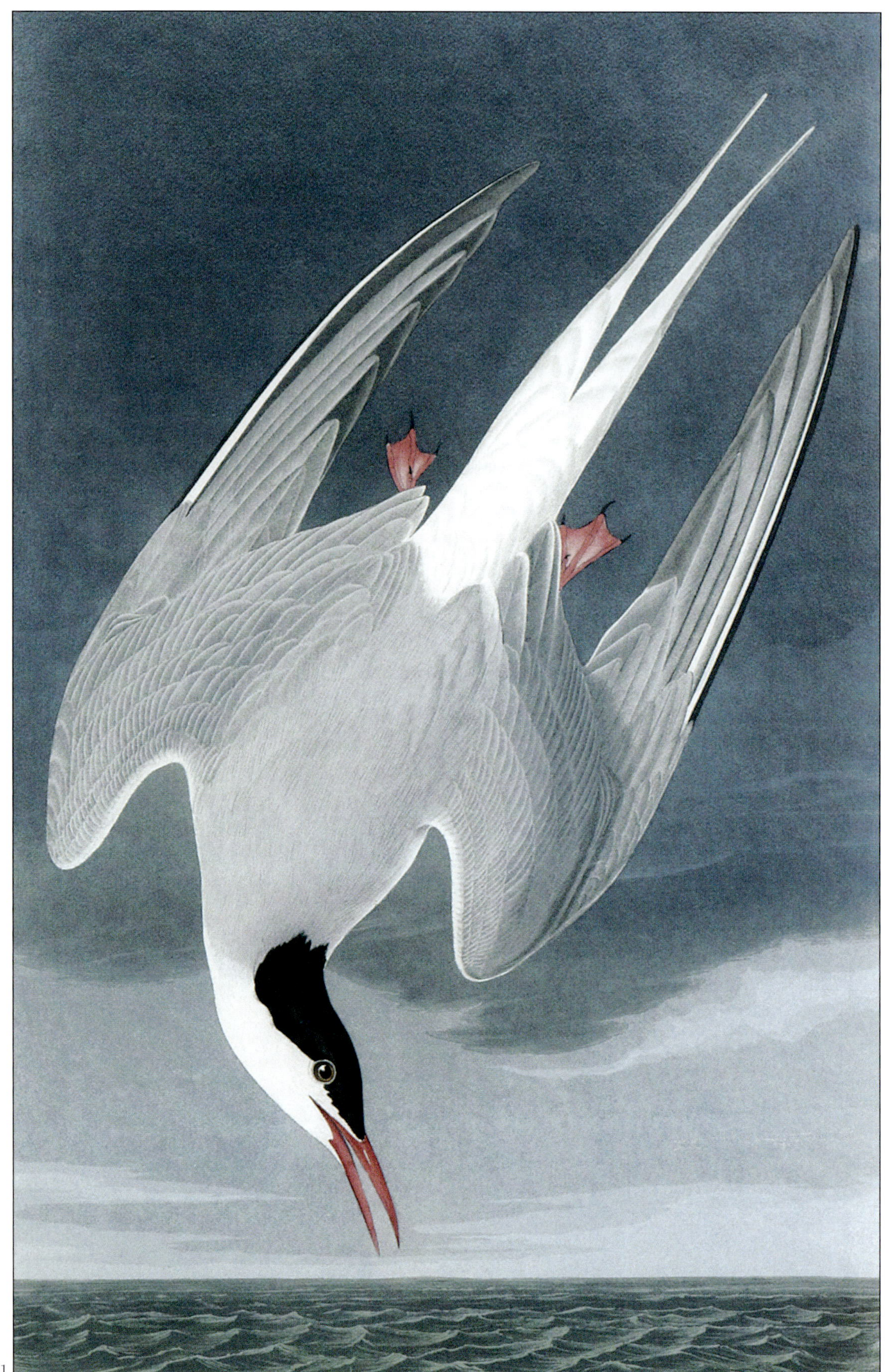

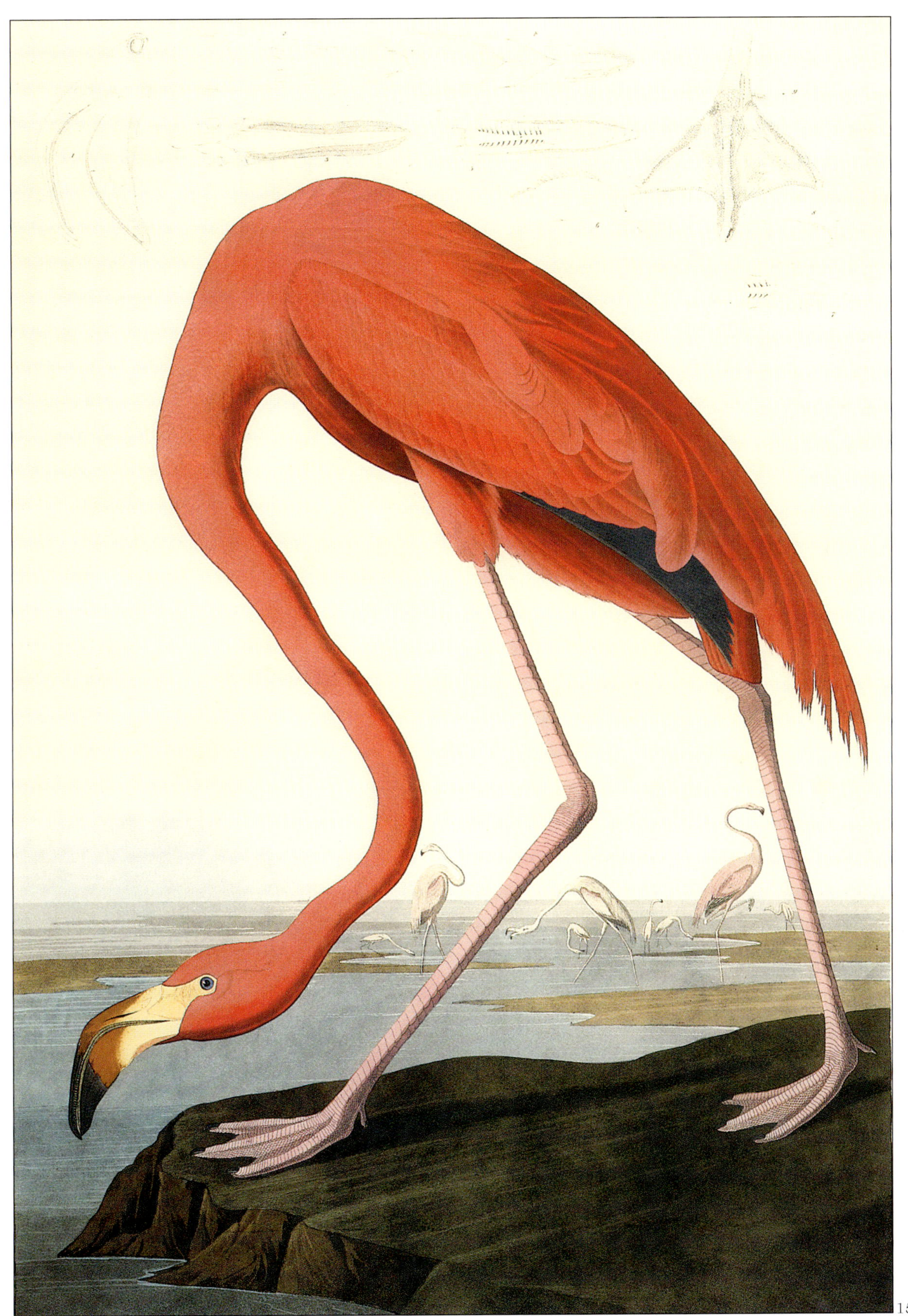

152

153

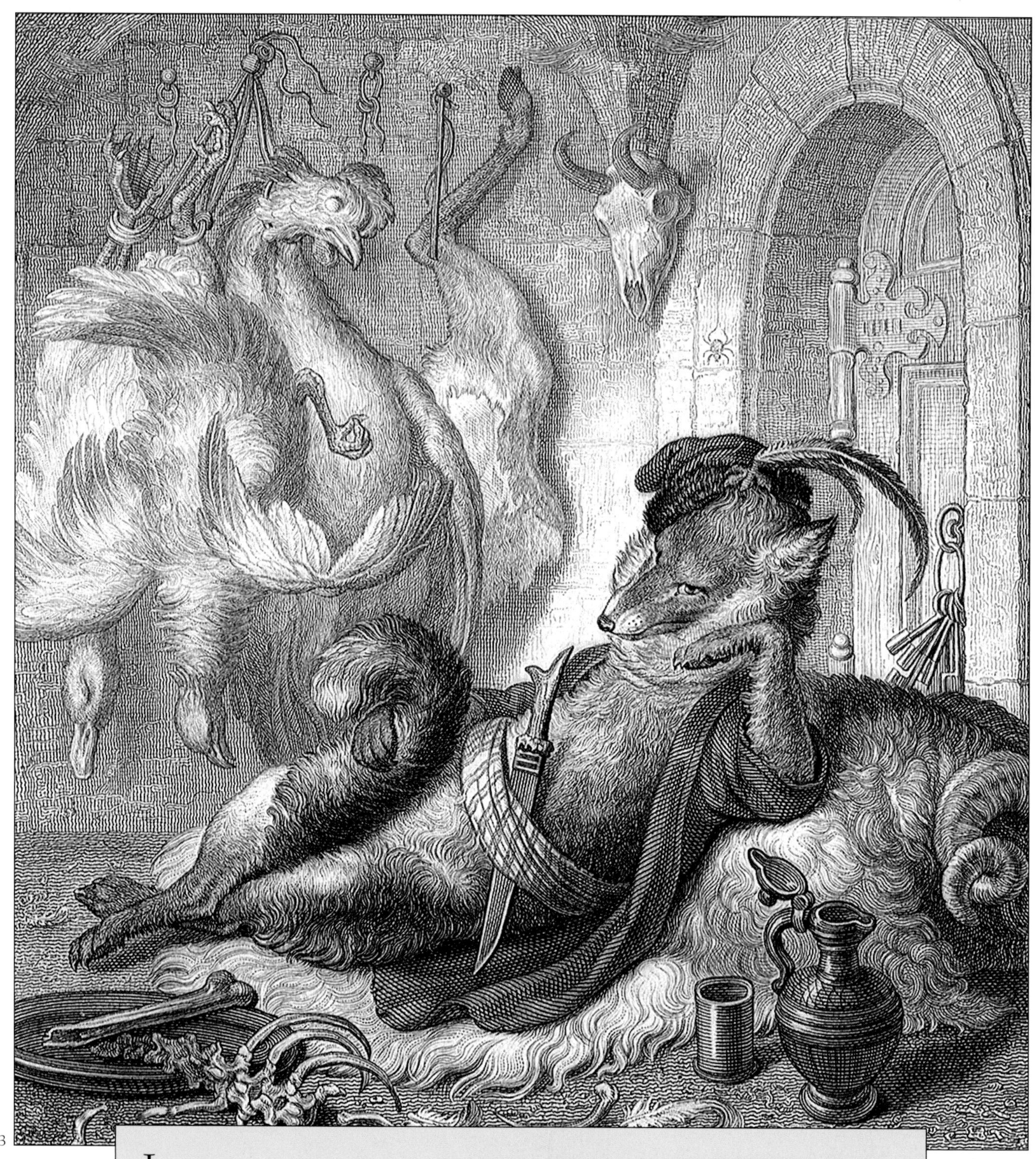

Images from *Reynard the Fox* by Wolfgang von Goethe, with drawings by Wilhelm von Kaulbach, engraved by R. Rahn and A. Schleich (Stuttgart and Tubingen: Cotta, 1846). Available online at DoverPictura.com.

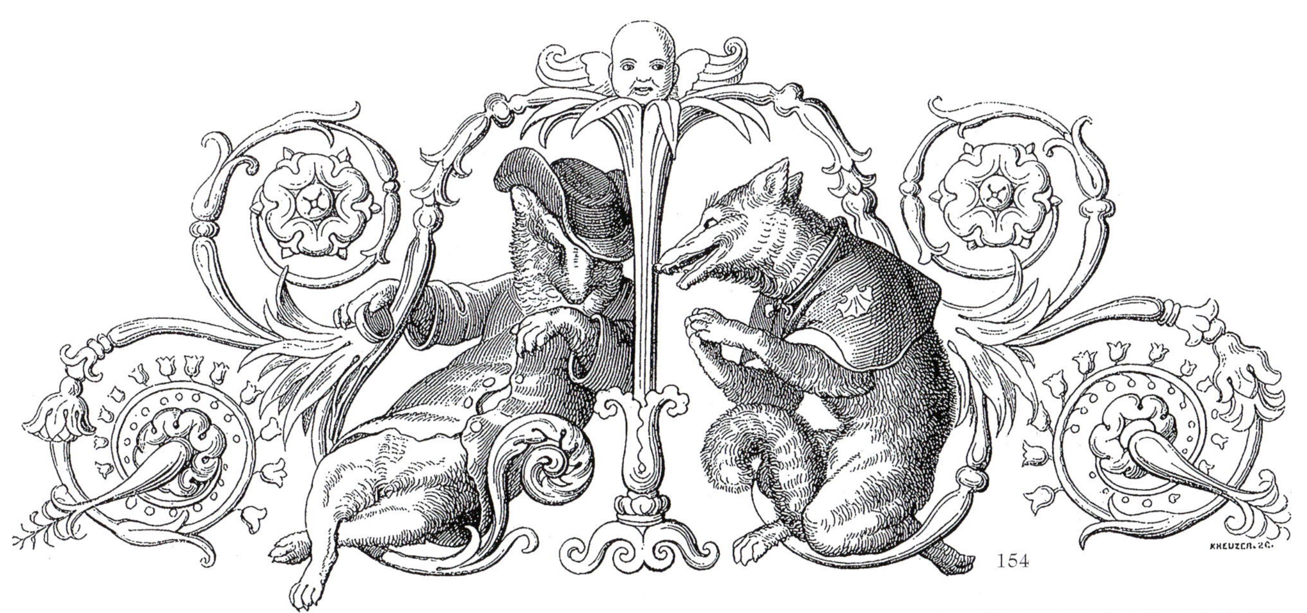

154

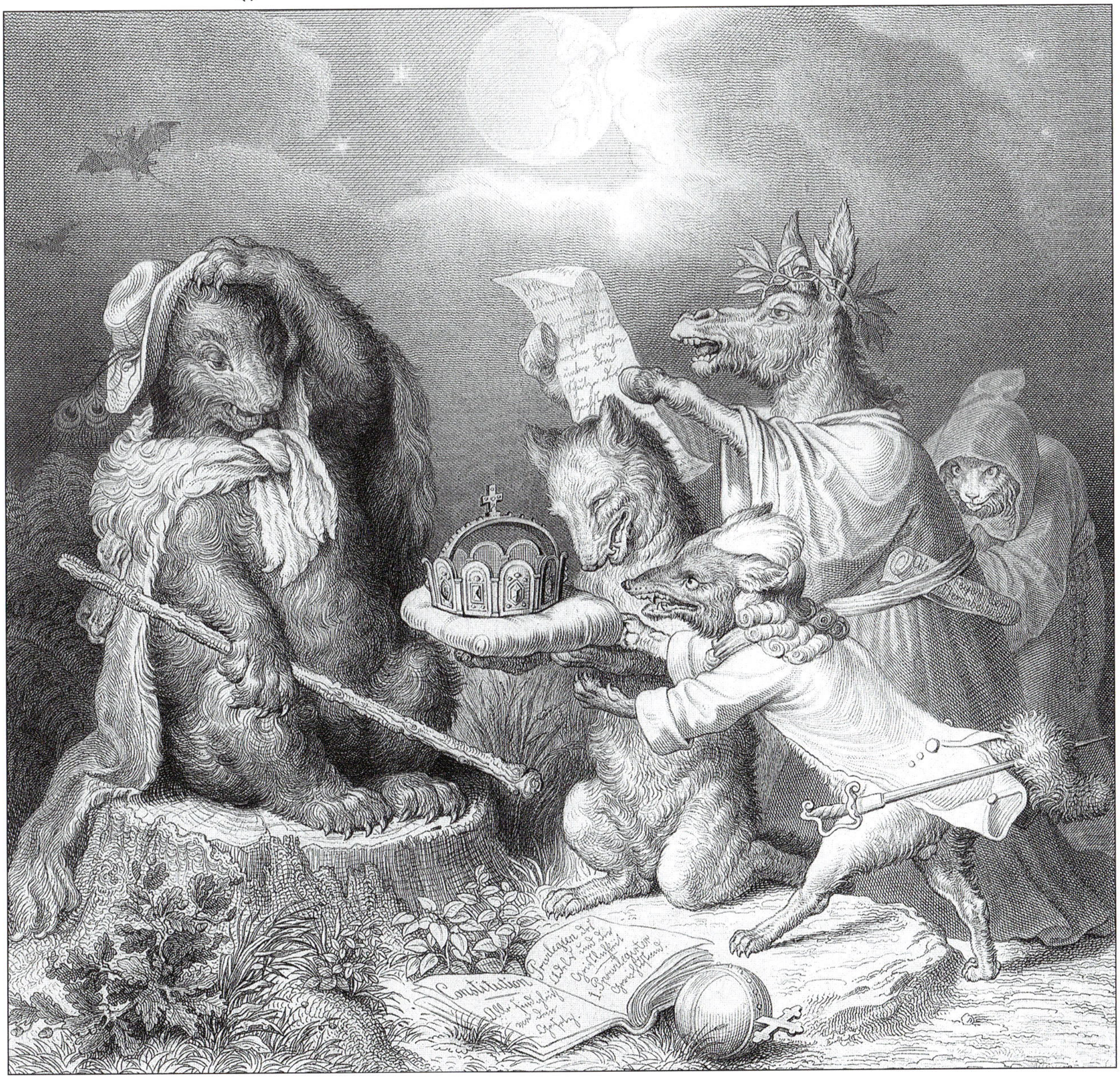

155

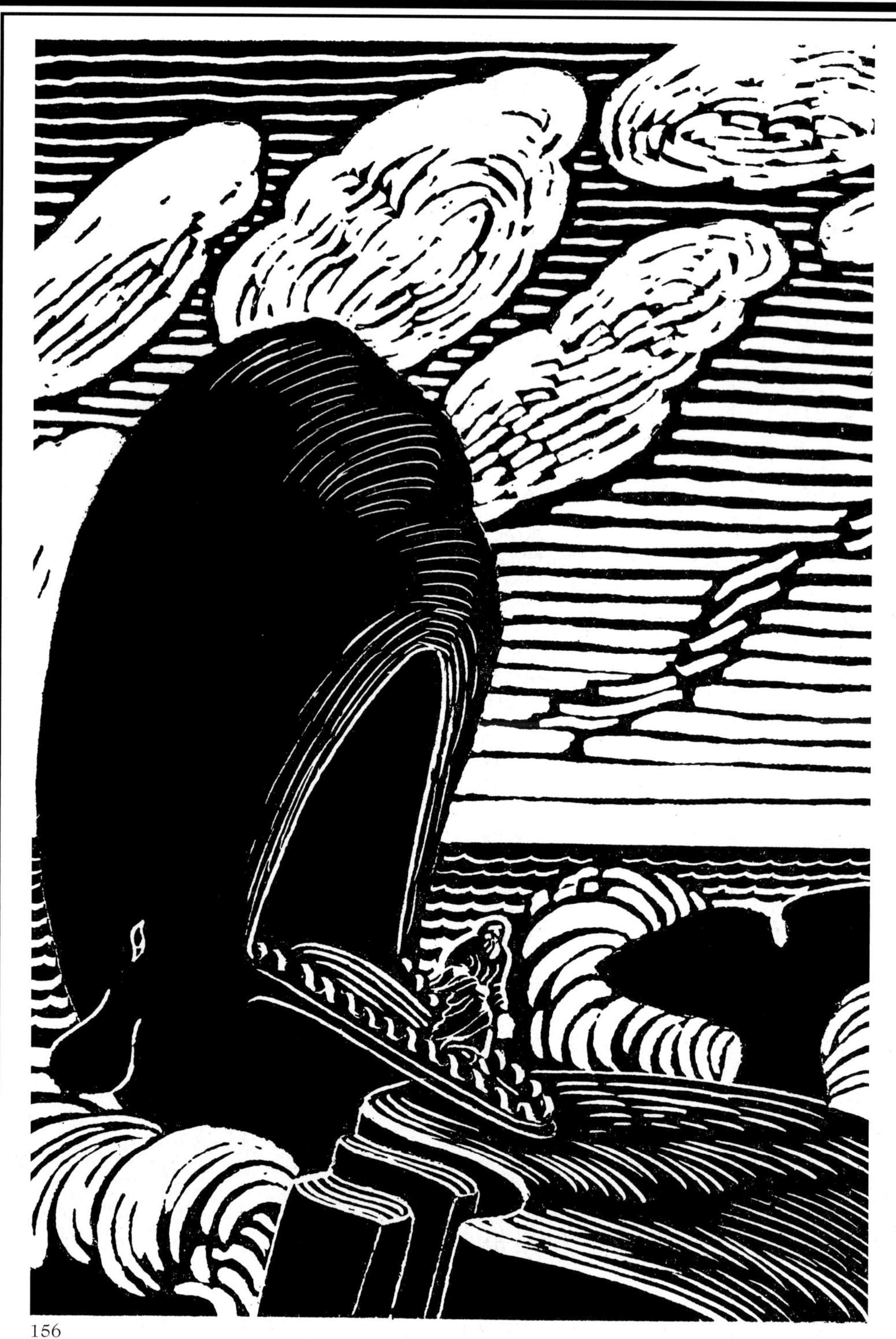

156

Images from *Moby-Dick, or, The Whale* by Herman Melville (New York: Harper and Brothers, 1851). Published by Dover as a *Calla Edition* in 2015, with all of the artwork by Raymond Bishop from the edition published by Albert & Charles Boni, Inc., New York, in 1933.

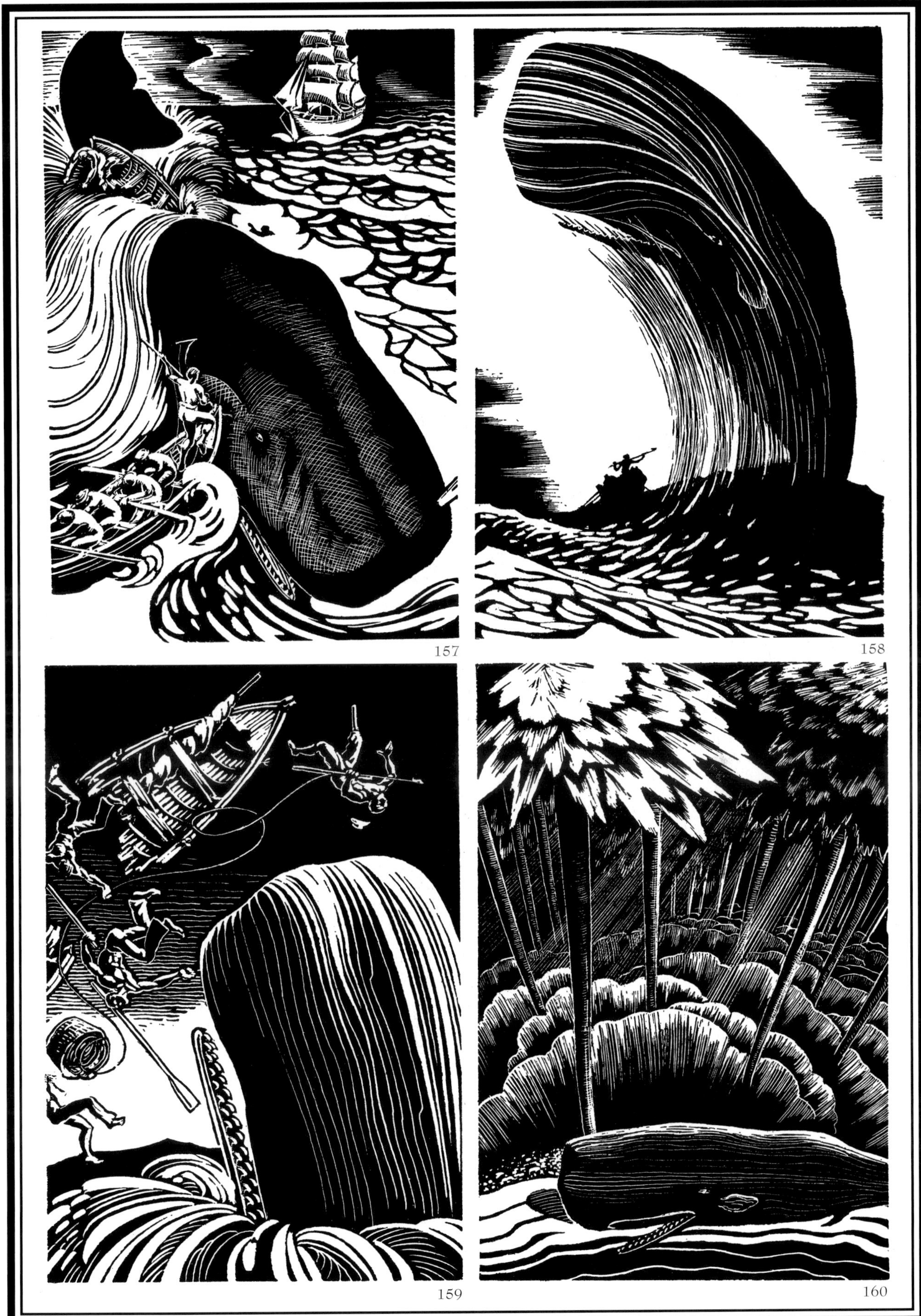

157

158

159

160

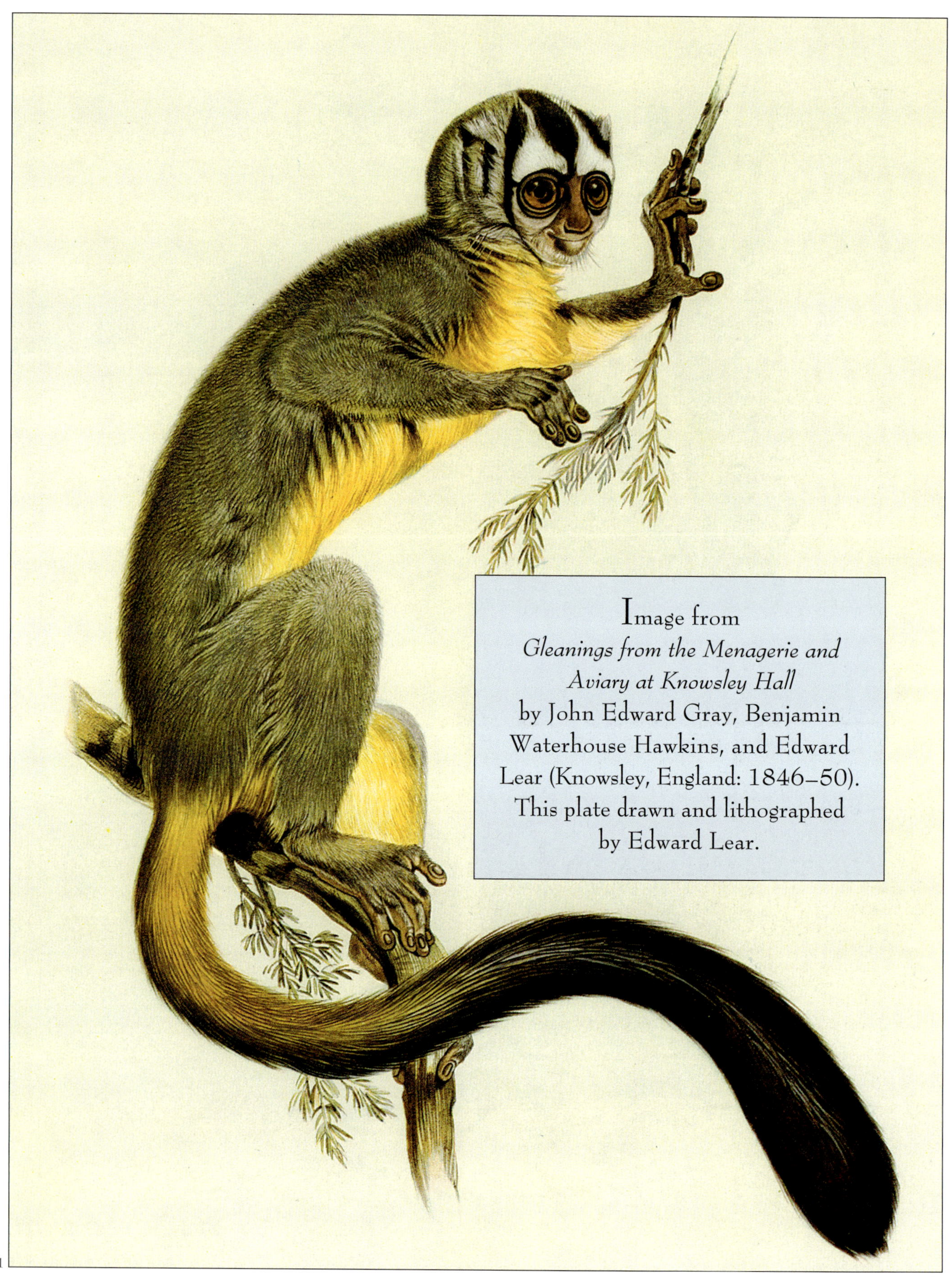

Image from
Gleanings from the Menagerie and Aviary at Knowsley Hall
by John Edward Gray, Benjamin Waterhouse Hawkins, and Edward Lear (Knowsley, England: 1846–50).
This plate drawn and lithographed by Edward Lear.

161

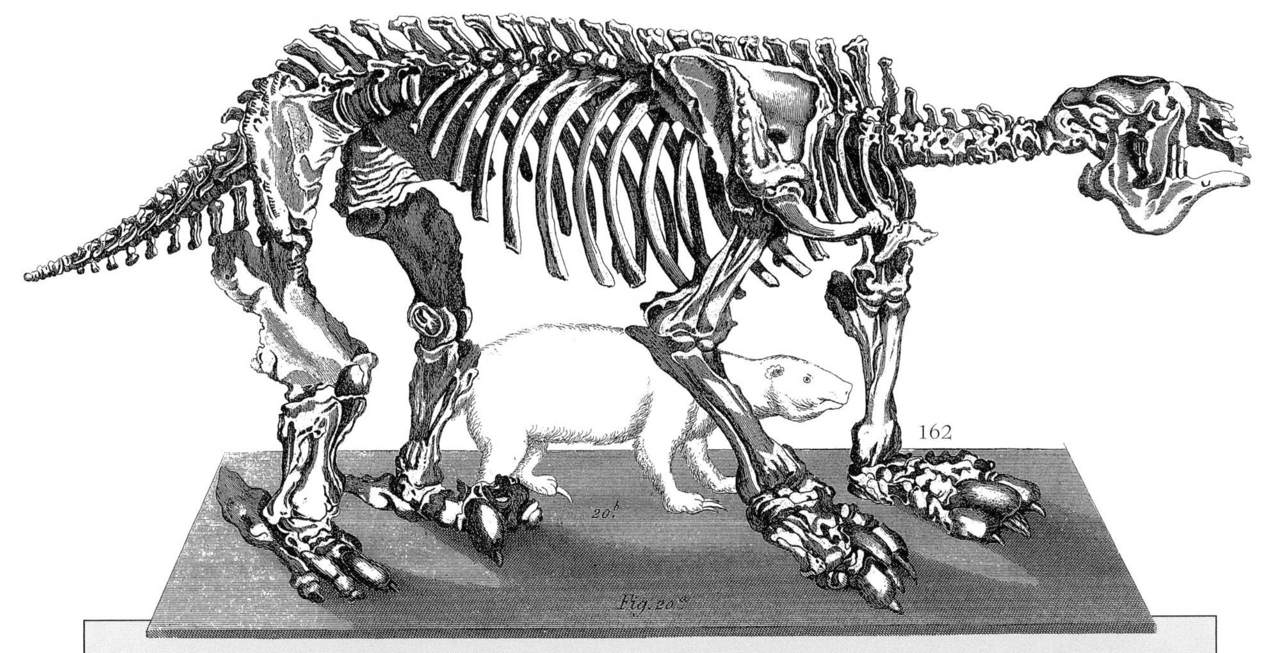

162

Images from a selection of engravings from *Iconographic Encyclopaedia of Science, Literature, and Art,* which was a translation of J. G. Heck's *Bilder-Atlas zum Conversations-Lexikon.* Illustrated by Five Hundred Steel Plates, Containing Upwards of Twelve Thousand Engravings (New York: Rudolph Garrigue, 1851). Reprinted by Dover as *Heck's Pictorial Archive of Nature and Science* (Mineola, NY, 1994).

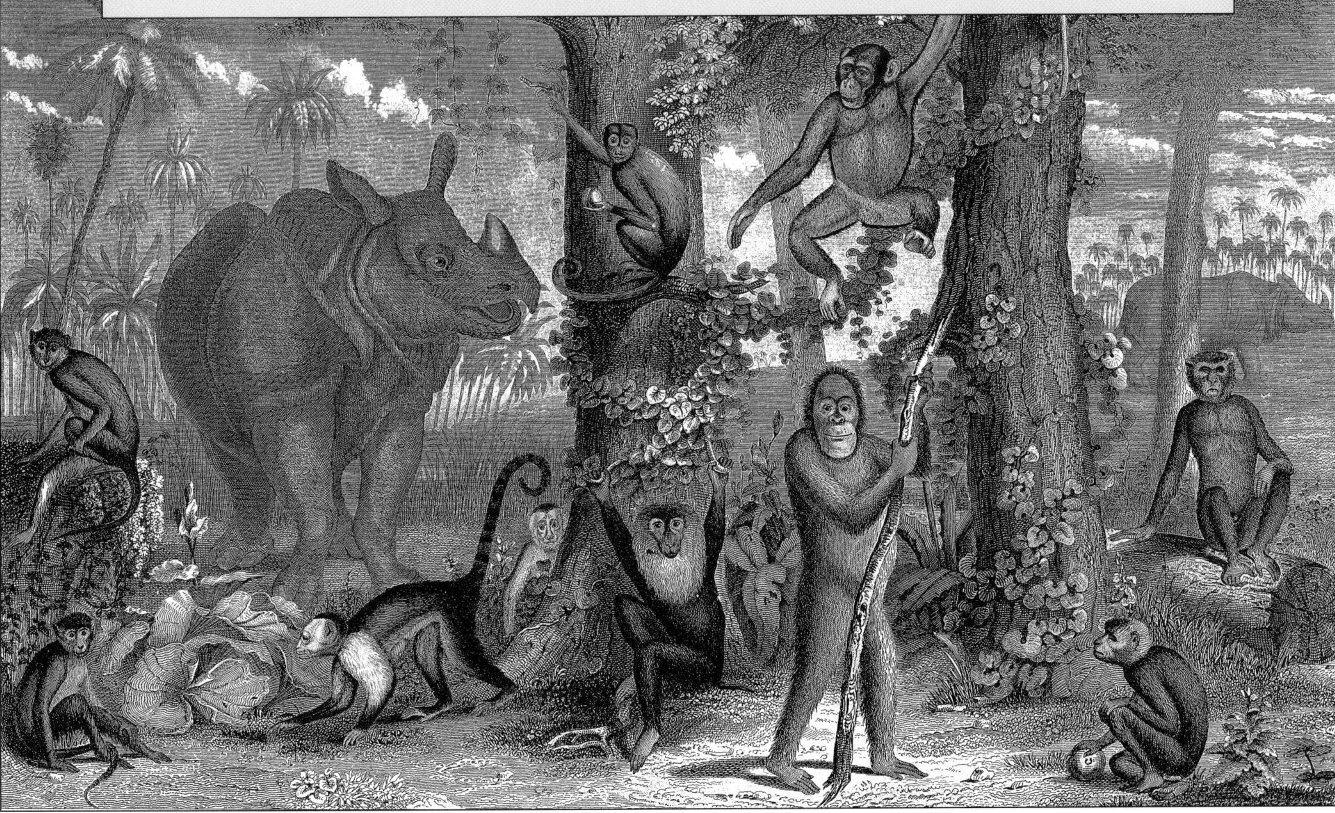

163

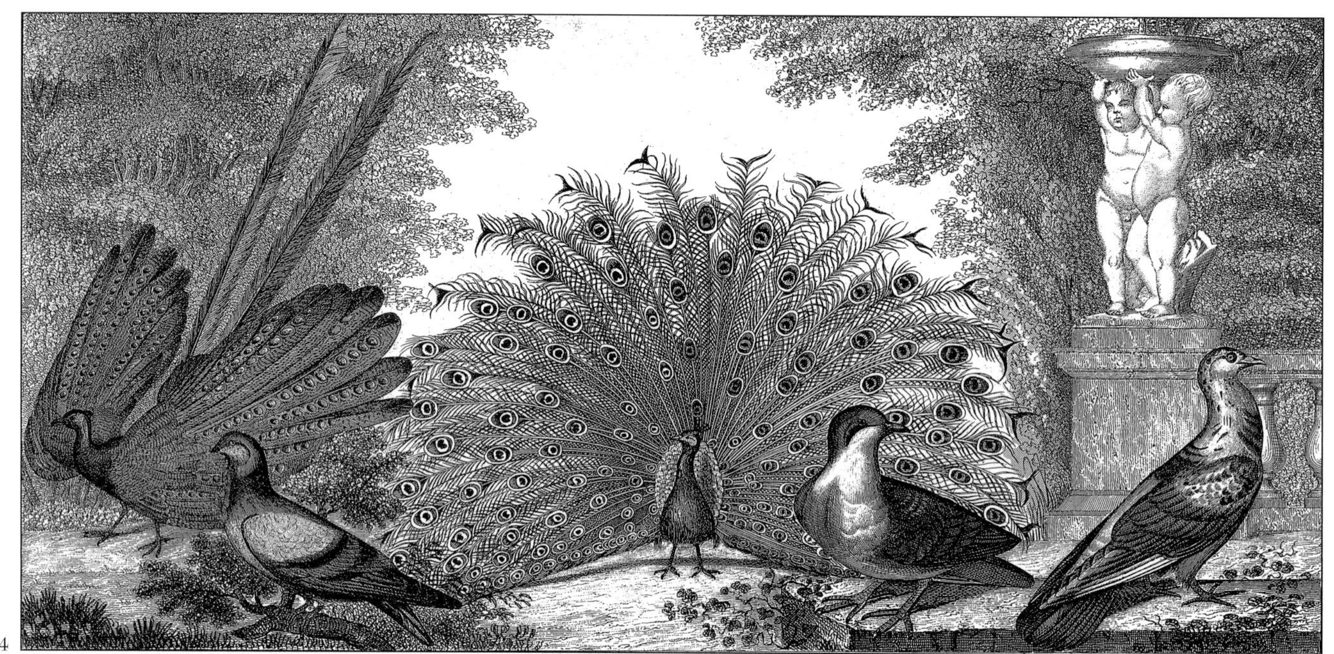
164

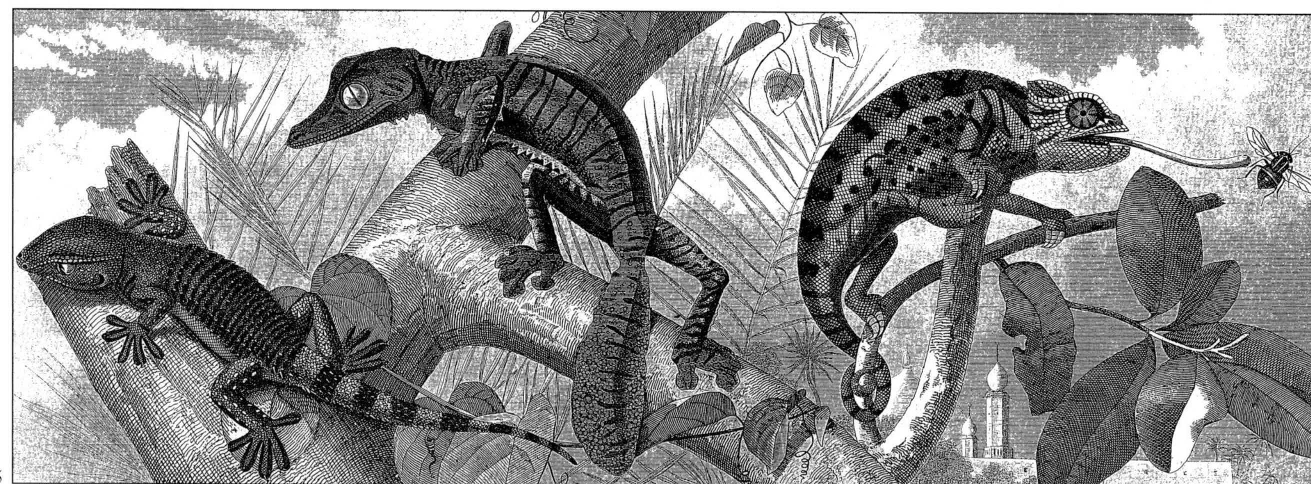
165

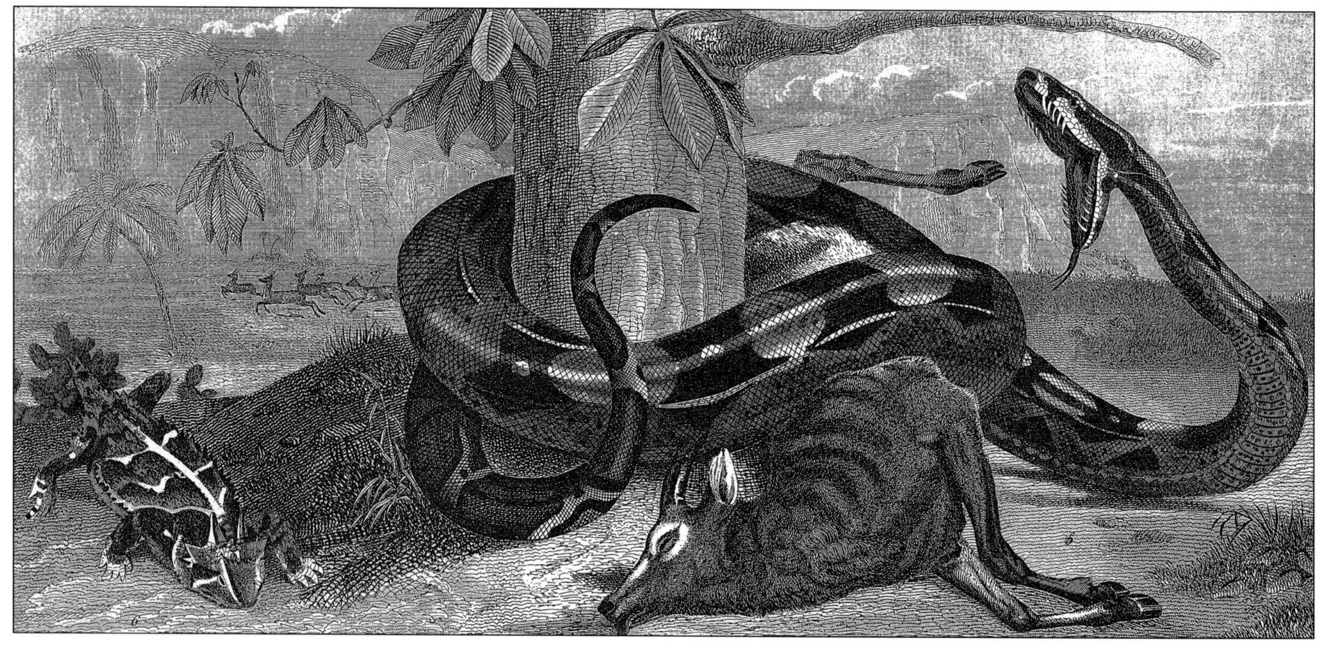
166

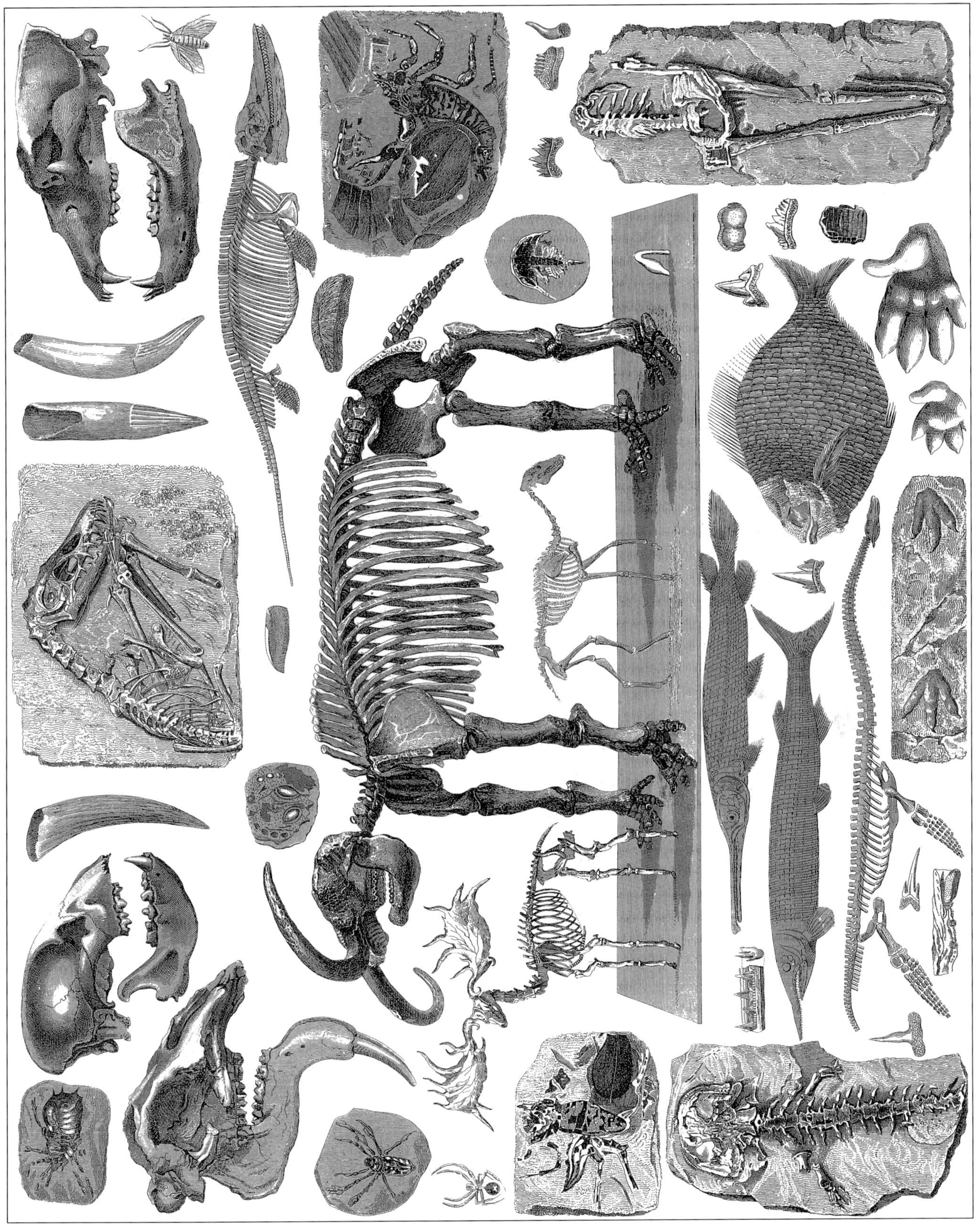

168

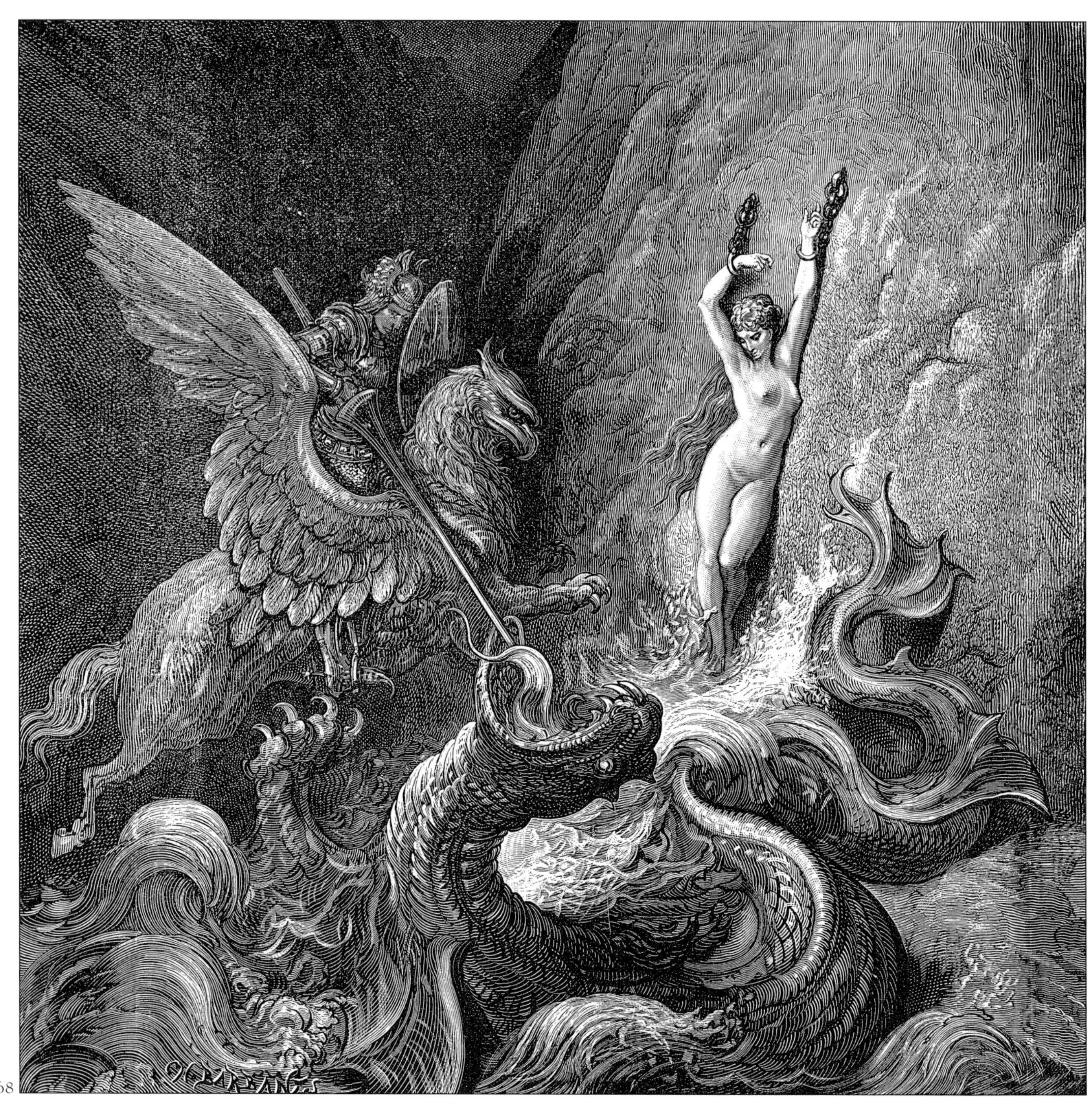

Images from various works illustrated by Gustave Doré, including *Oeuvres de François Rabelais, or Gargantua and Pantagruel* (Paris: J. Bry Ainé, 1854), *Orlando Furioso* by Lodovico Ariosto (Milan: Treves, 1881), and *Fables de la Fontaine* by Jean de la Fontaine (Paris: Hachette, 1868). Published by Dover as *Doré's Dragons, Demons and Monsters* by Gustave Doré, edited by Carol Belanger Grafton (Mineola, NY, 2006).

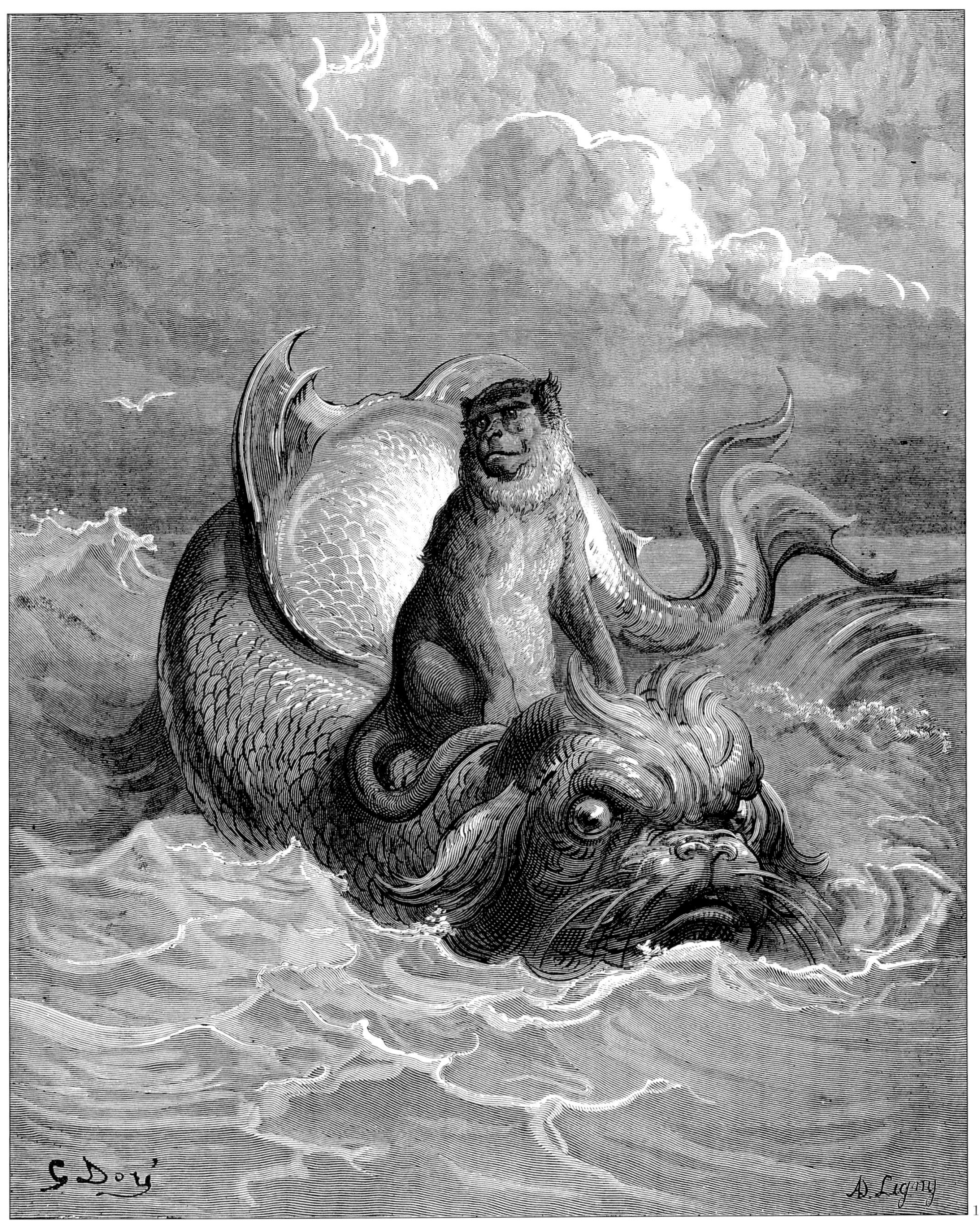

169

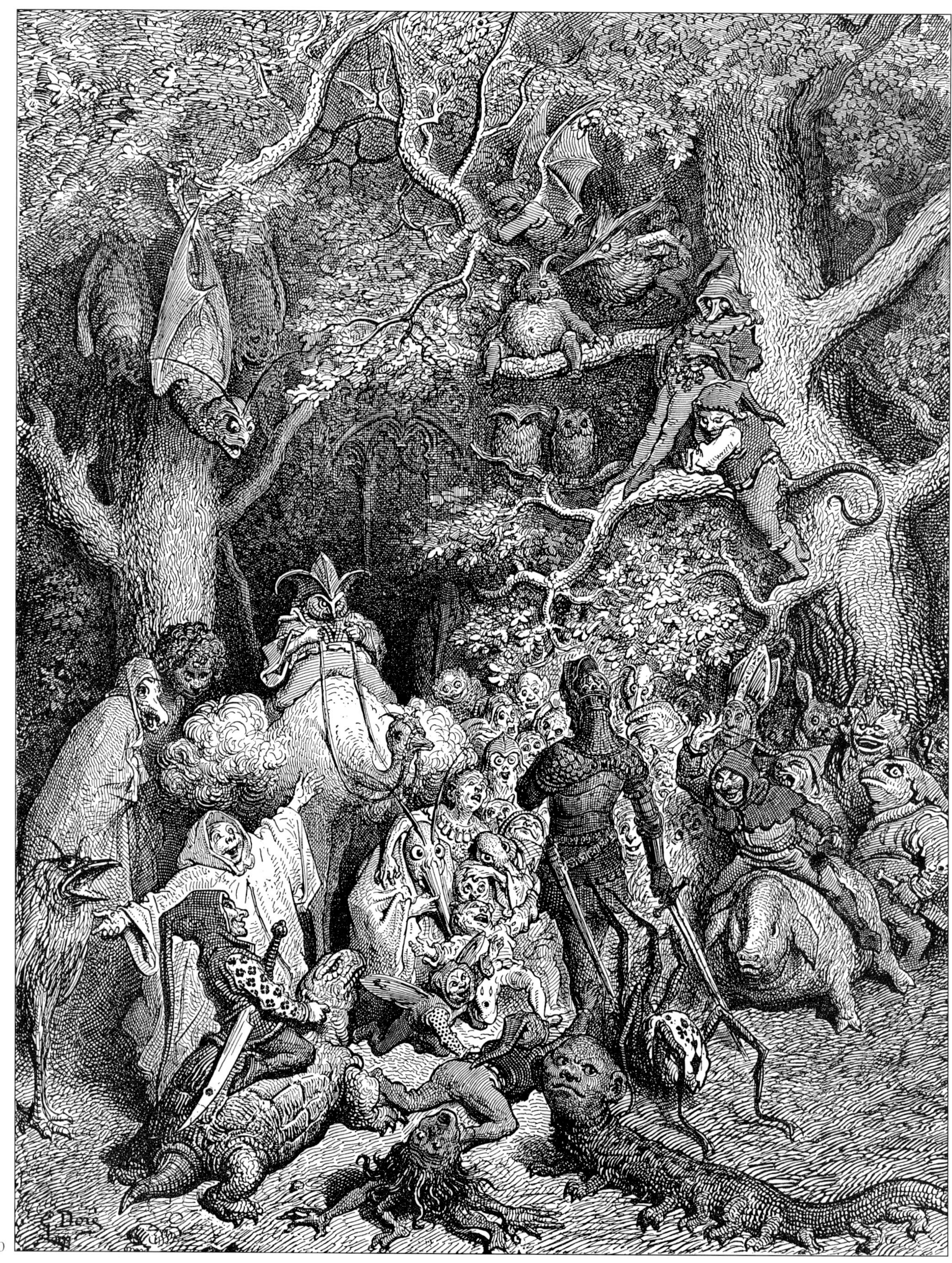

170

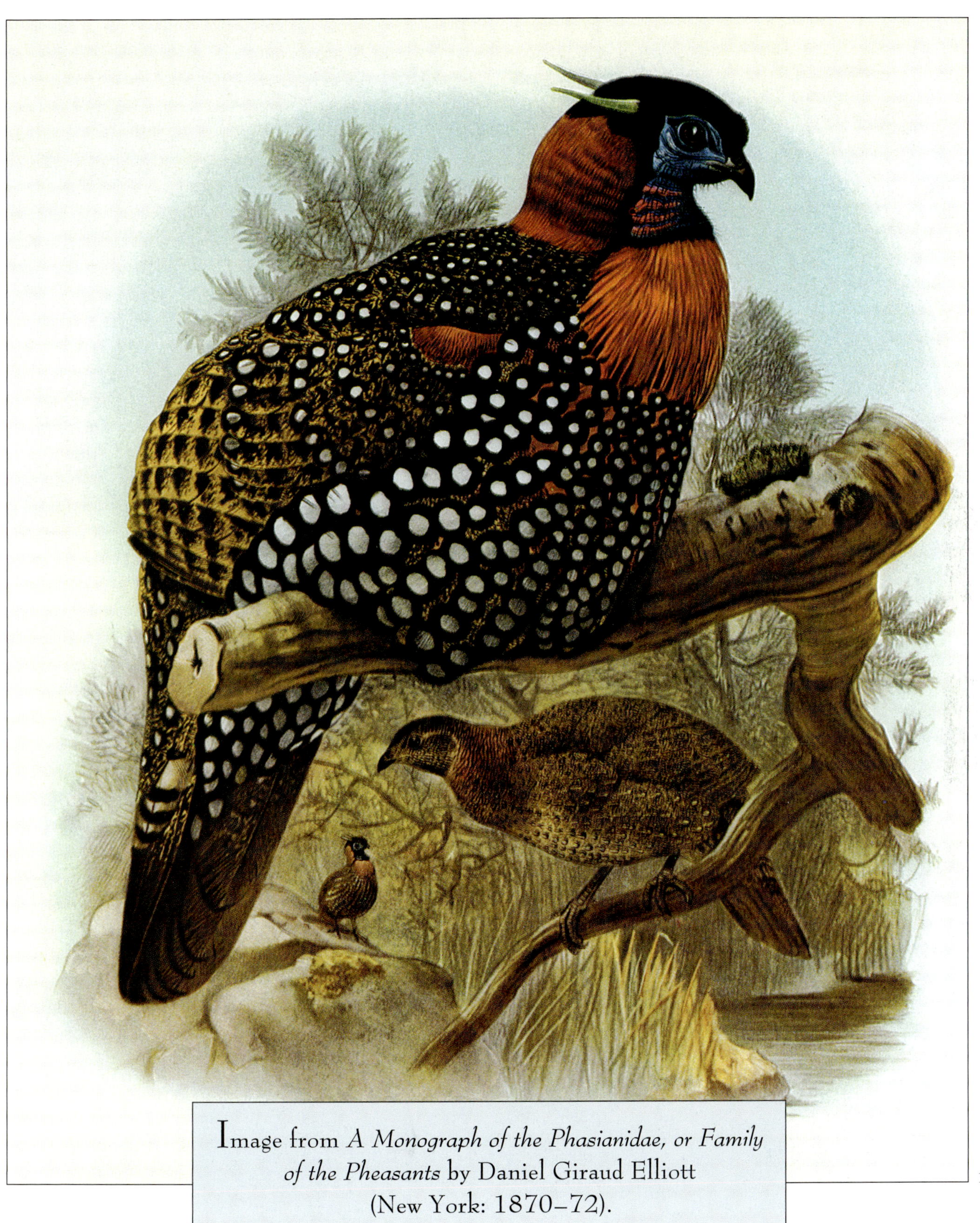

171

Image from *A Monograph of the Phasianidae, or Family of the Pheasants* by Daniel Giraud Elliott (New York: 1870–72).

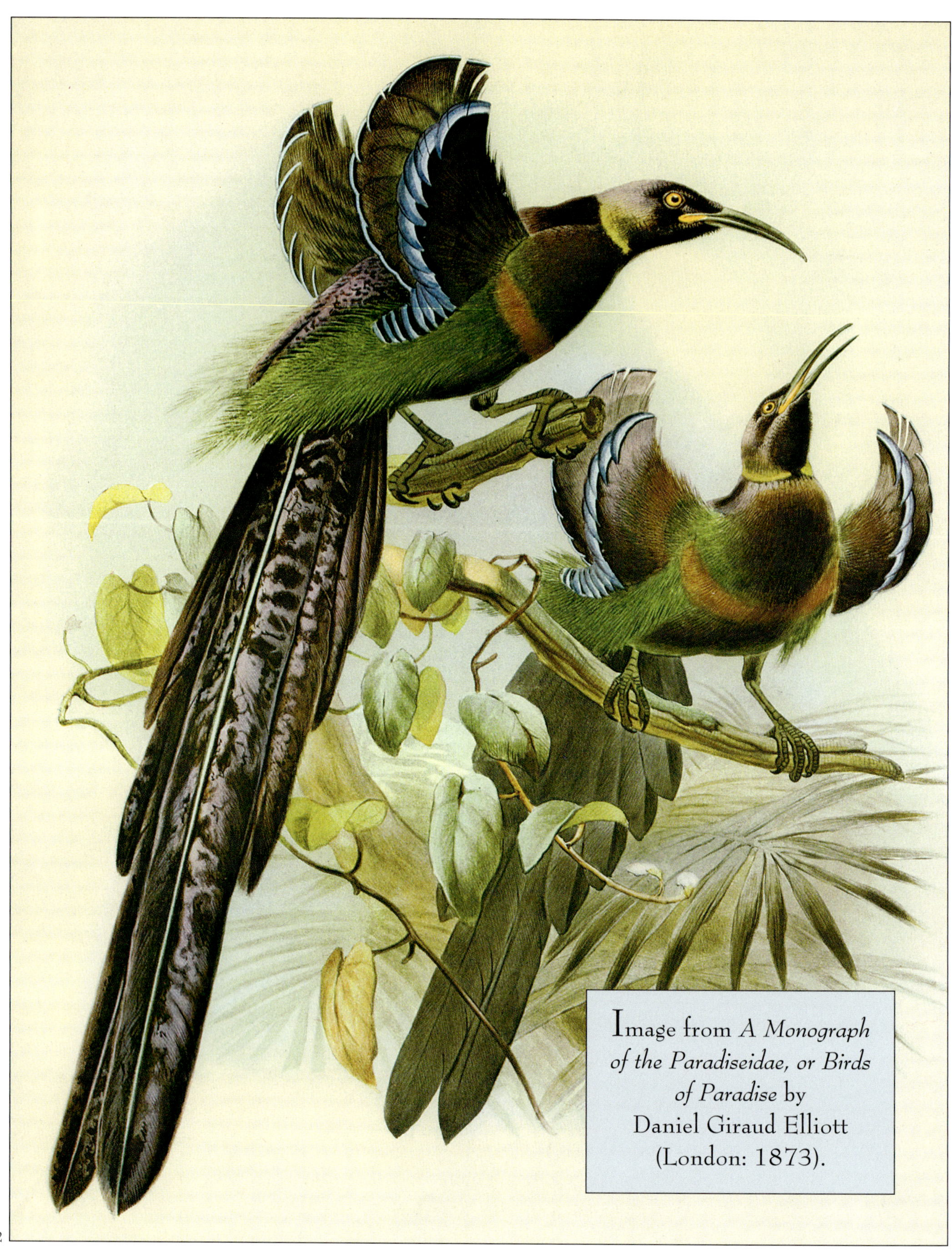

Image from *A Monograph of the Paradiseidae, or Birds of Paradise* by Daniel Giraud Elliott (London: 1873).

172

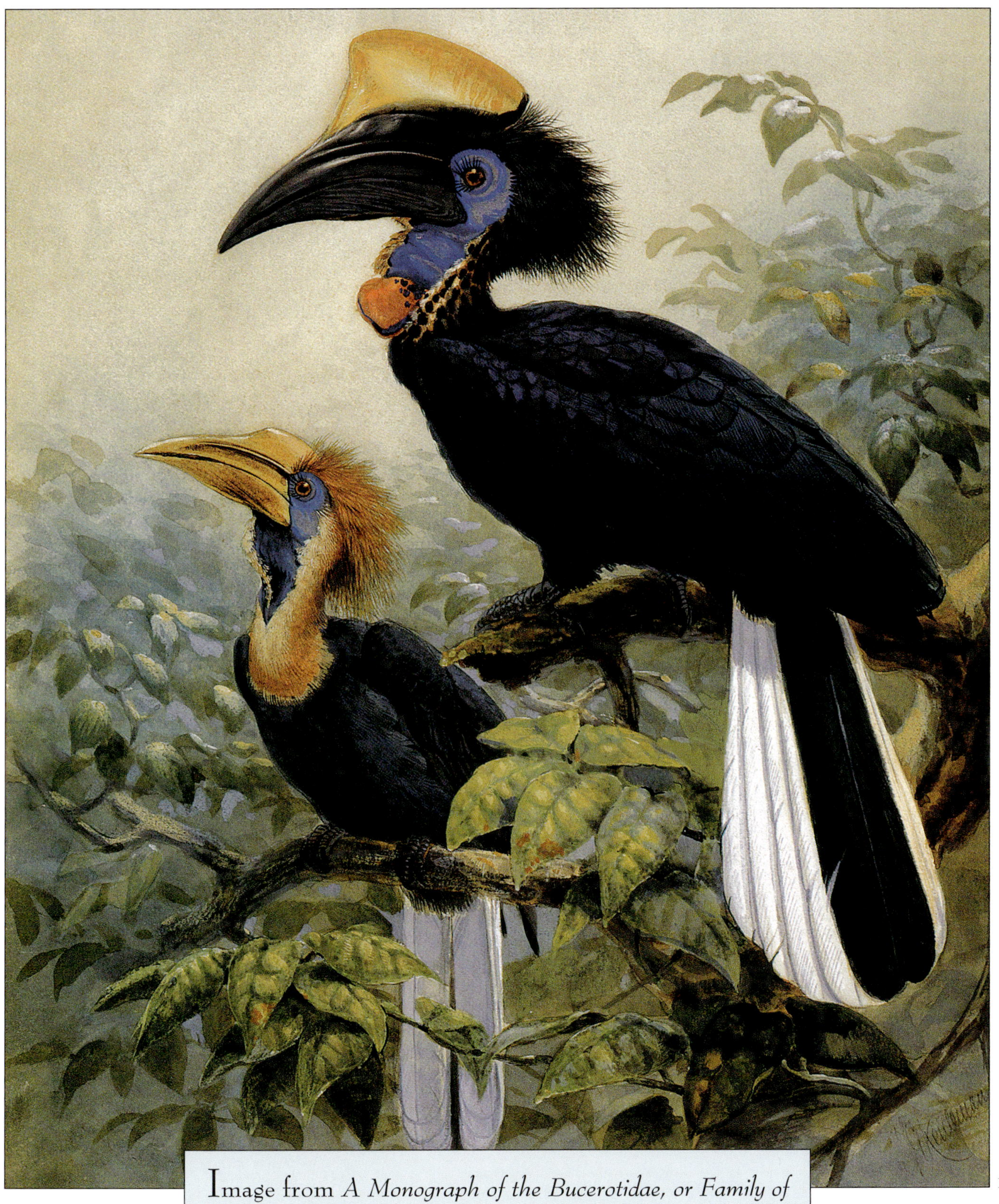

Image from *A Monograph of the Bucerotidae, or Family of the Hornbills* by Daniel Giraud Elliott. Painted by John Gerrard Keulemans (c. 1876–82). 173

Images from *Scènes de la vie privée et publique des animaux* and *Les Animaux*. (Paris: J. Hetzel et Paulin, 1842, 1868) and *Un Autre Monde* (Paris: H. Fournier, 1844). Published by Dover as *Dover Digital Design Source #5: Grandville's Animals* (Mineola, NY, 2010).

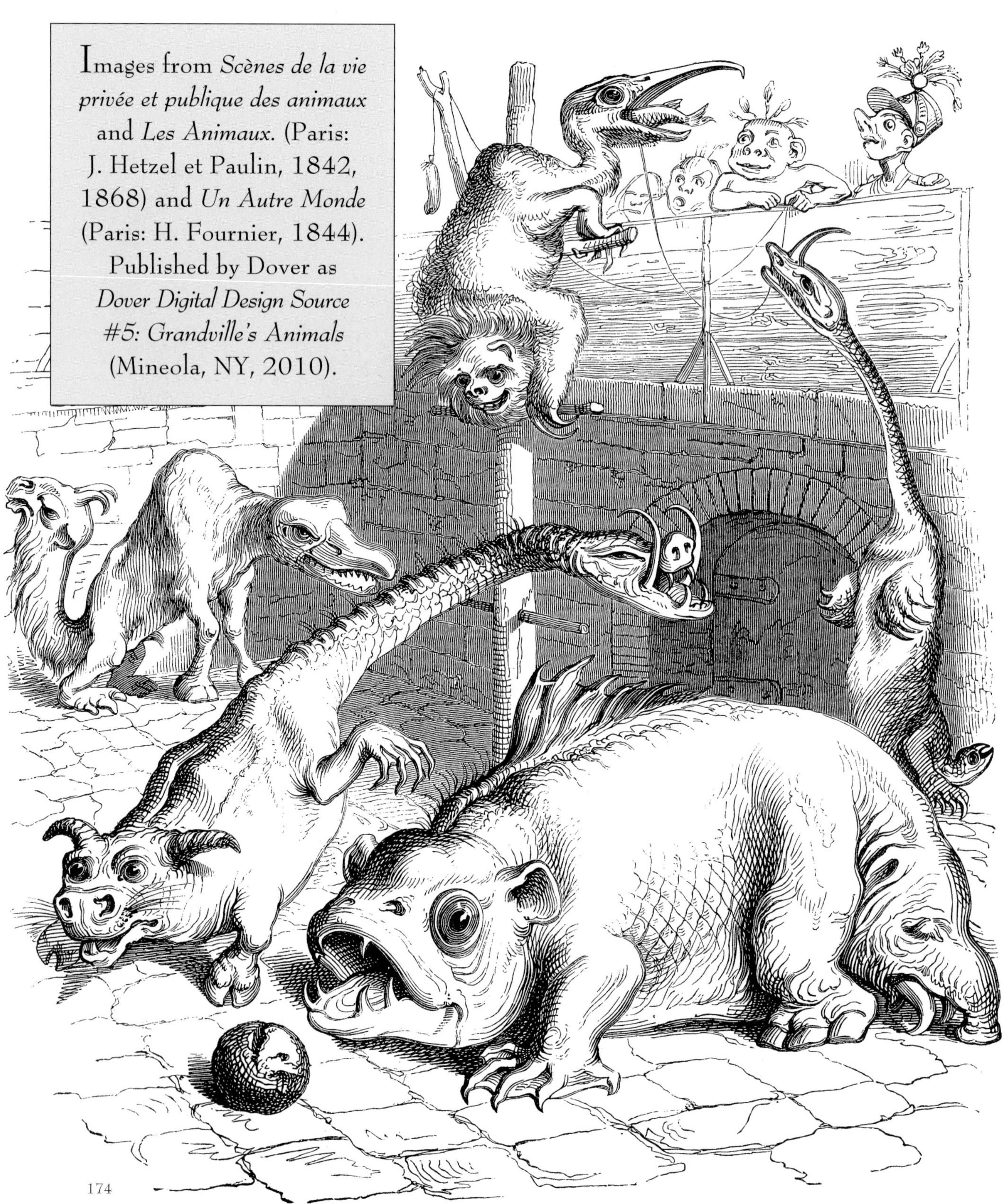

174

The pit of "doublivores" (animals that can eat at both ends) at the zoo.

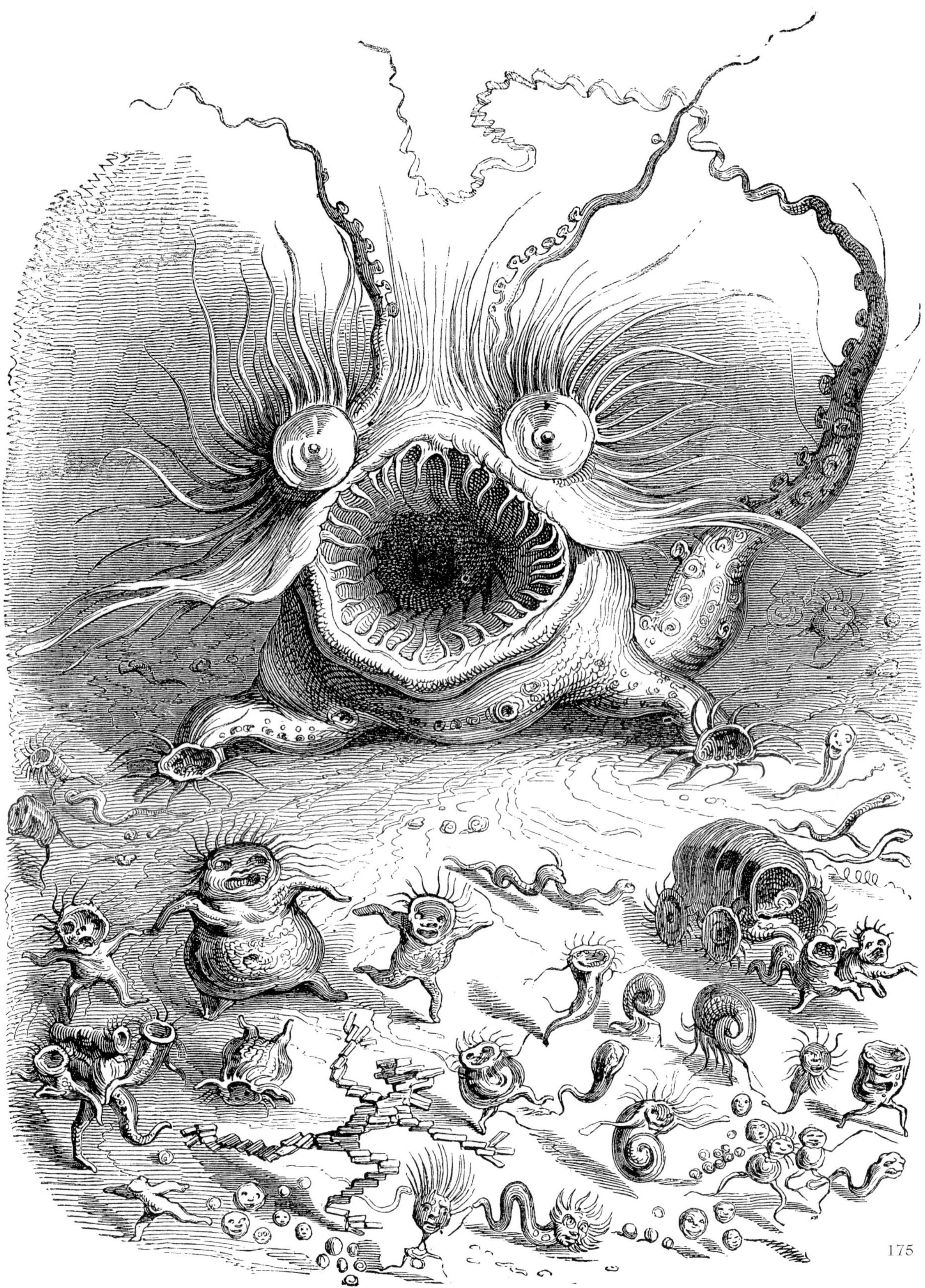

175

A volvox epidemic strikes the near-microscopic world of the scale insects.

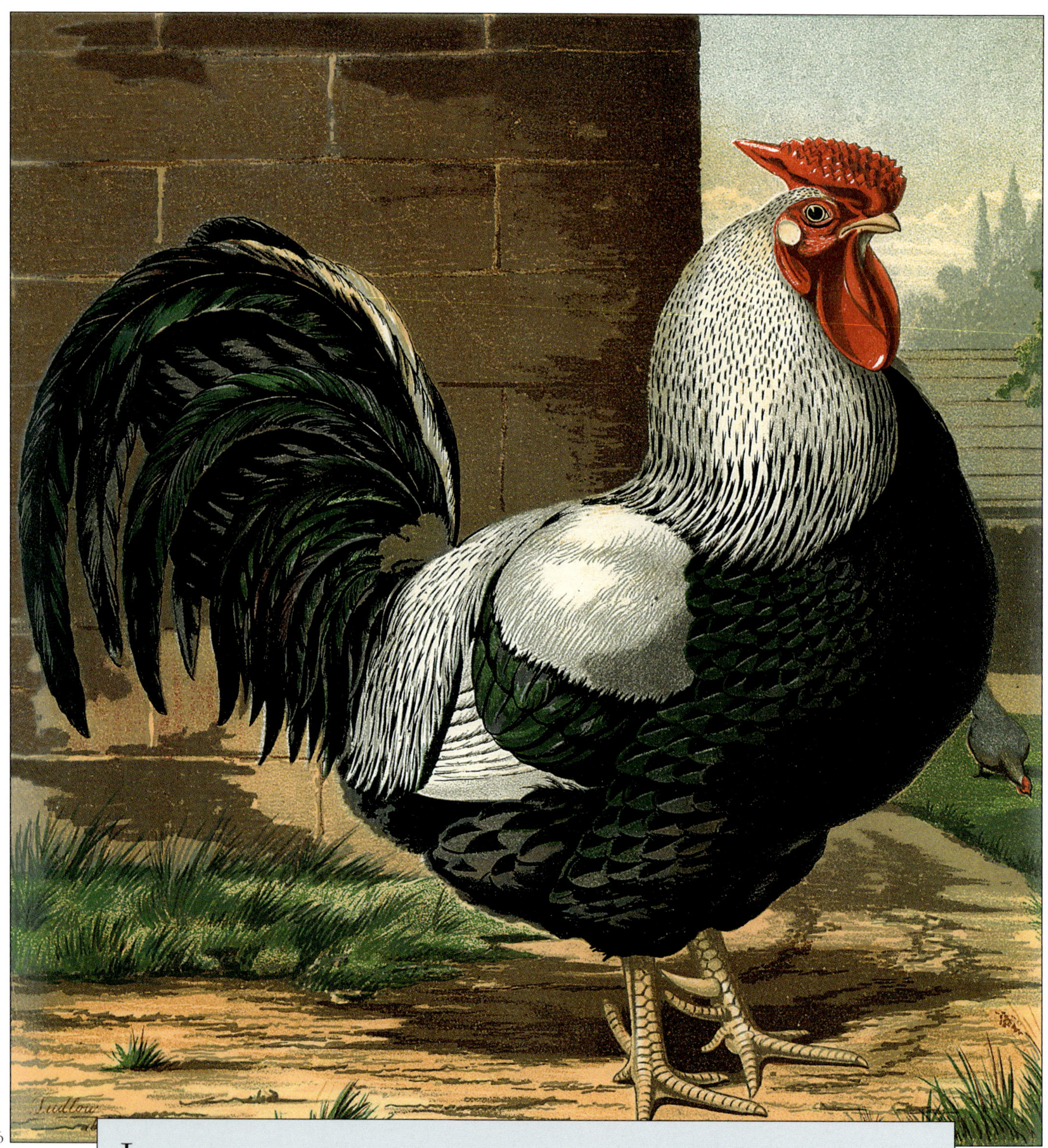

176

Images from *The Illustrated Book of Poultry, with Practical Schedules for Judging* by Lewis Wright (London: Cassell, Petter, Galpin & Co., 1880). Available online at DoverPictura.com as *The Book of Poultry.*

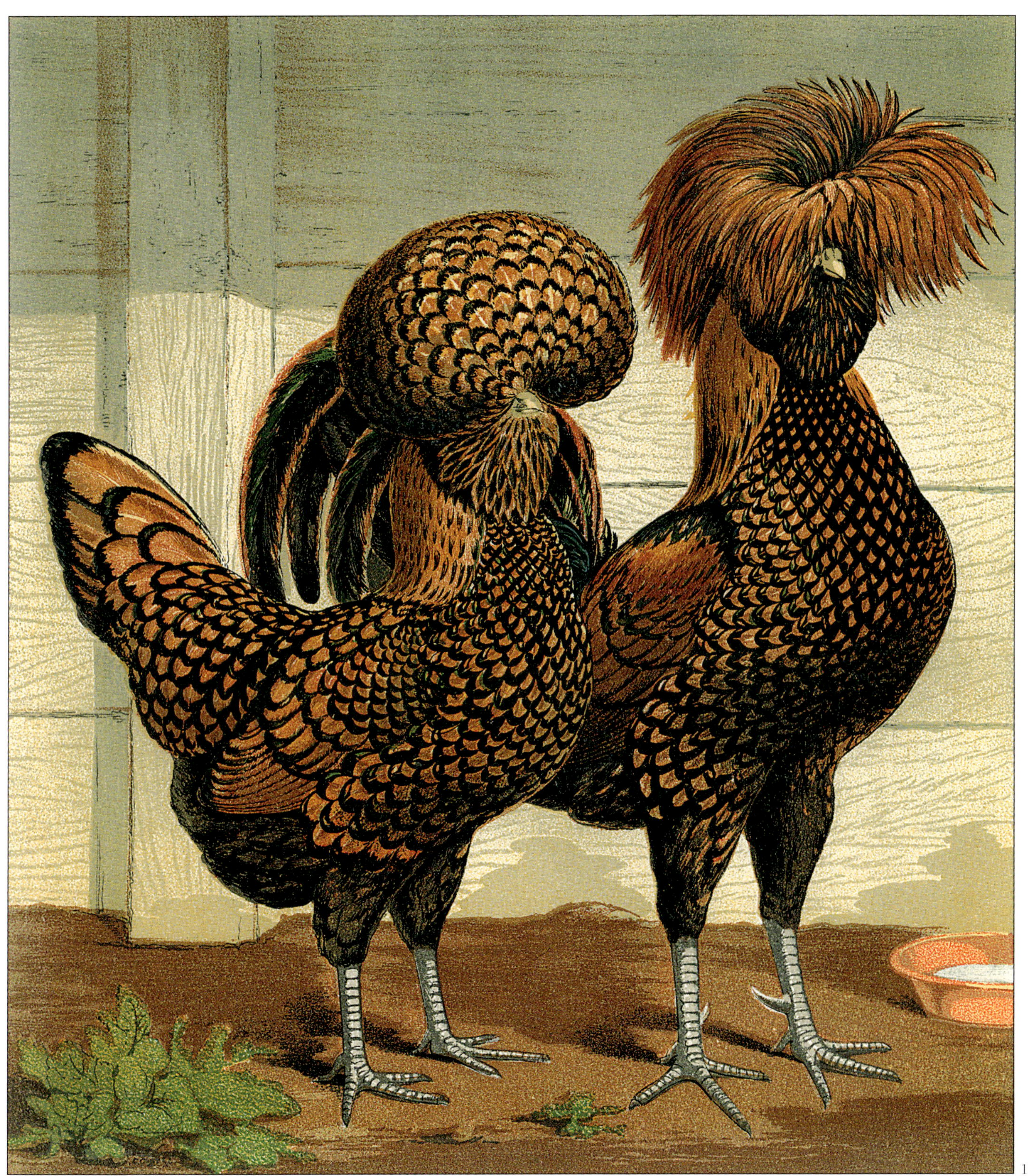

177

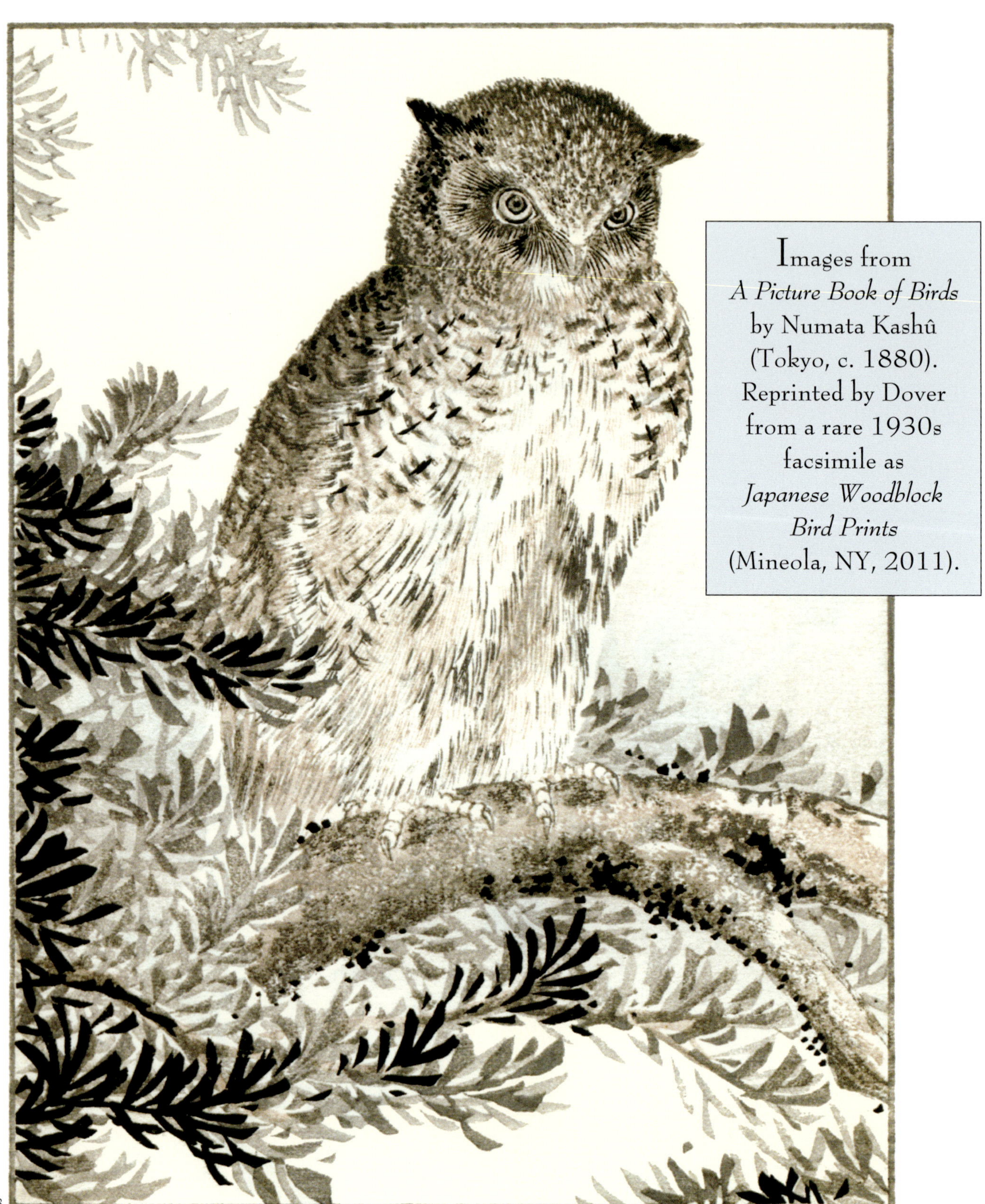

Images from
A Picture Book of Birds
by Numata Kashû
(Tokyo, c. 1880).
Reprinted by Dover
from a rare 1930s
facsimile as
*Japanese Woodblock
Bird Prints*
(Mineola, NY, 2011).

178

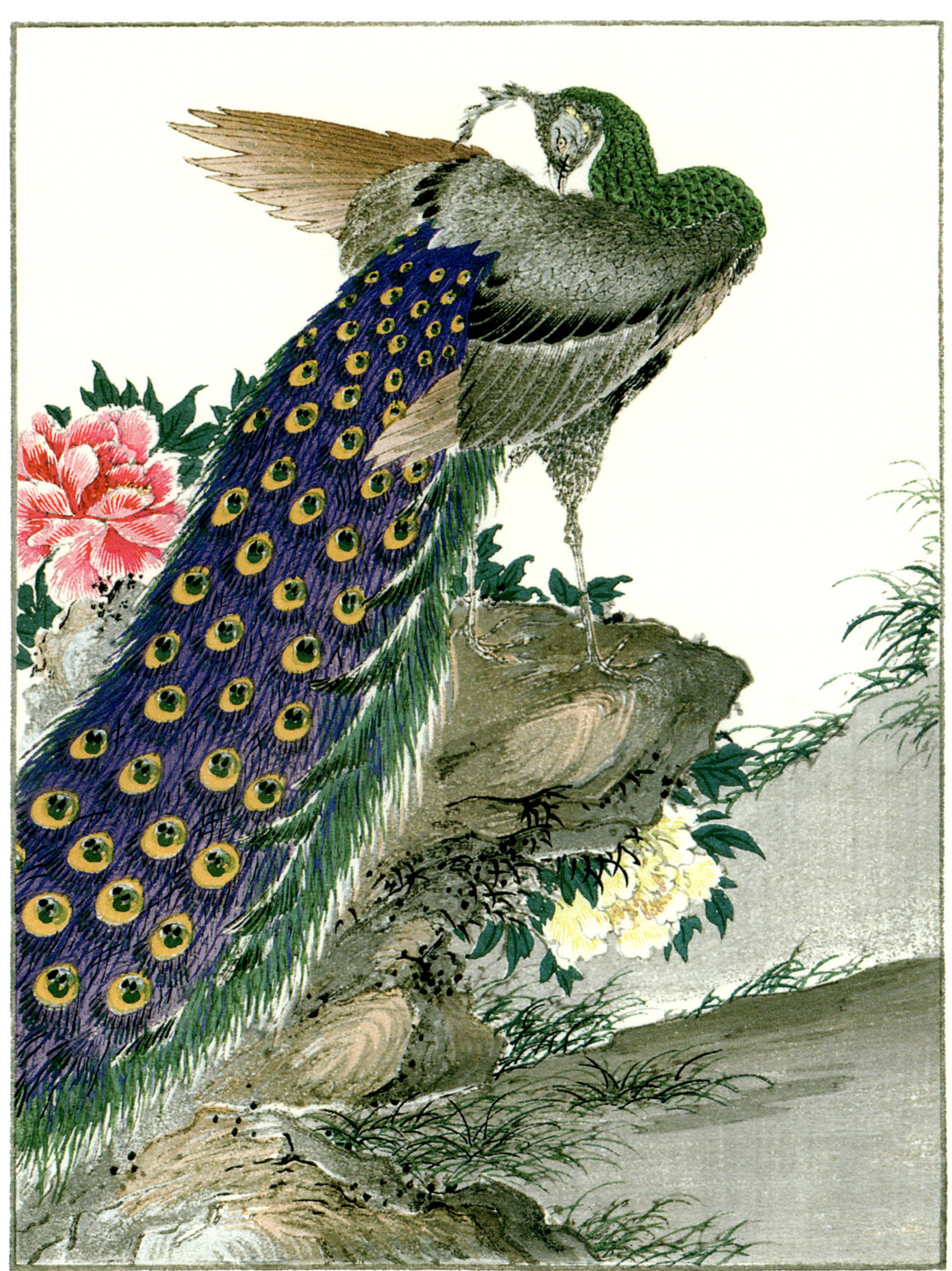

179

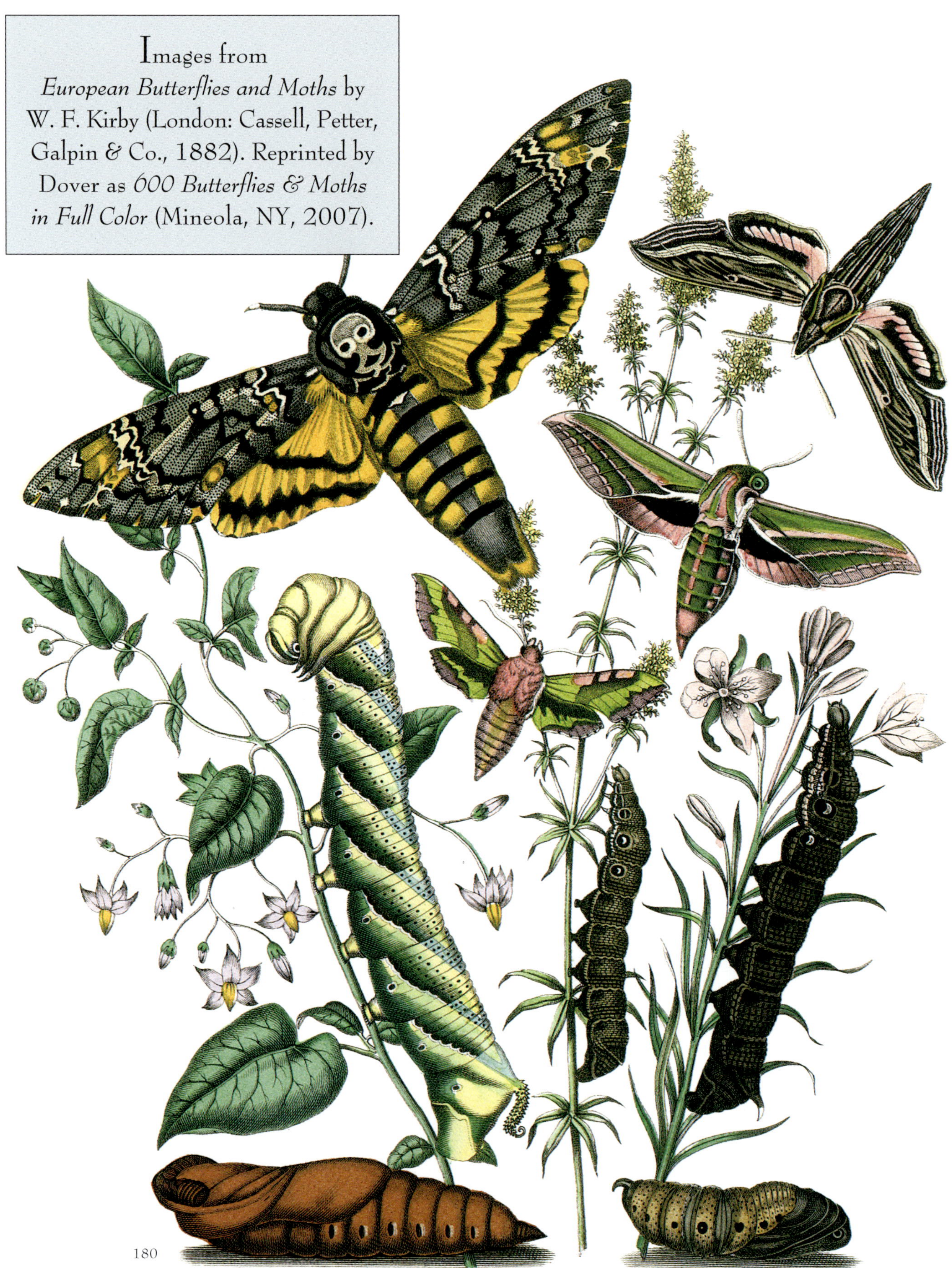

Images from
European Butterflies and Moths by W. F. Kirby (London: Cassell, Petter, Galpin & Co., 1882). Reprinted by Dover as *600 Butterflies & Moths in Full Color* (Mineola, NY, 2007).

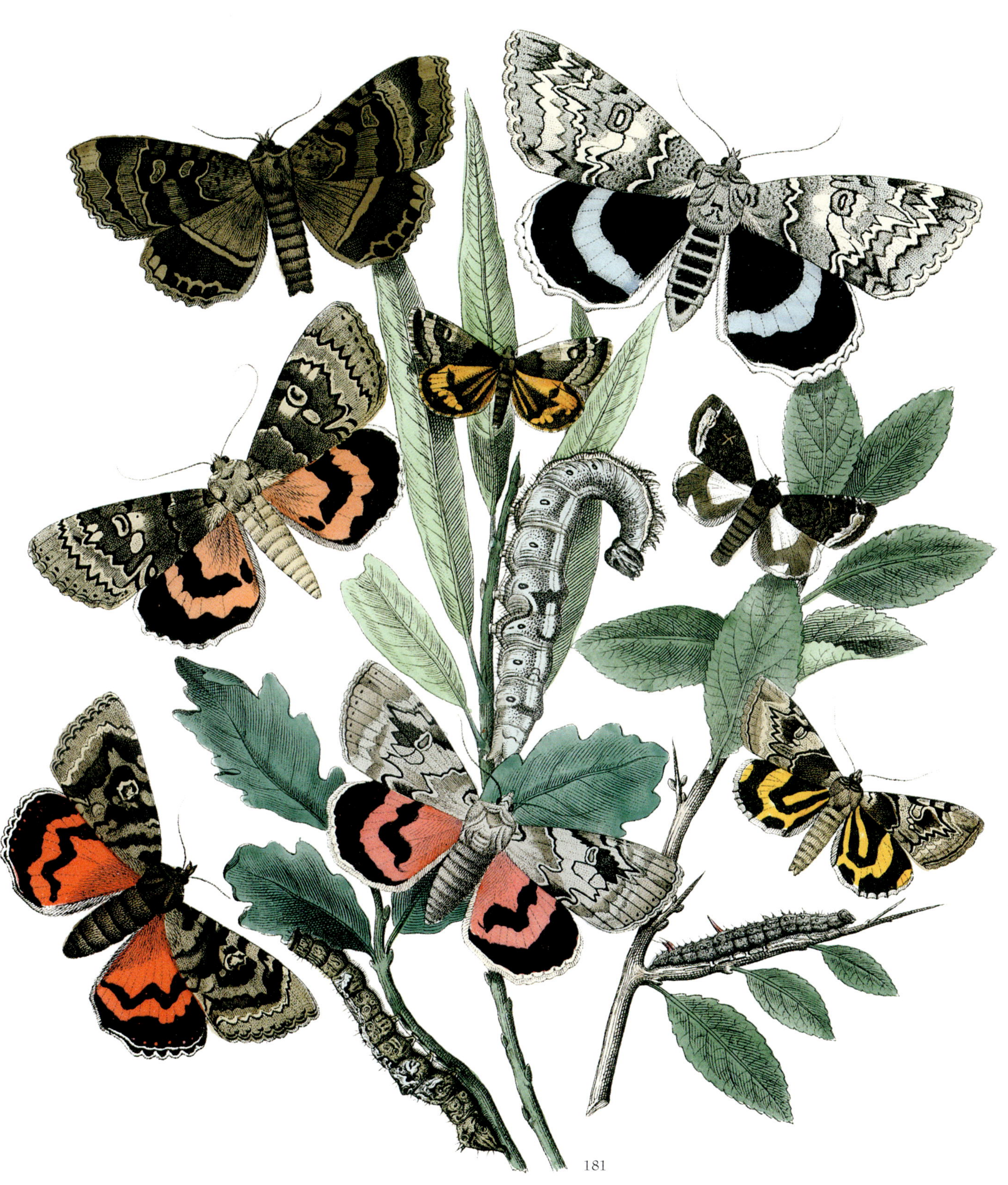

181

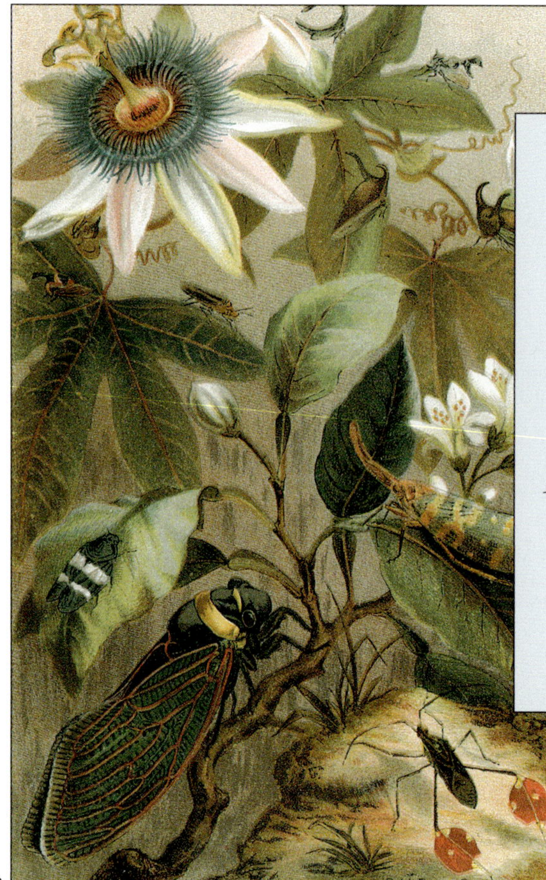

182

Images from *Animate Creation; Popular Edition of "Our Living World," a Natural History* by The Rev. J. G. Wood. Revised and Adapted to *American Zoology* by Joseph B. Holder, M.D. (New York: Selmar Hess, 1885).

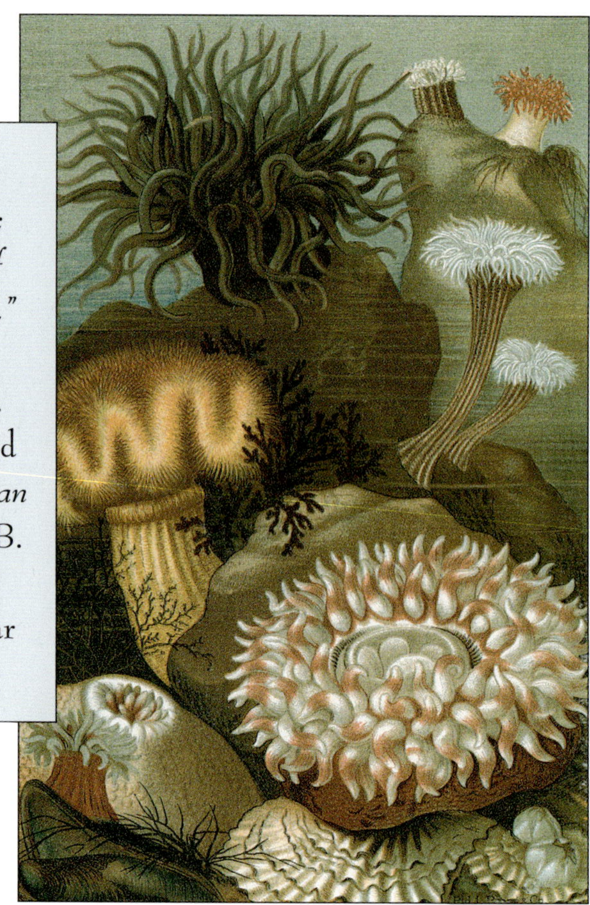

183

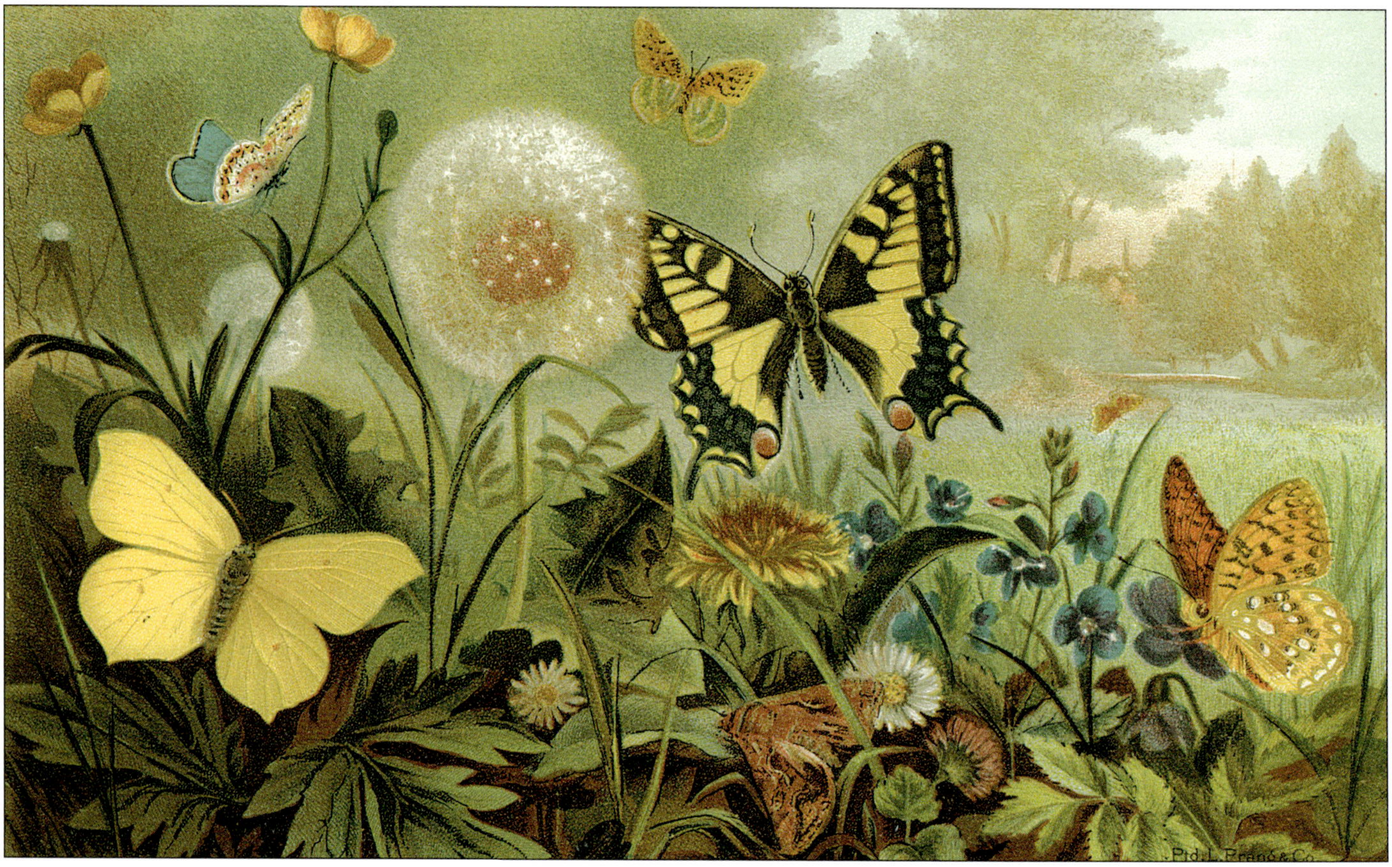

184

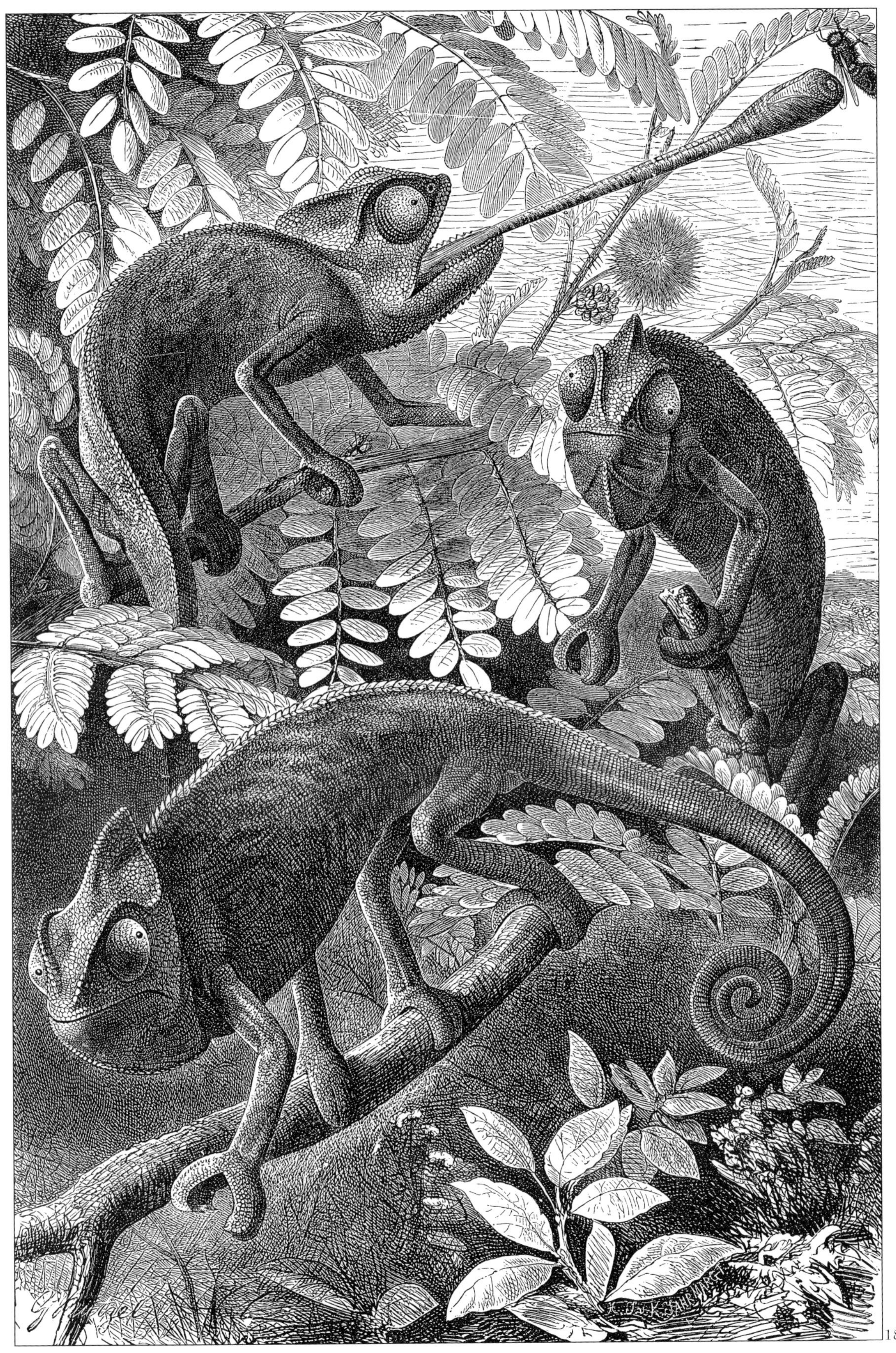

185

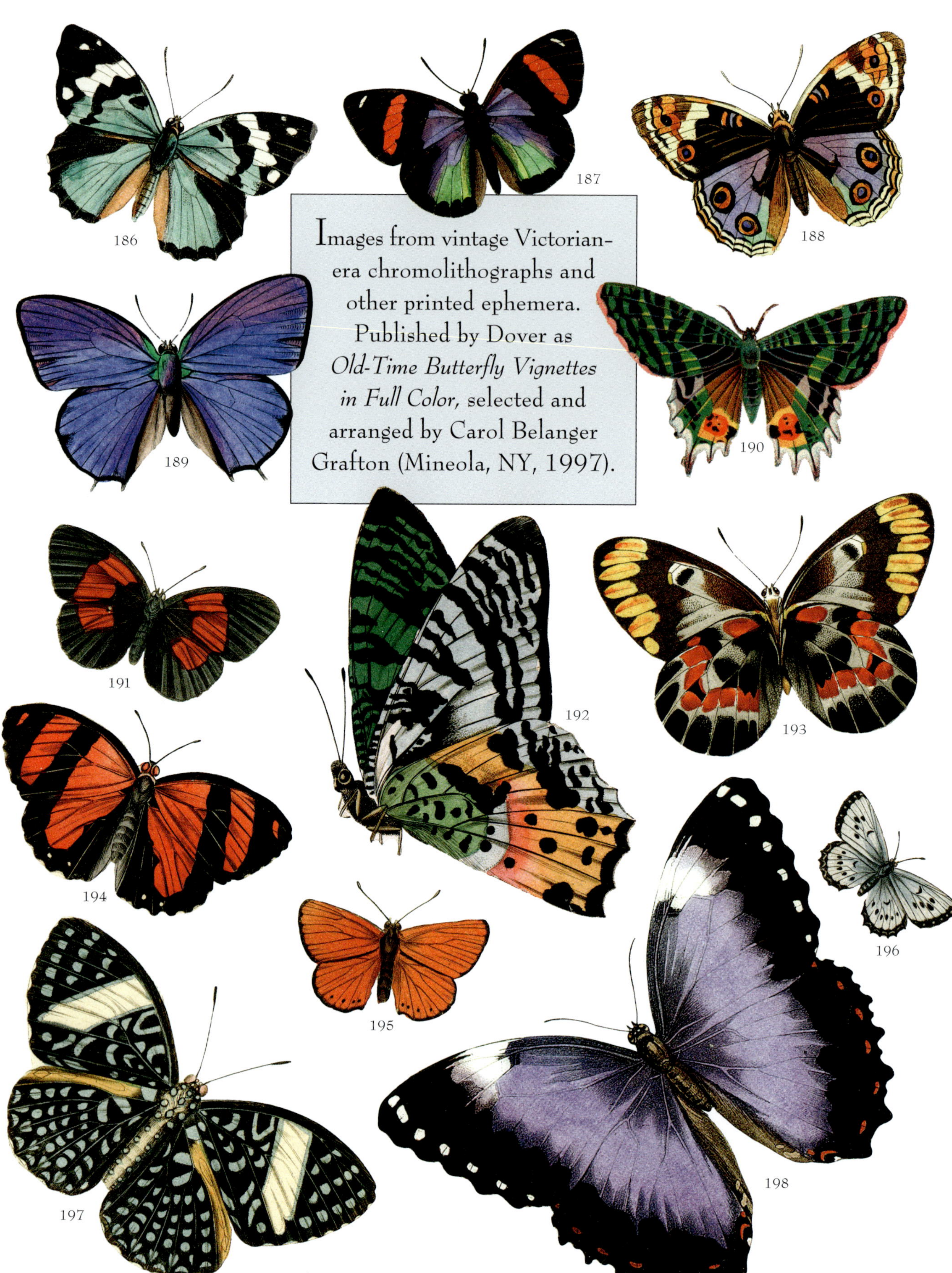

Images from vintage Victorian-era chromolithographs and other printed ephemera. Published by Dover as *Old-Time Butterfly Vignettes in Full Color*, selected and arranged by Carol Belanger Grafton (Mineola, NY, 1997).

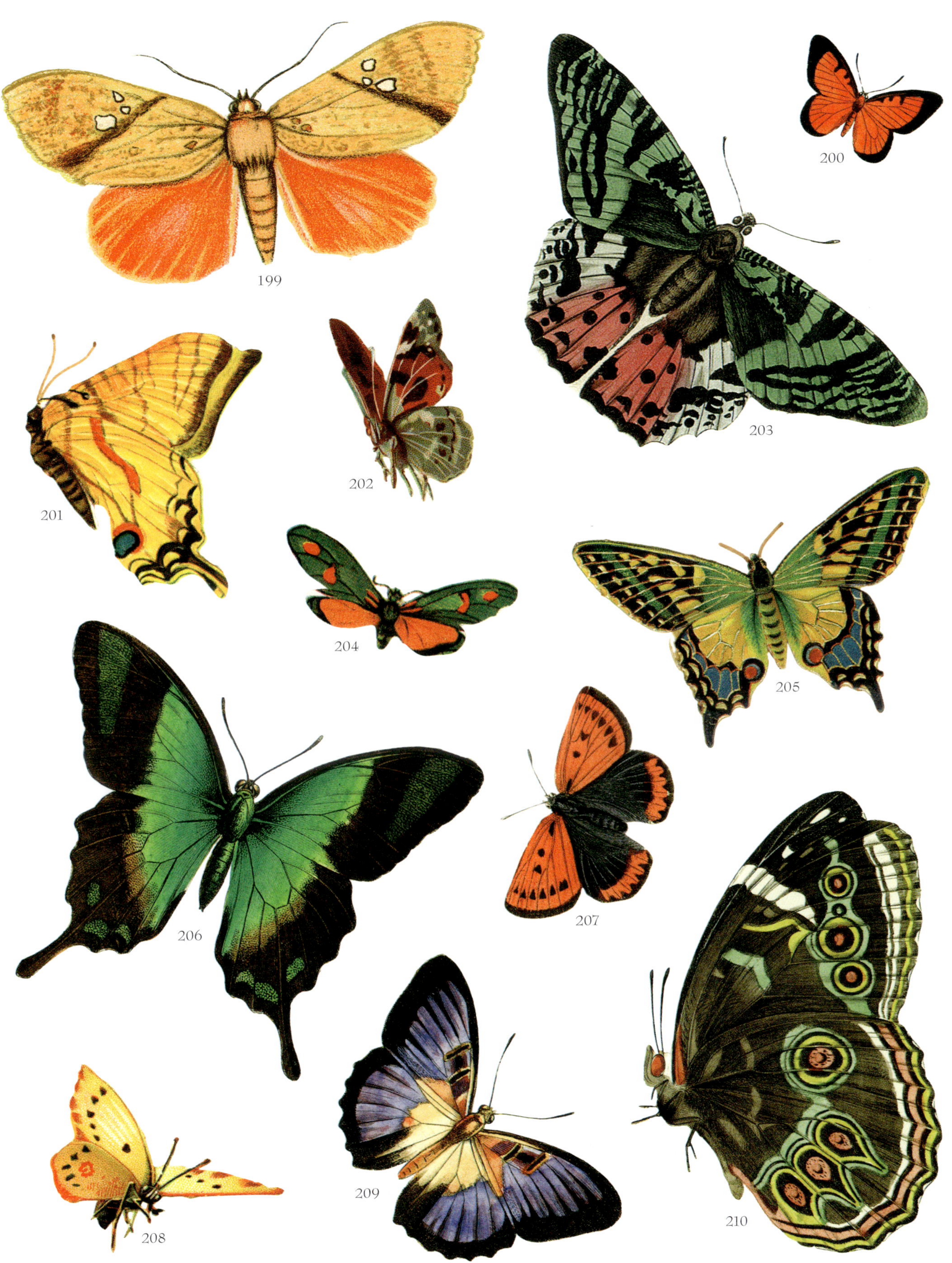
199
200
201
202
203
204
205
206
207
208
209
210

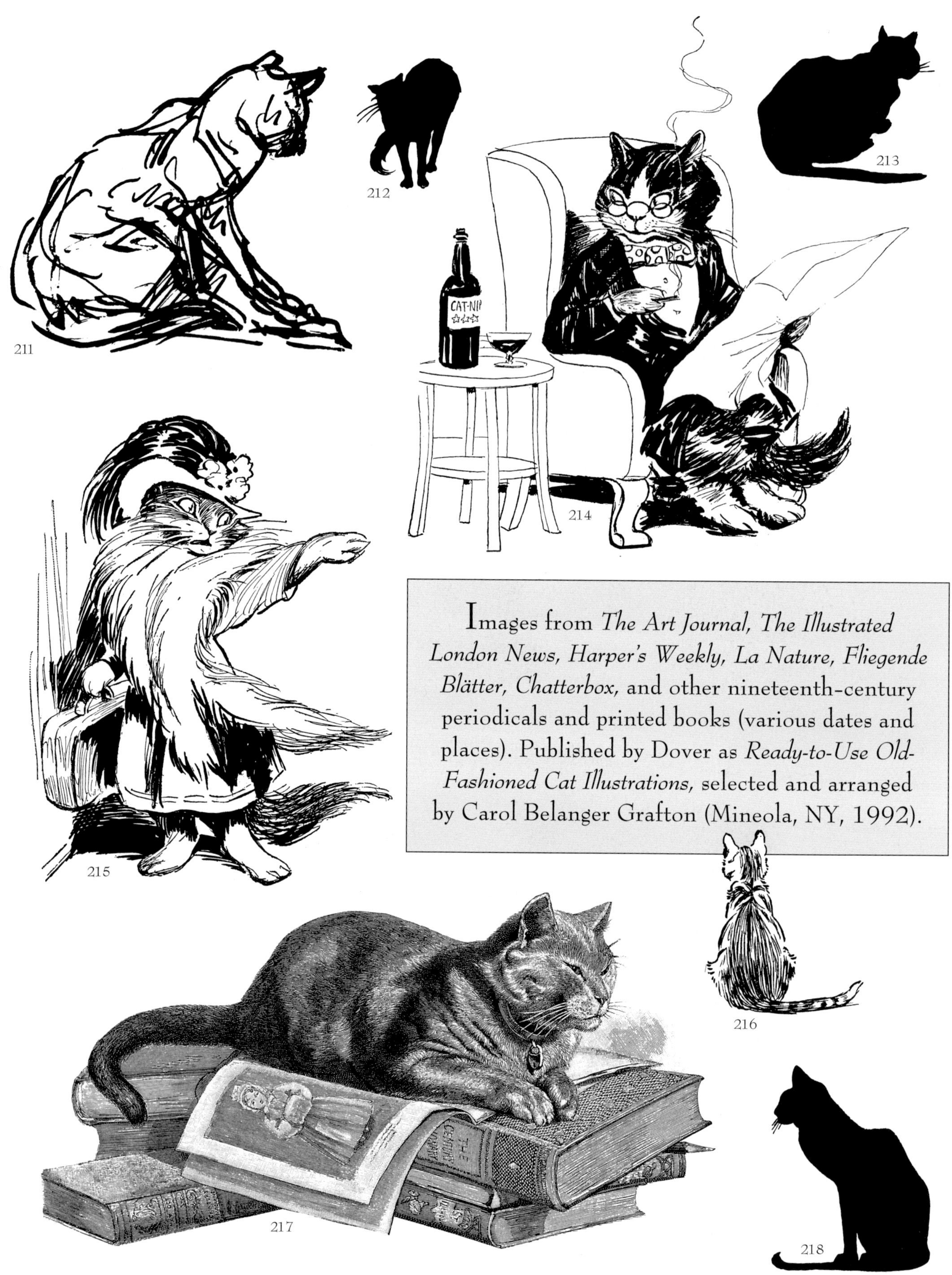

211

212

213

214

215

216

217

218

Images from *The Art Journal, The Illustrated London News, Harper's Weekly, La Nature, Fliegende Blätter, Chatterbox,* and other nineteenth-century periodicals and printed books (various dates and places). Published by Dover as *Ready-to-Use Old-Fashioned Cat Illustrations,* selected and arranged by Carol Belanger Grafton (Mineola, NY, 1992).

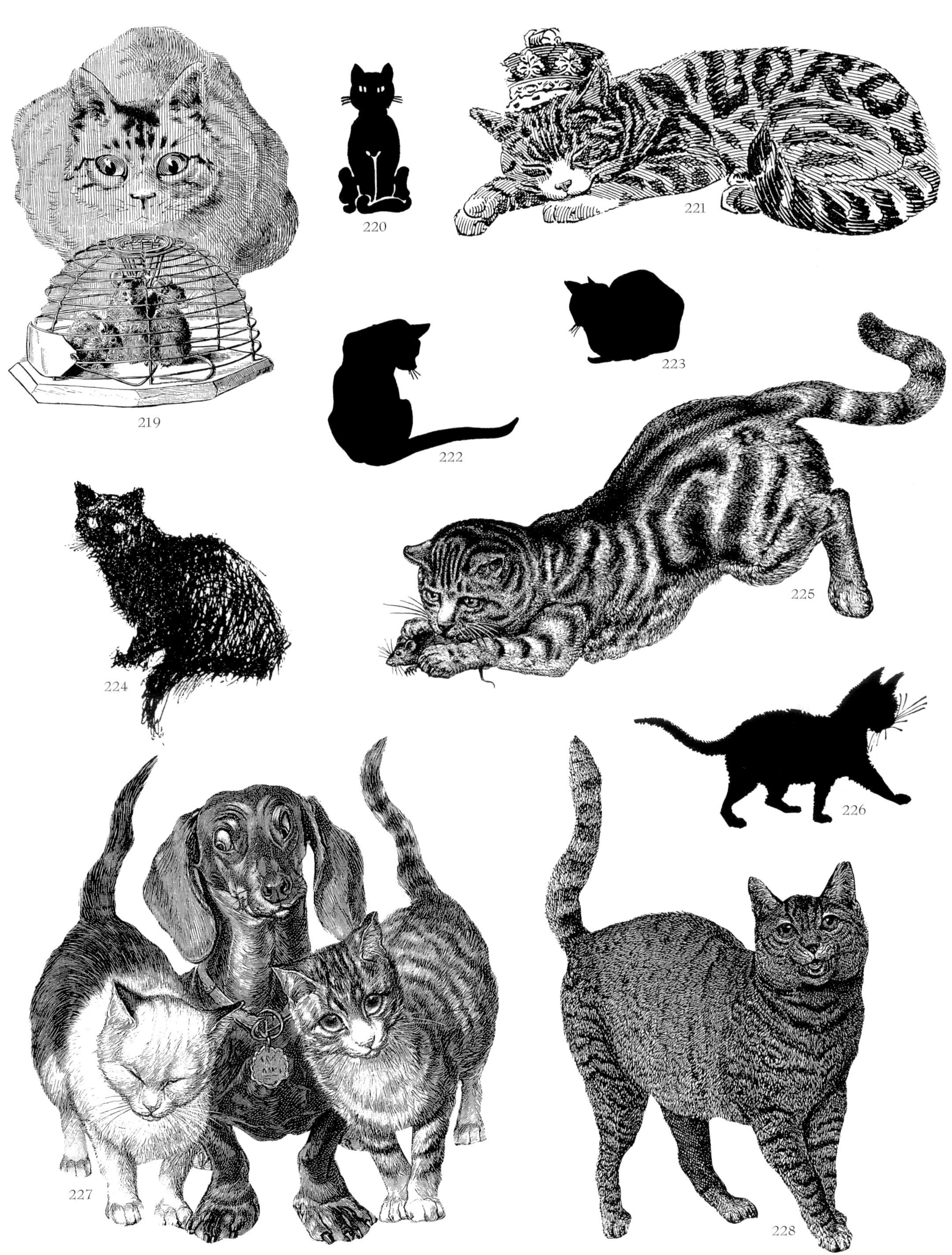
219
220
221
222
223
224
225
226
227
228

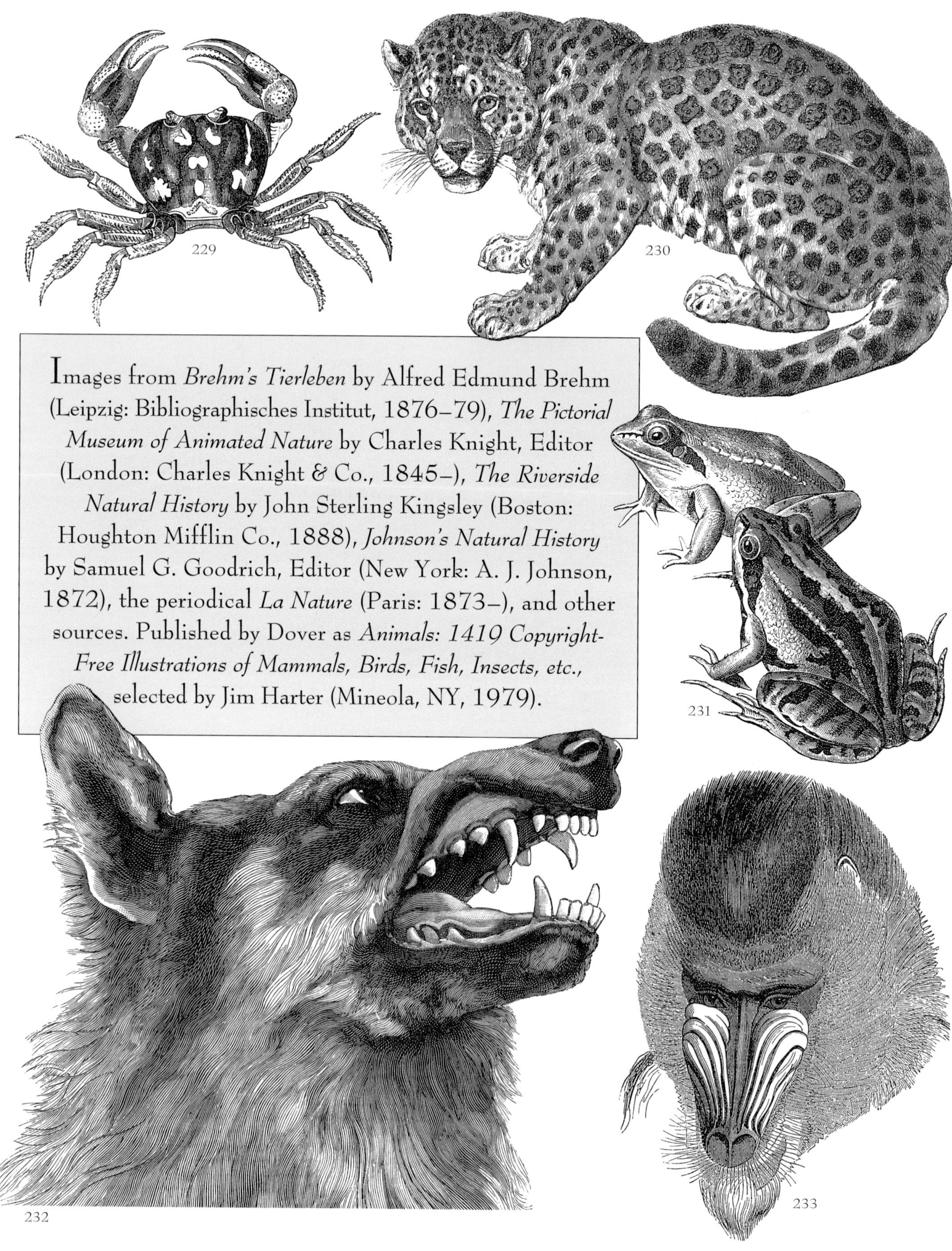

Images from *Brehm's Tierleben* by Alfred Edmund Brehm (Leipzig: Bibliographisches Institut, 1876–79), *The Pictorial Museum of Animated Nature* by Charles Knight, Editor (London: Charles Knight & Co., 1845–), *The Riverside Natural History* by John Sterling Kingsley (Boston: Houghton Mifflin Co., 1888), *Johnson's Natural History* by Samuel G. Goodrich, Editor (New York: A. J. Johnson, 1872), the periodical *La Nature* (Paris: 1873–), and other sources. Published by Dover as *Animals: 1419 Copyright-Free Illustrations of Mammals, Birds, Fish, Insects, etc.*, selected by Jim Harter (Mineola, NY, 1979).

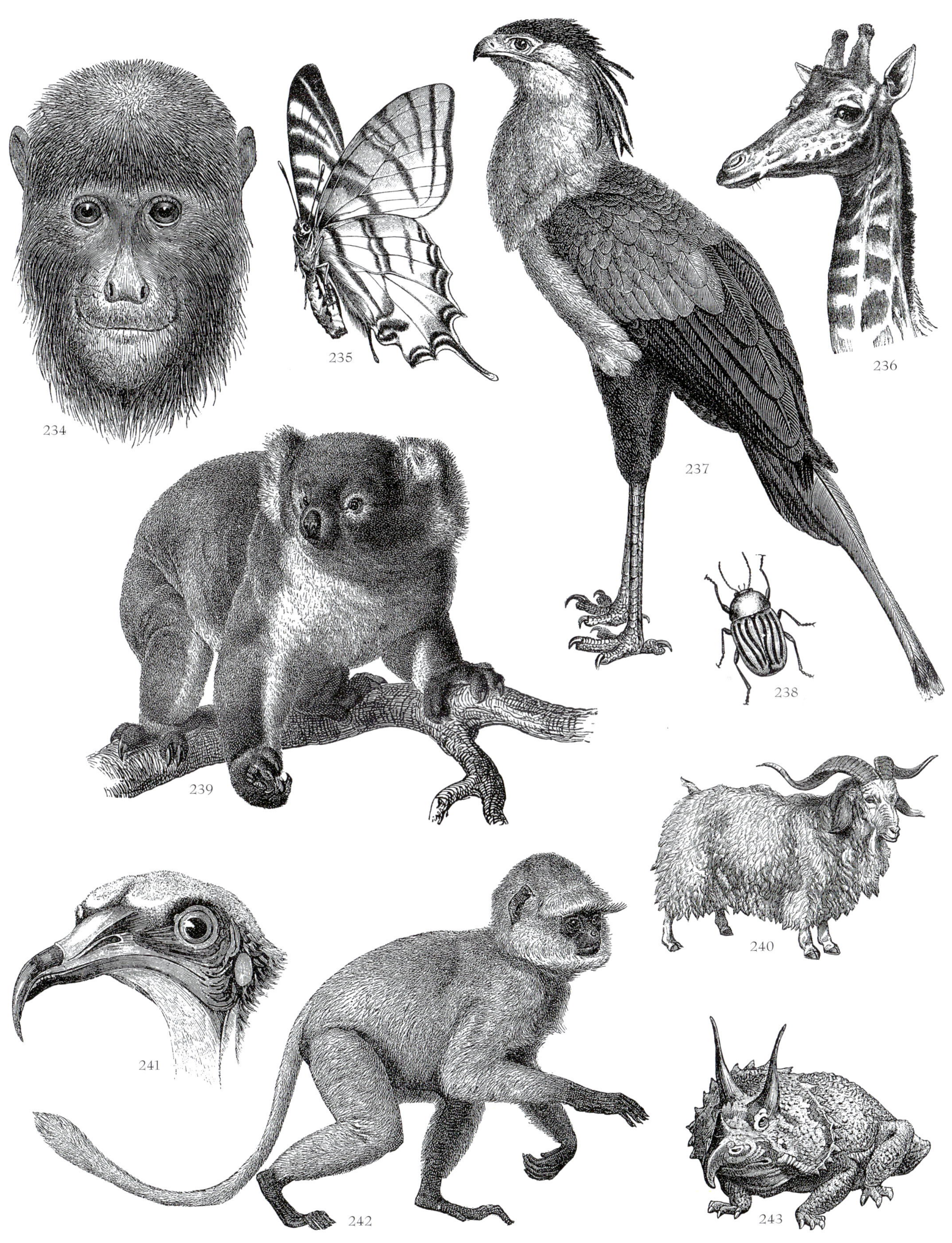

234
235
236
237
238
239
240
241
242
243

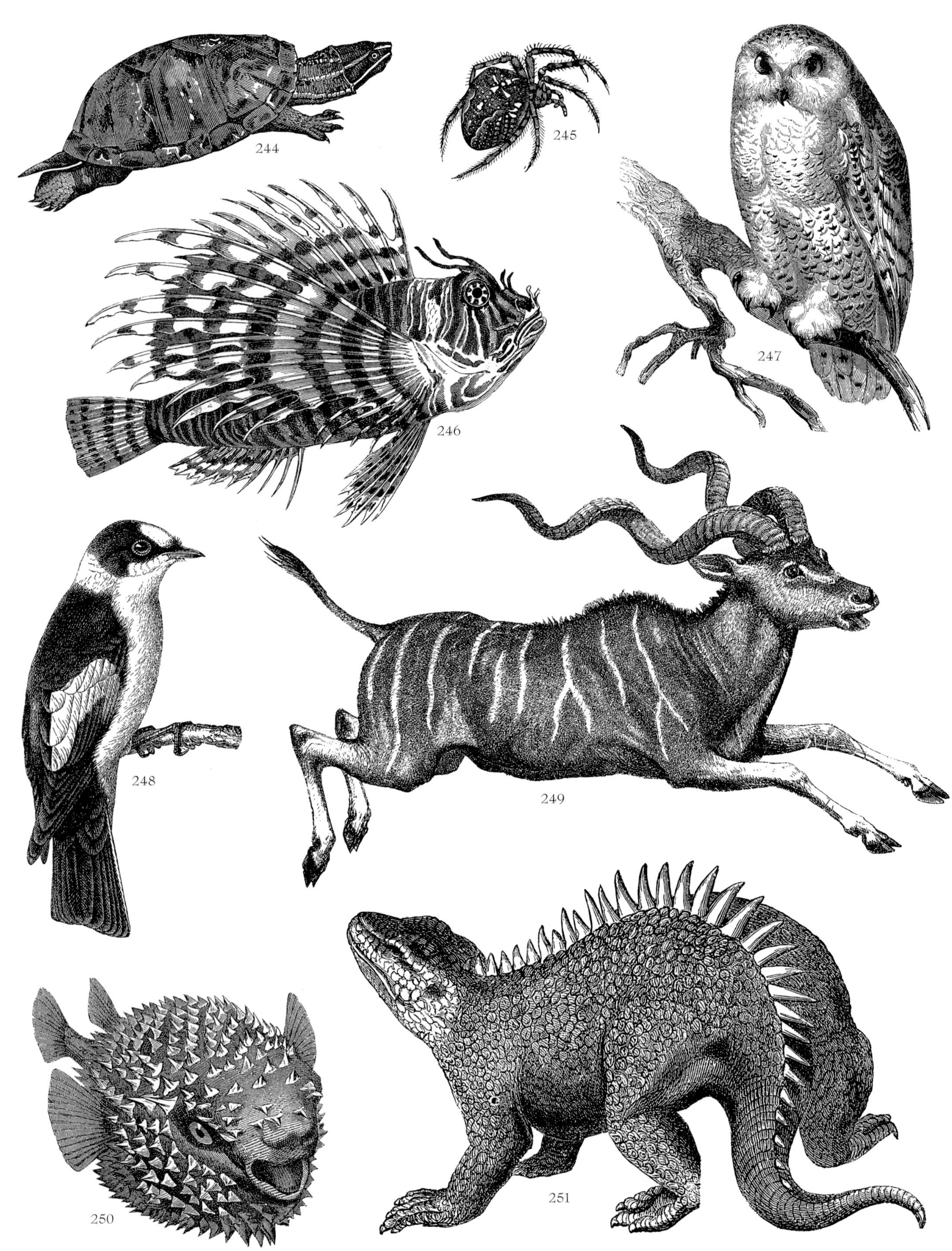

244
245
246
247
248
249
250
251

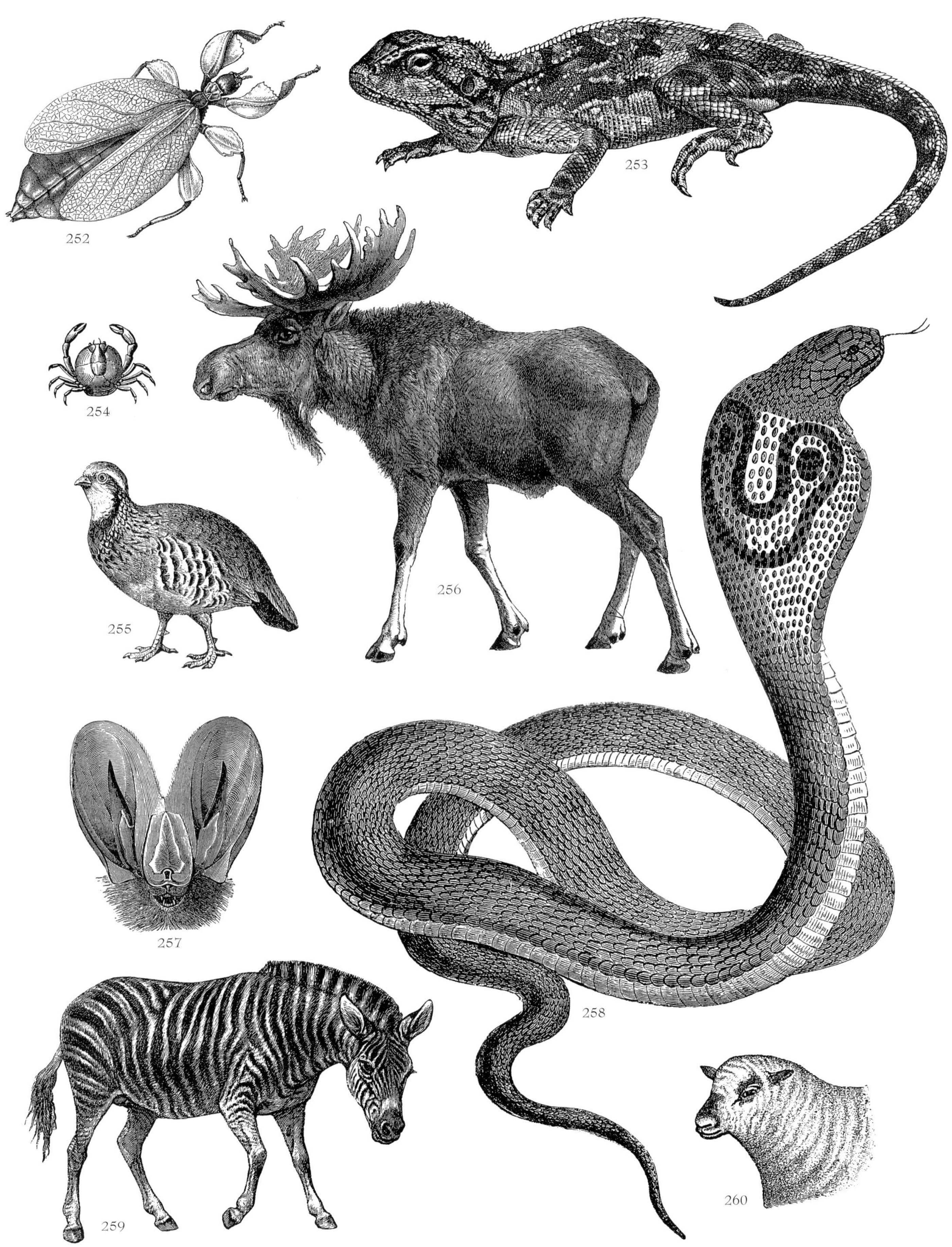
252
253
254
255
256
257
258
259
260

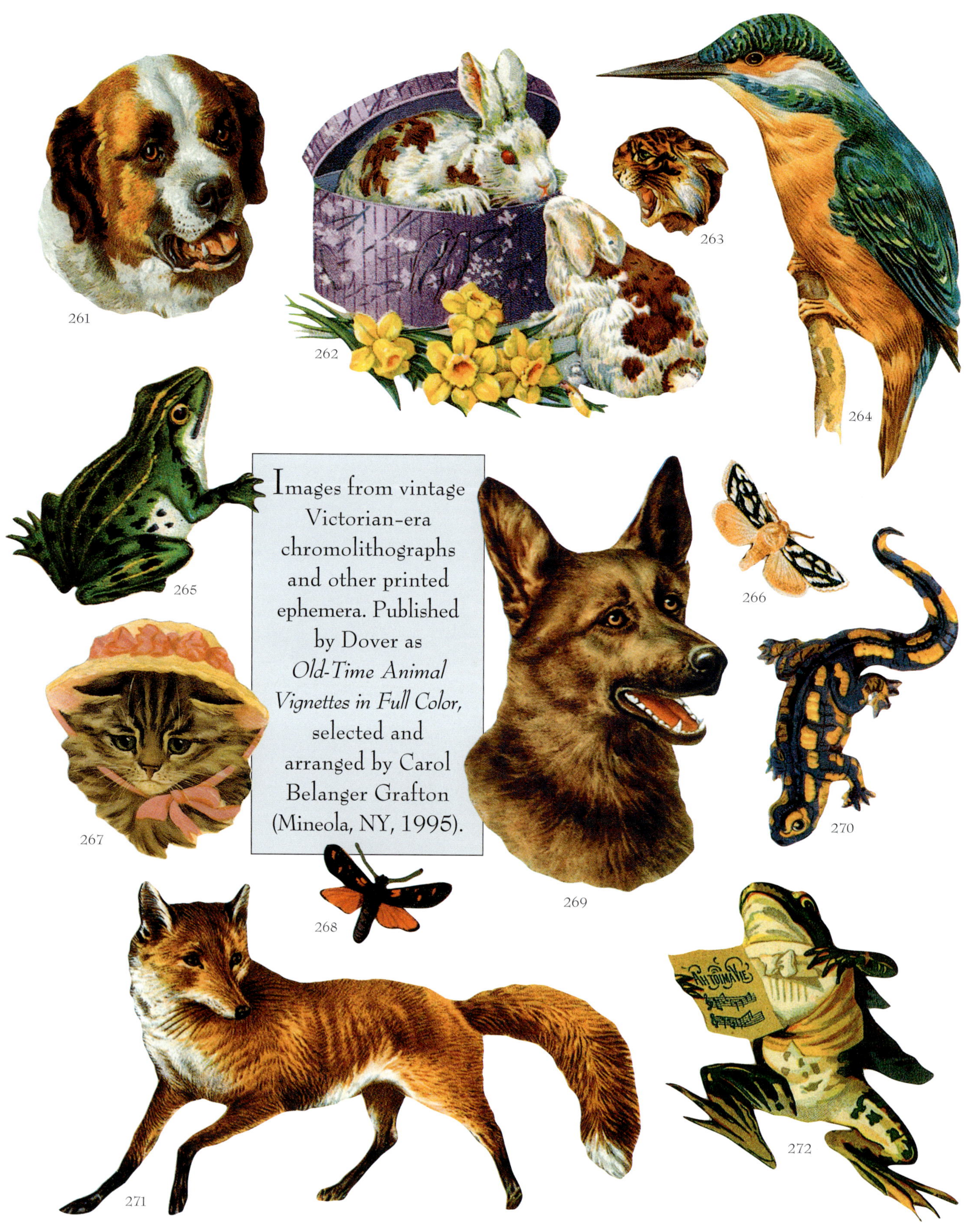

Images from vintage Victorian-era chromolithographs and other printed ephemera. Published by Dover as *Old-Time Animal Vignettes in Full Color,* selected and arranged by Carol Belanger Grafton (Mineola, NY, 1995).

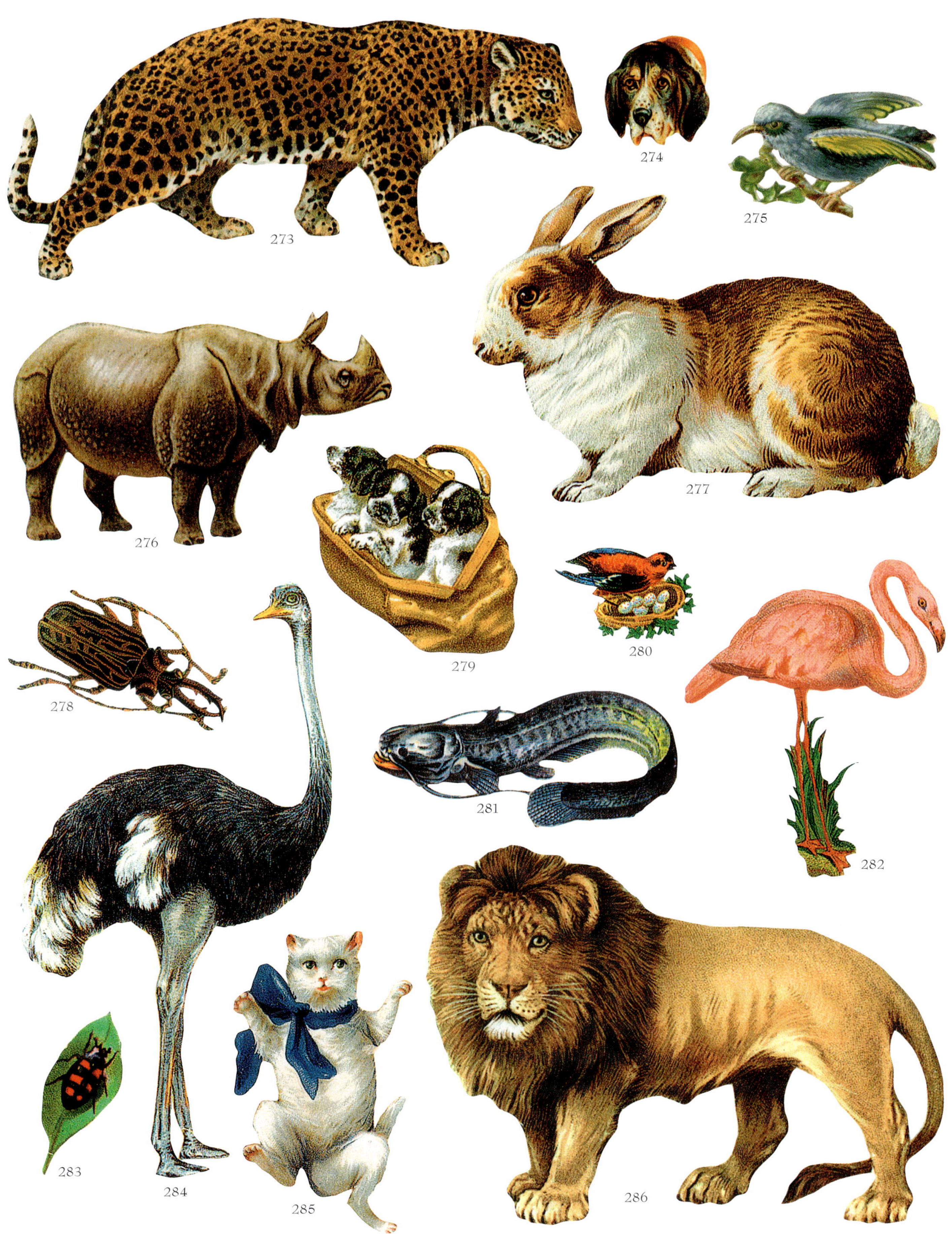
273
274
275
276
277
278
279
280
281
282
283
284
285
286

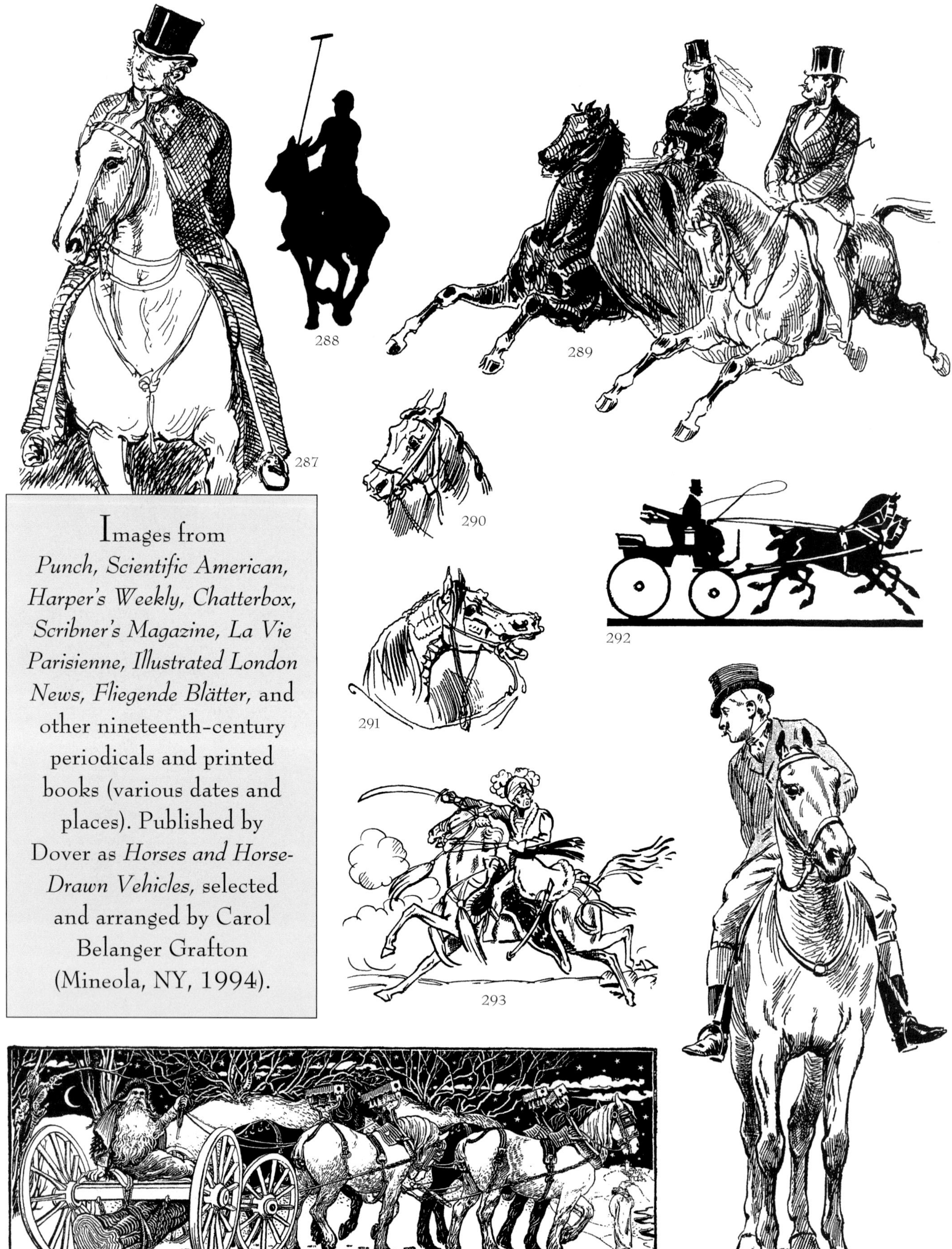

287

288

289

290

291

292

293

294

295

Images from *Punch, Scientific American, Harper's Weekly, Chatterbox, Scribner's Magazine, La Vie Parisienne, Illustrated London News, Fliegende Blätter,* and other nineteenth-century periodicals and printed books (various dates and places). Published by Dover as *Horses and Horse-Drawn Vehicles,* selected and arranged by Carol Belanger Grafton (Mineola, NY, 1994).

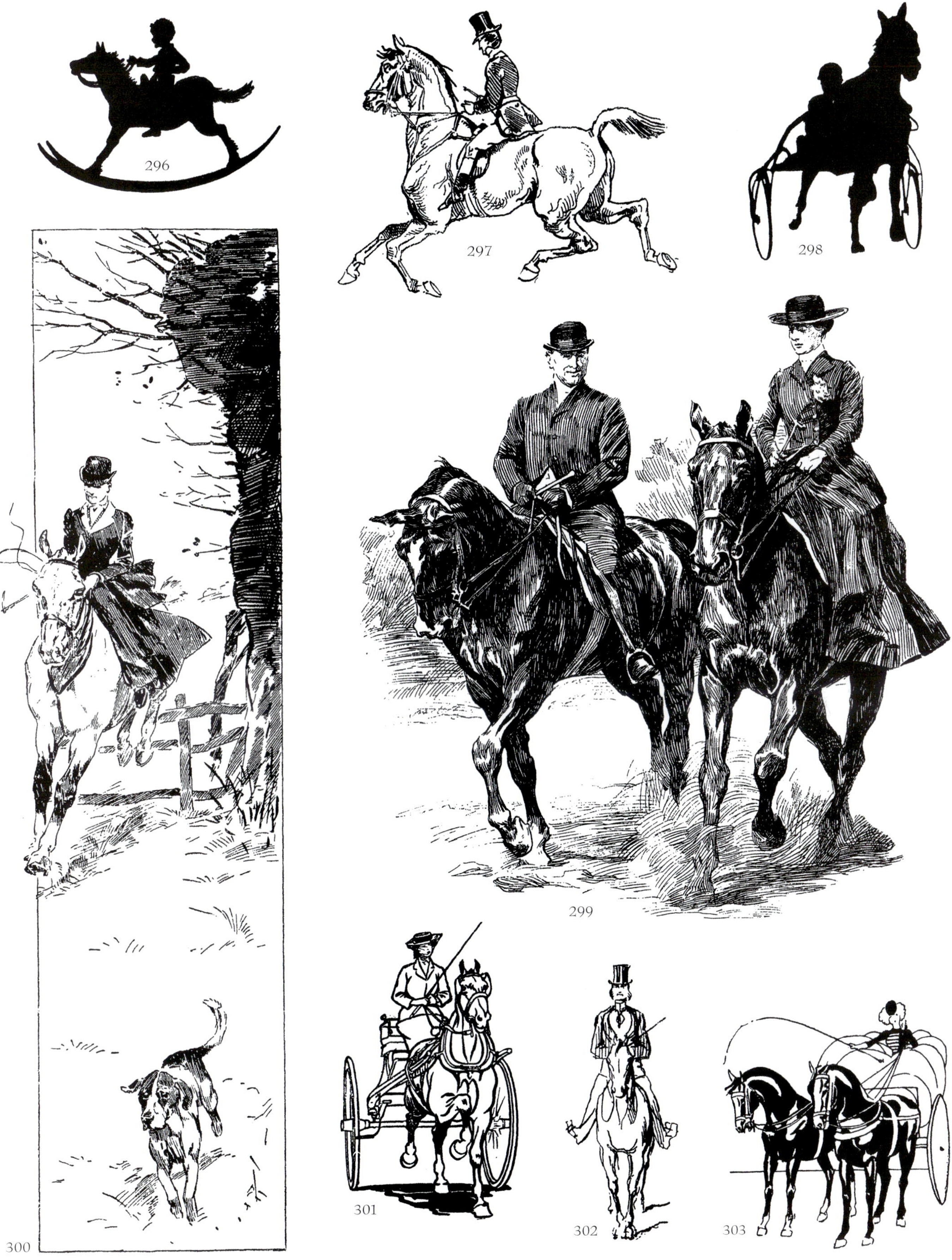
296 297 298 299 300 301 302 303

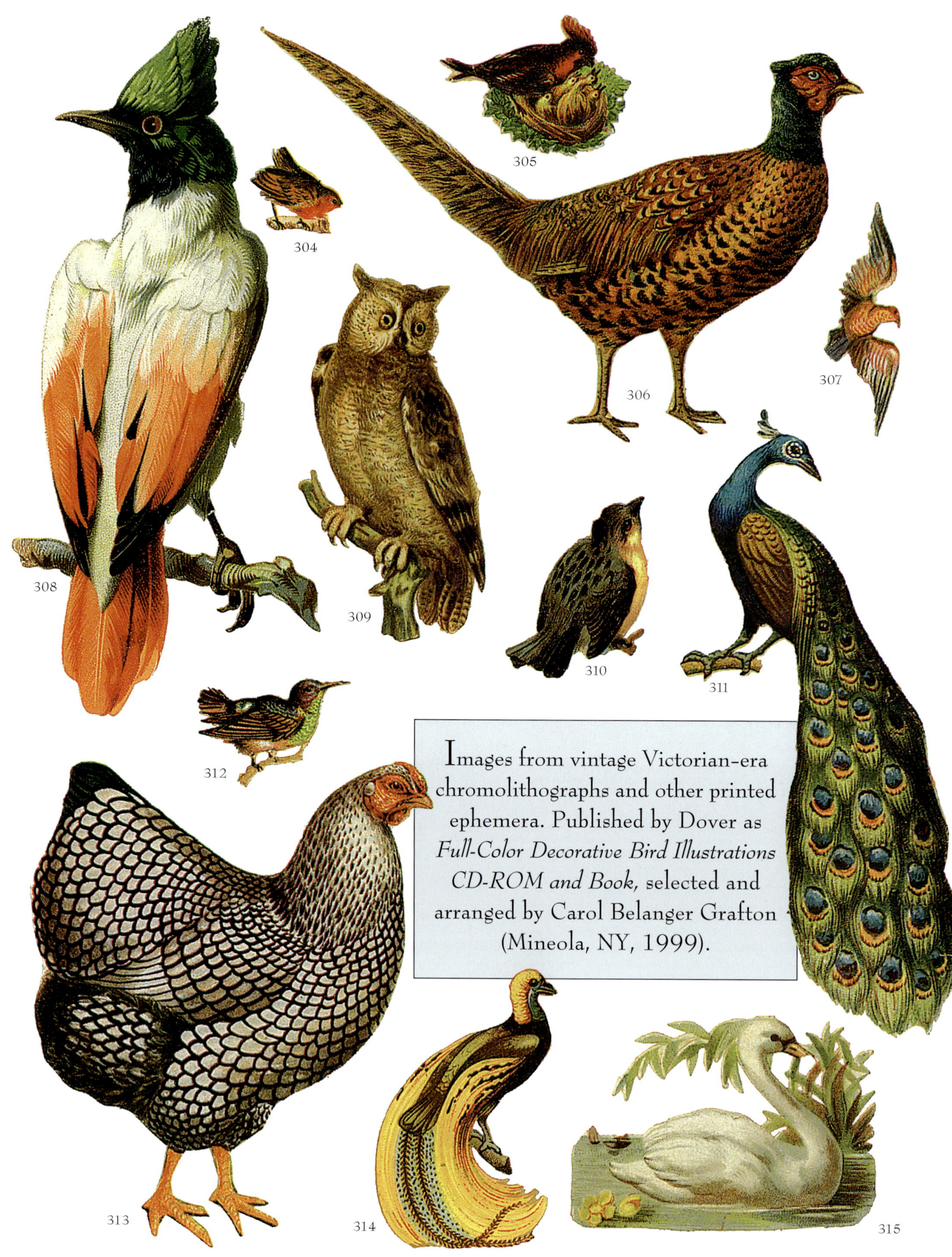

Images from vintage Victorian-era chromolithographs and other printed ephemera. Published by Dover as *Full-Color Decorative Bird Illustrations CD-ROM and Book,* selected and arranged by Carol Belanger Grafton (Mineola, NY, 1999).

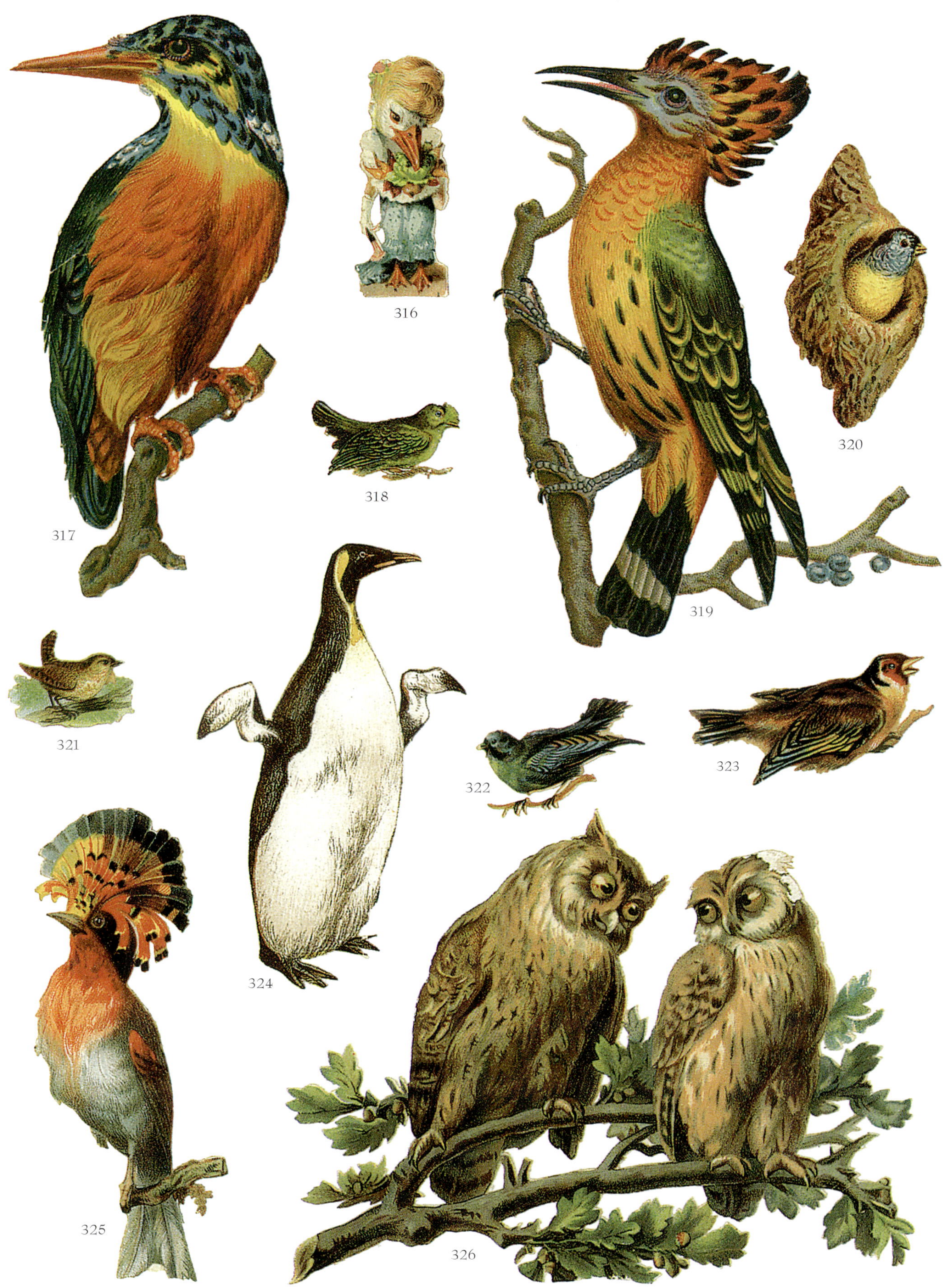
316
317
318
319
320
321
322
323
324
325
326

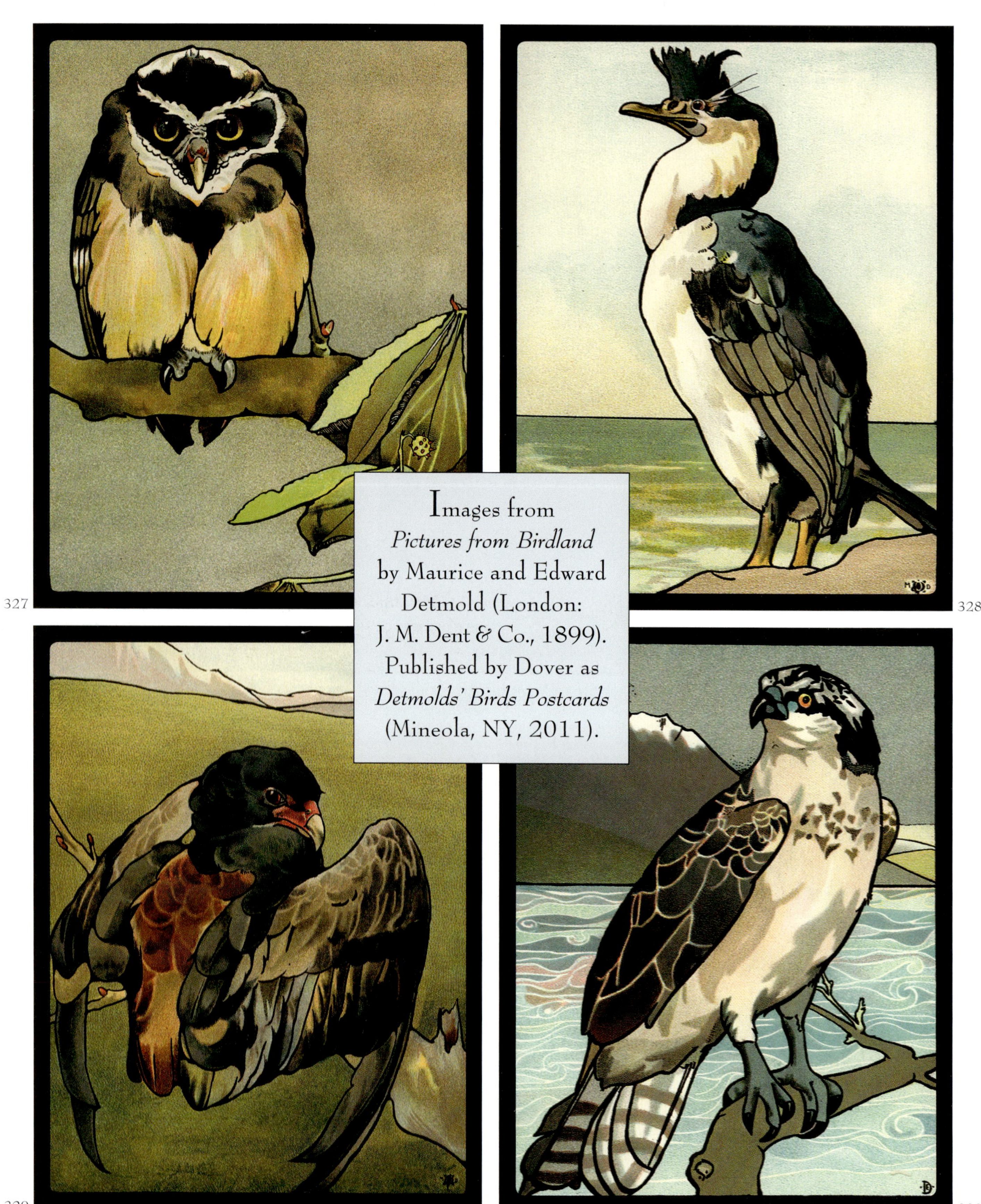

327 328 329 330

Images from
Pictures from Birdland
by Maurice and Edward
Detmold (London:
J. M. Dent & Co., 1899).
Published by Dover as
Detmolds' Birds Postcards
(Mineola, NY, 2011).

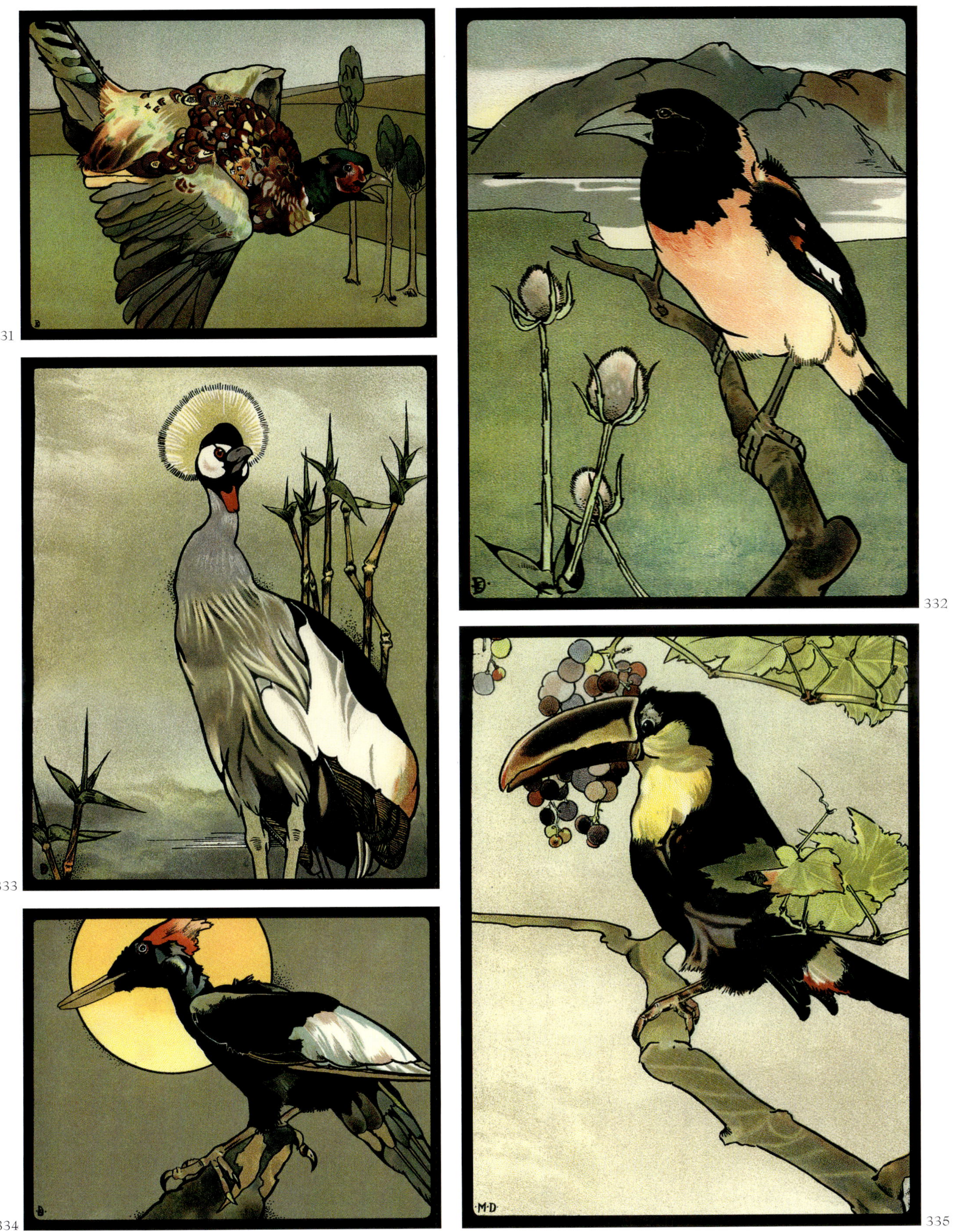

331 332 333 334 335

Images from *Grand Animal ABC Book,* with pictures from the watercolors of the animal painter August Specht and with text by M. Kohler (Konstanz, Germany: Book and Art Publisher Carl Hirsch A.G., c. 1900).

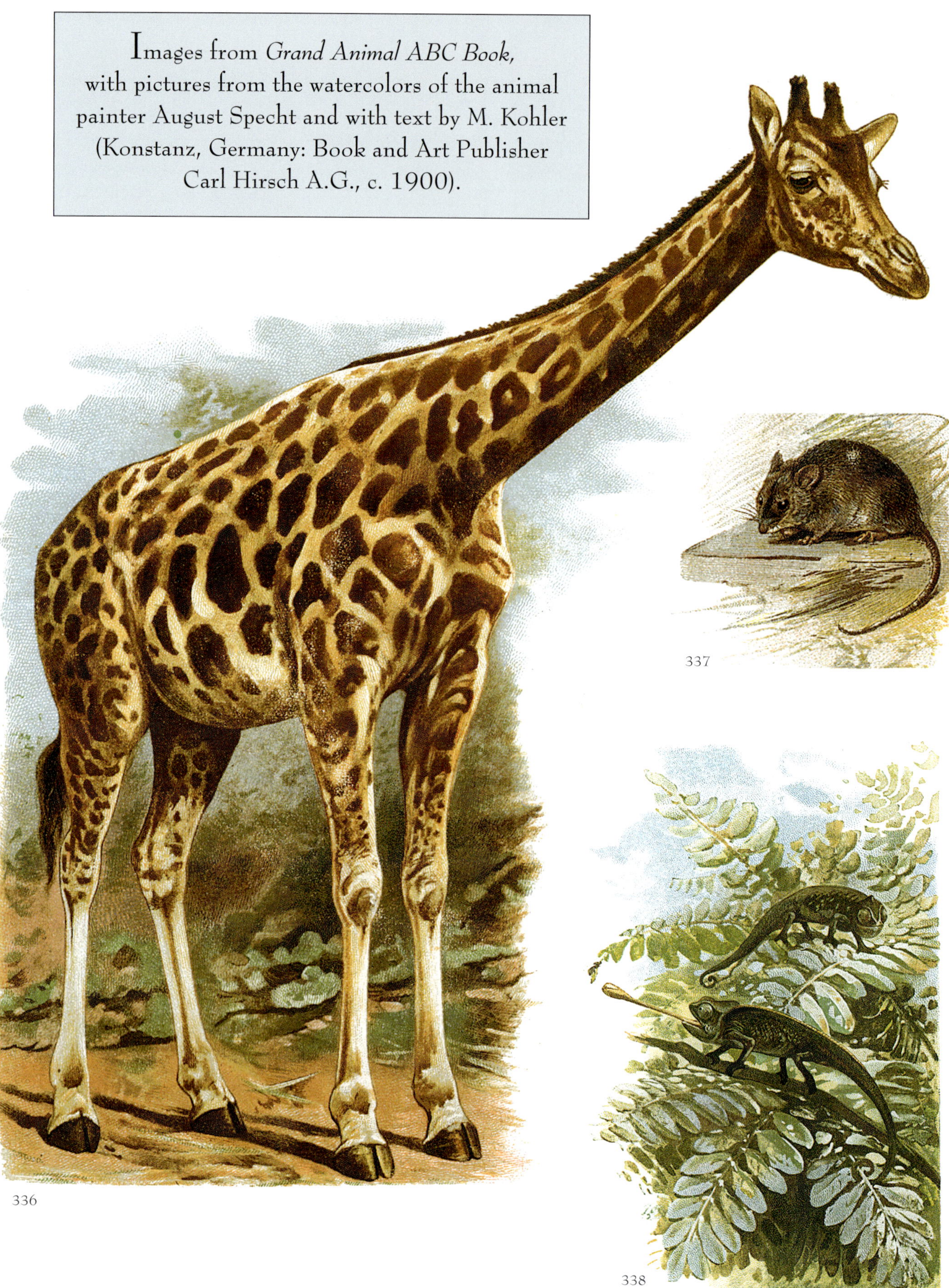

336

337

338

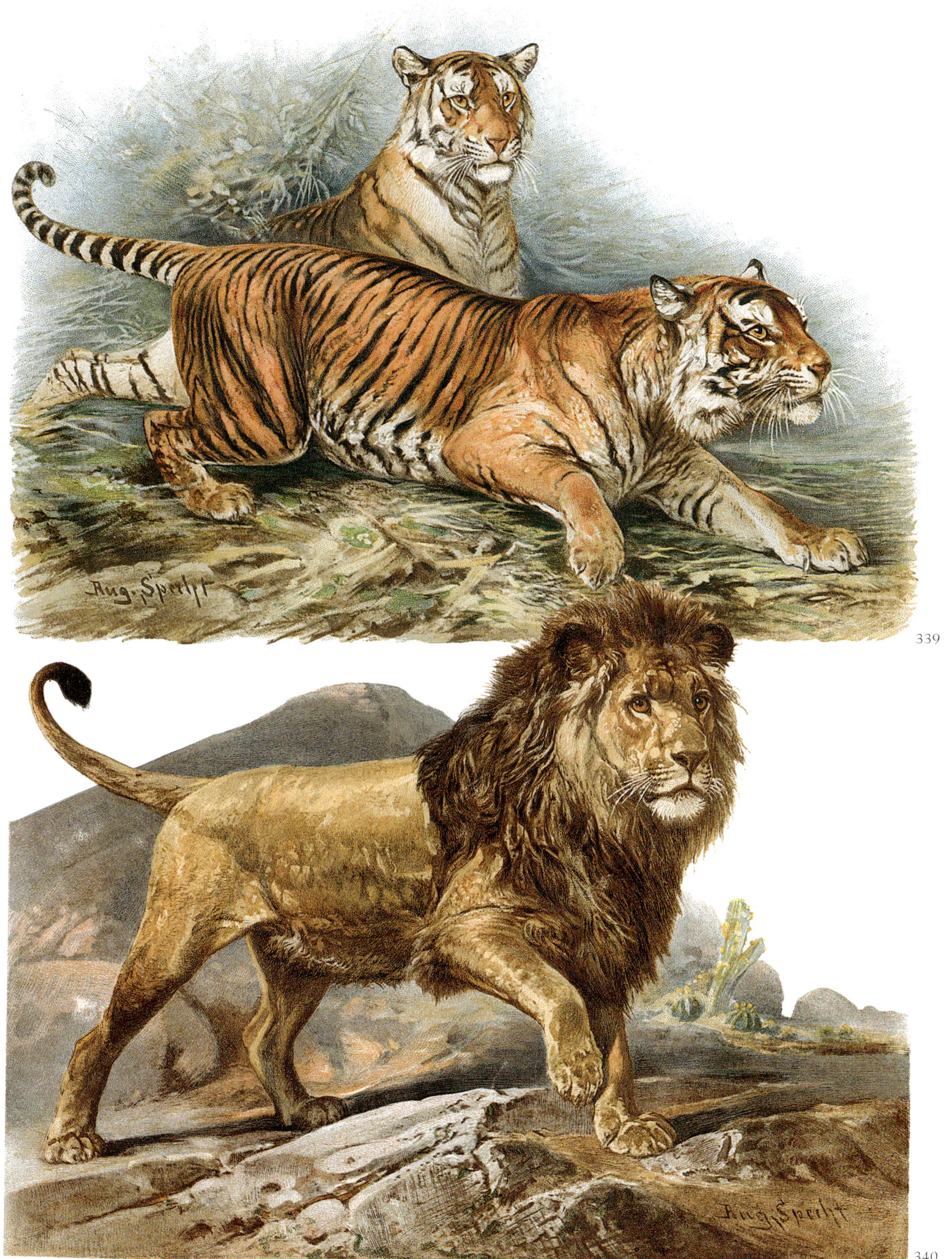

339

340

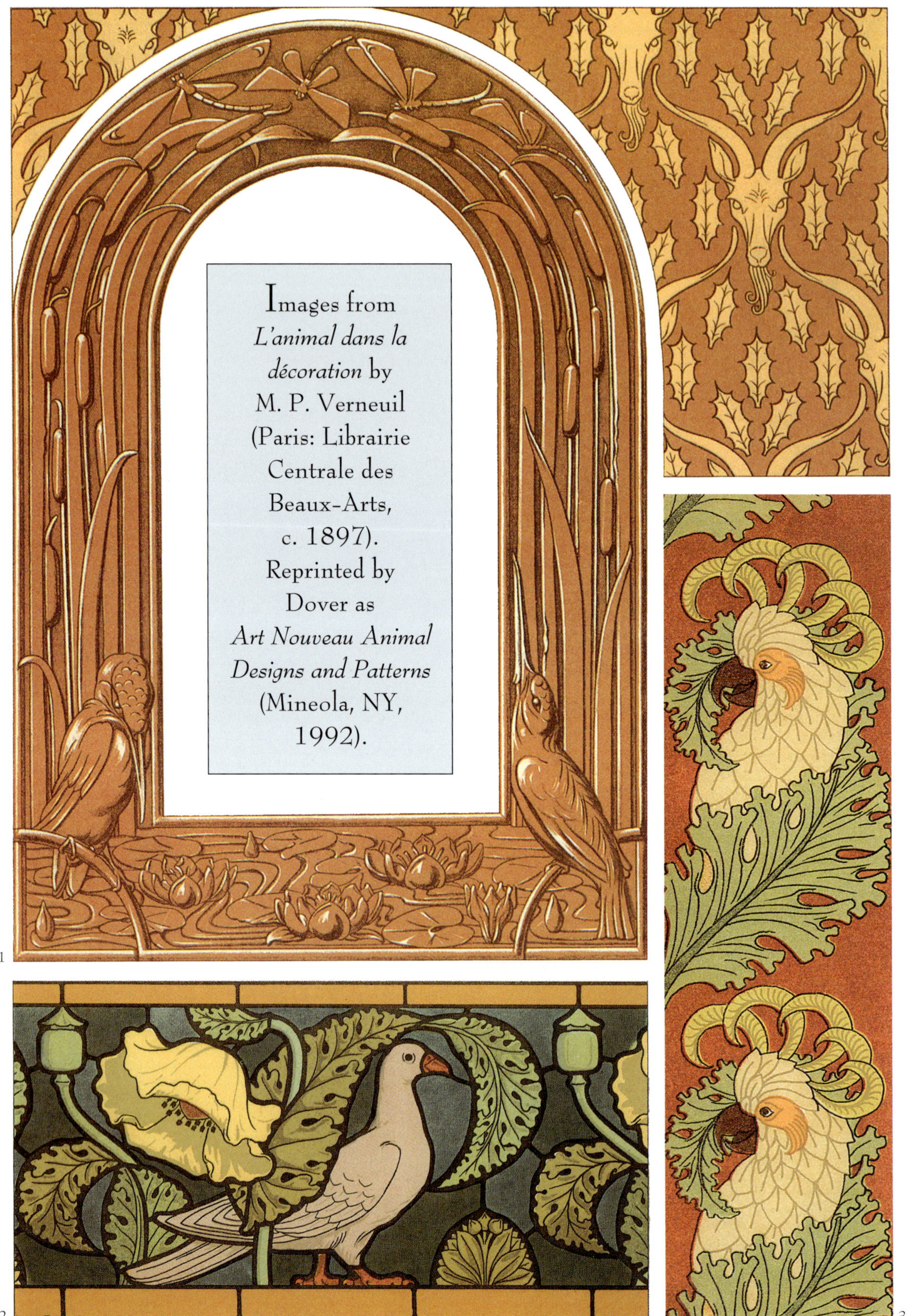

Images from *L'animal dans la décoration* by M. P. Verneuil (Paris: Librairie Centrale des Beaux-Arts, c. 1897). Reprinted by Dover as *Art Nouveau Animal Designs and Patterns* (Mineola, NY, 1992).

341

342

343

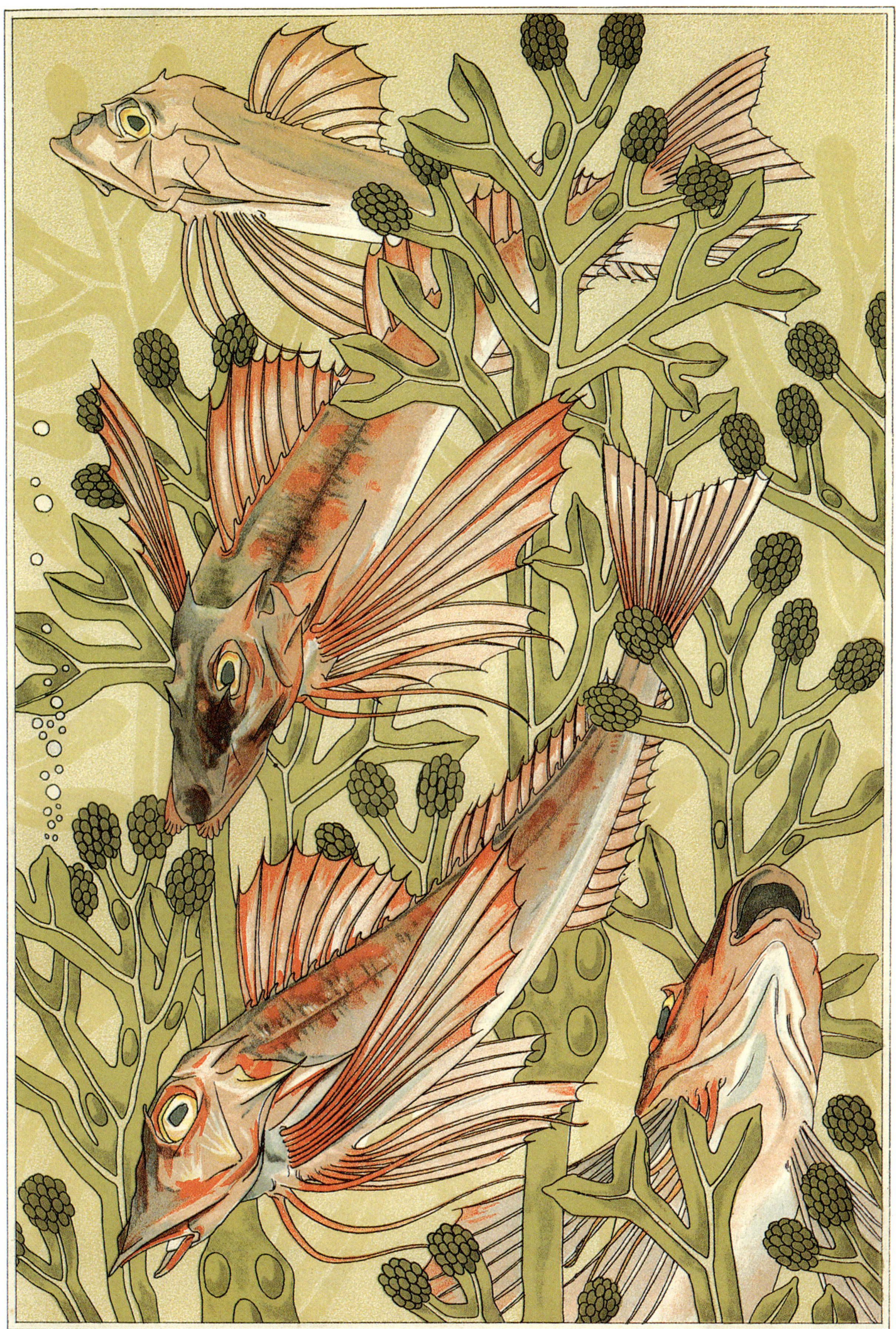

344

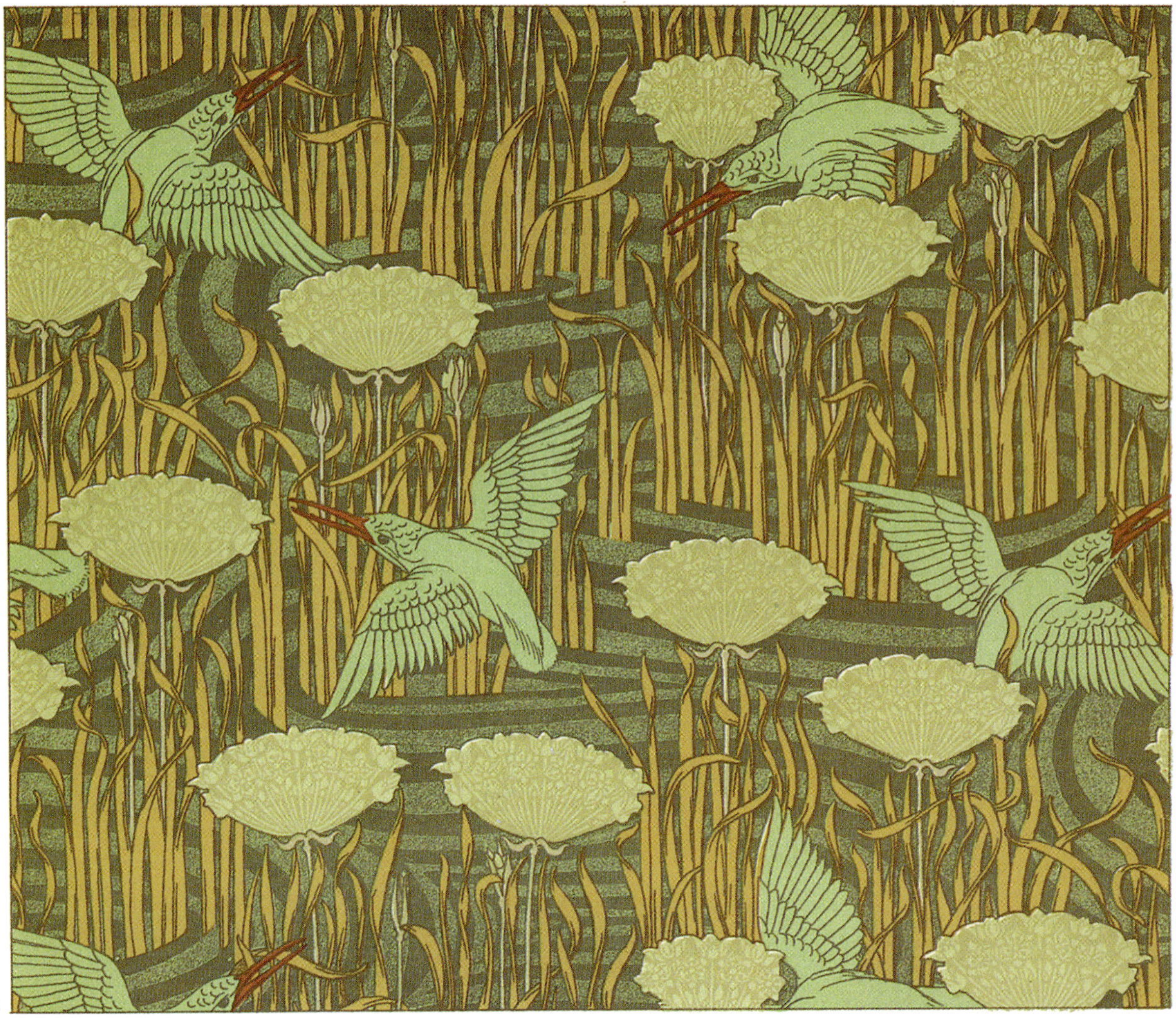

345

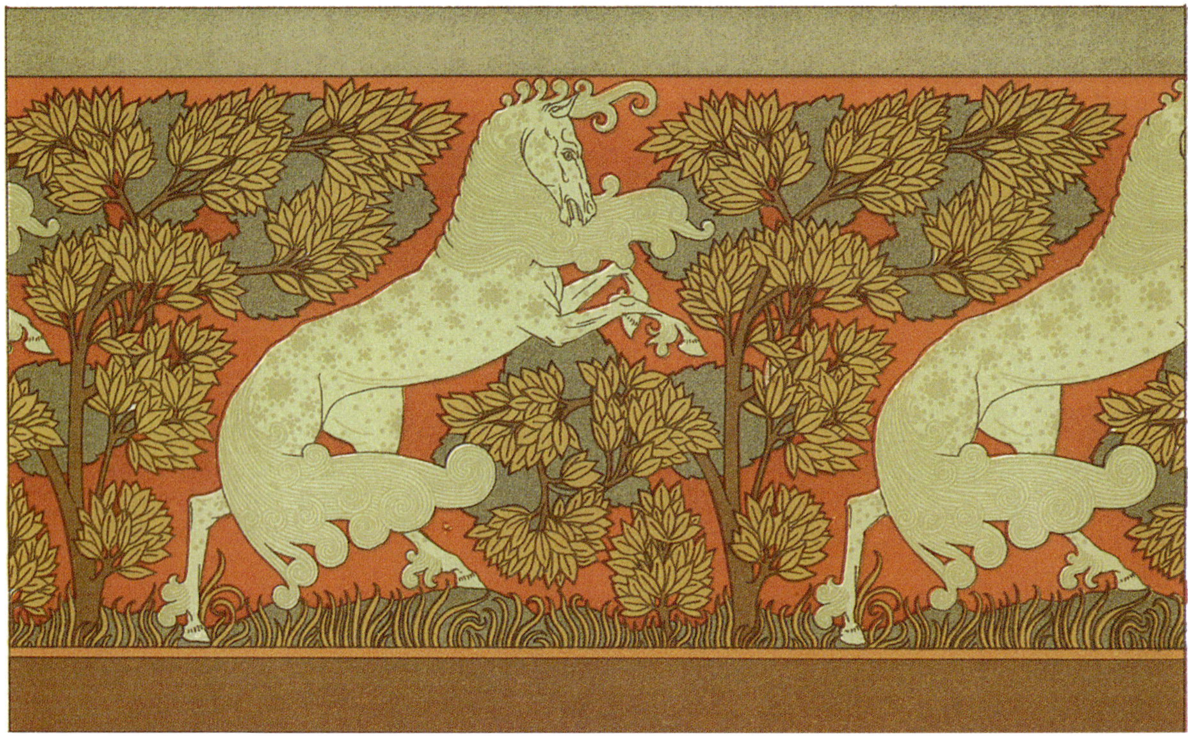

346

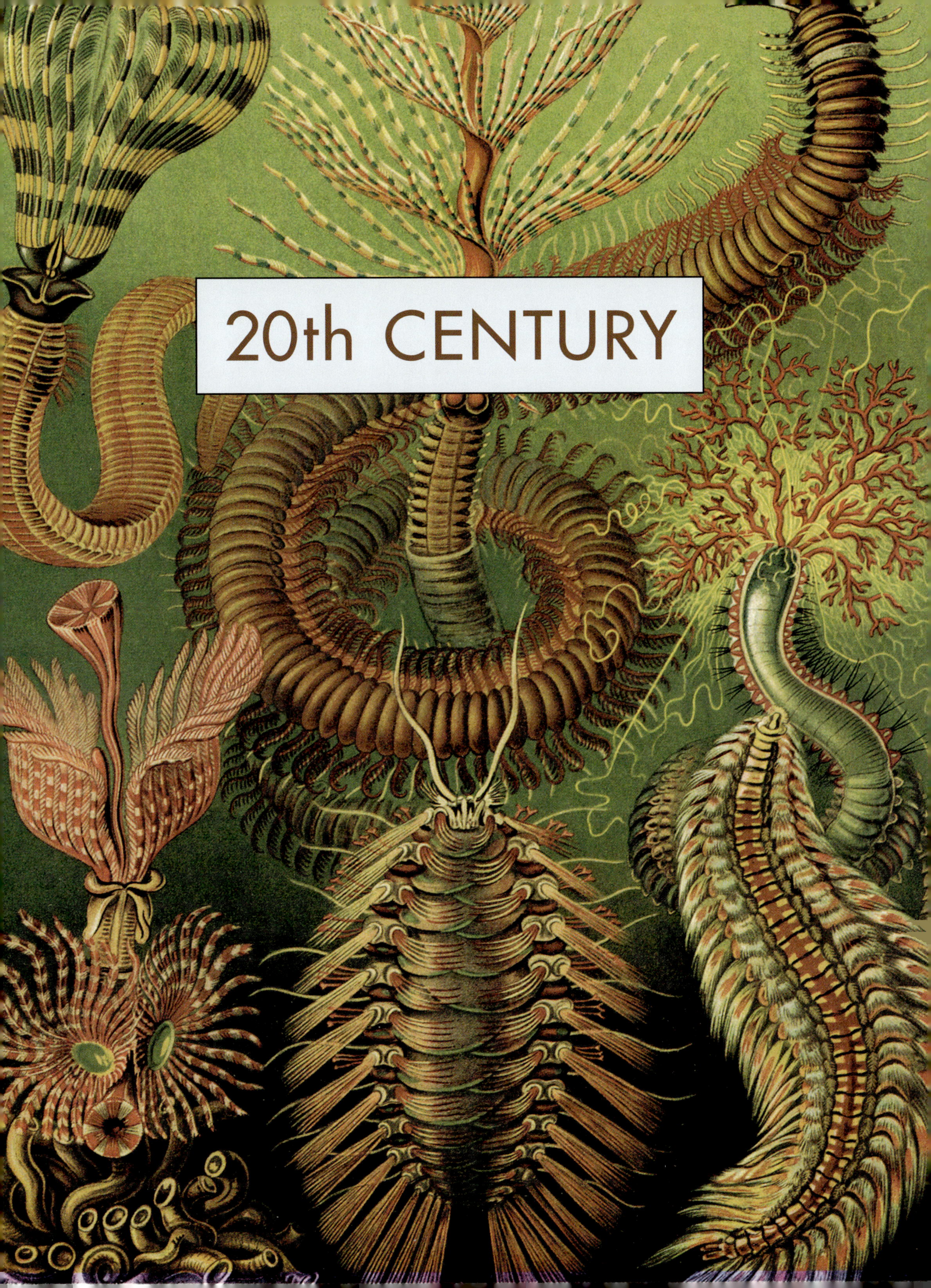

20th CENTURY

348

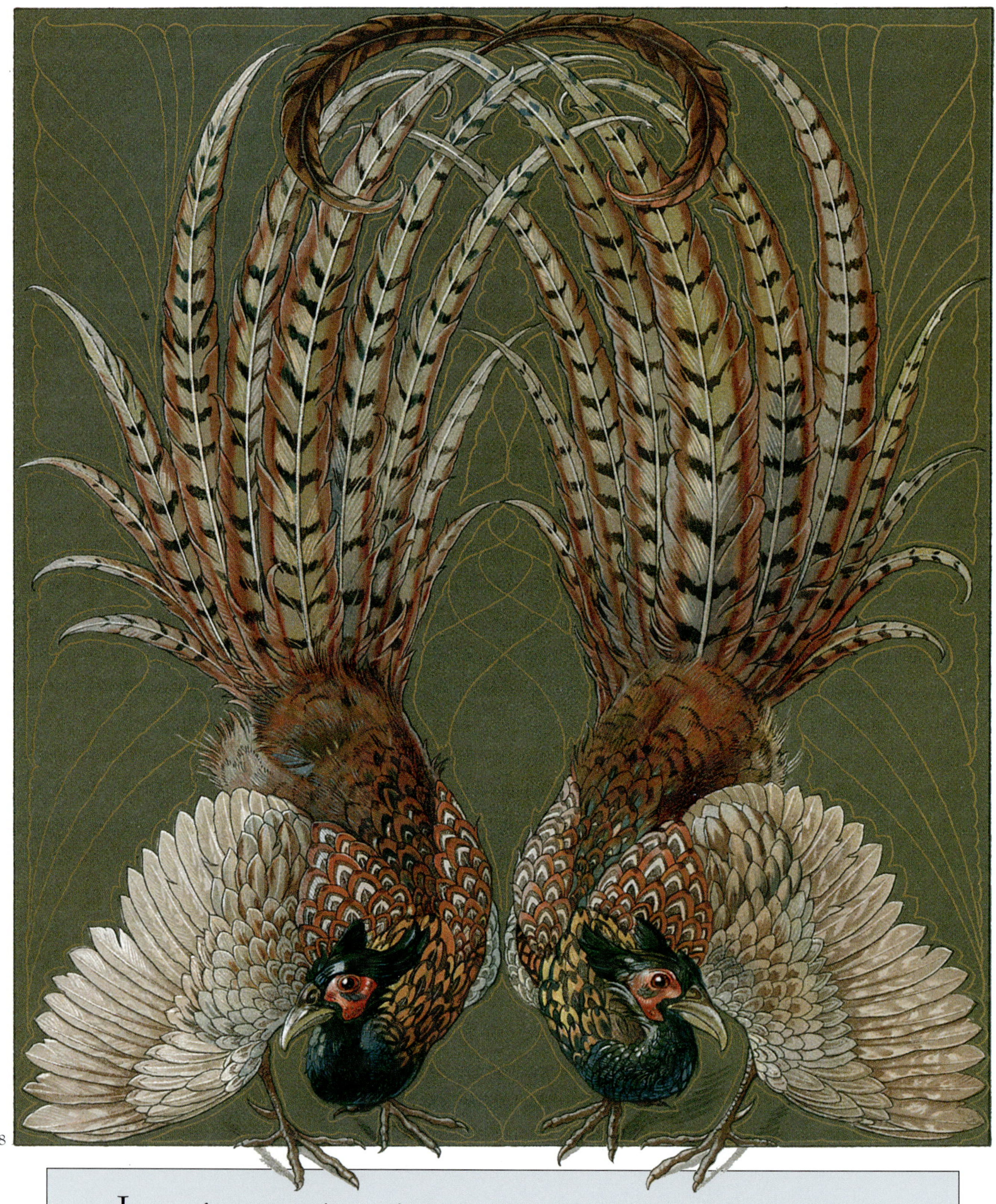

Images from *Das Thier in der Decorativen Kunst, Serie 1–2* by Anton Seder (Vienna: Gerlach & Schenk, 1896; Gerlach & Wiedling, 1909). Available online at DoverPictura.com as *Dragons, Birds and Incredible Sea Creatures.*

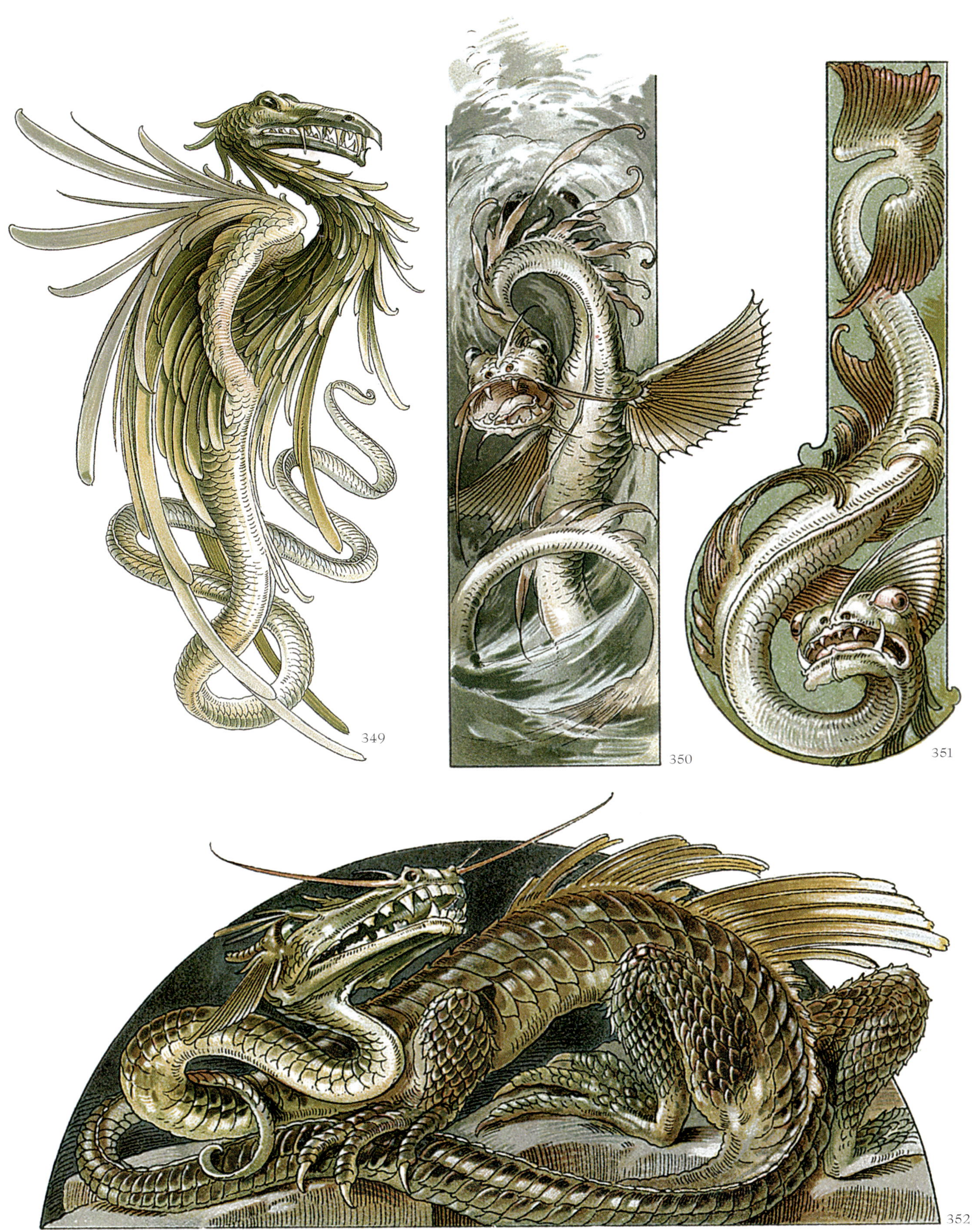
349
350
351
352

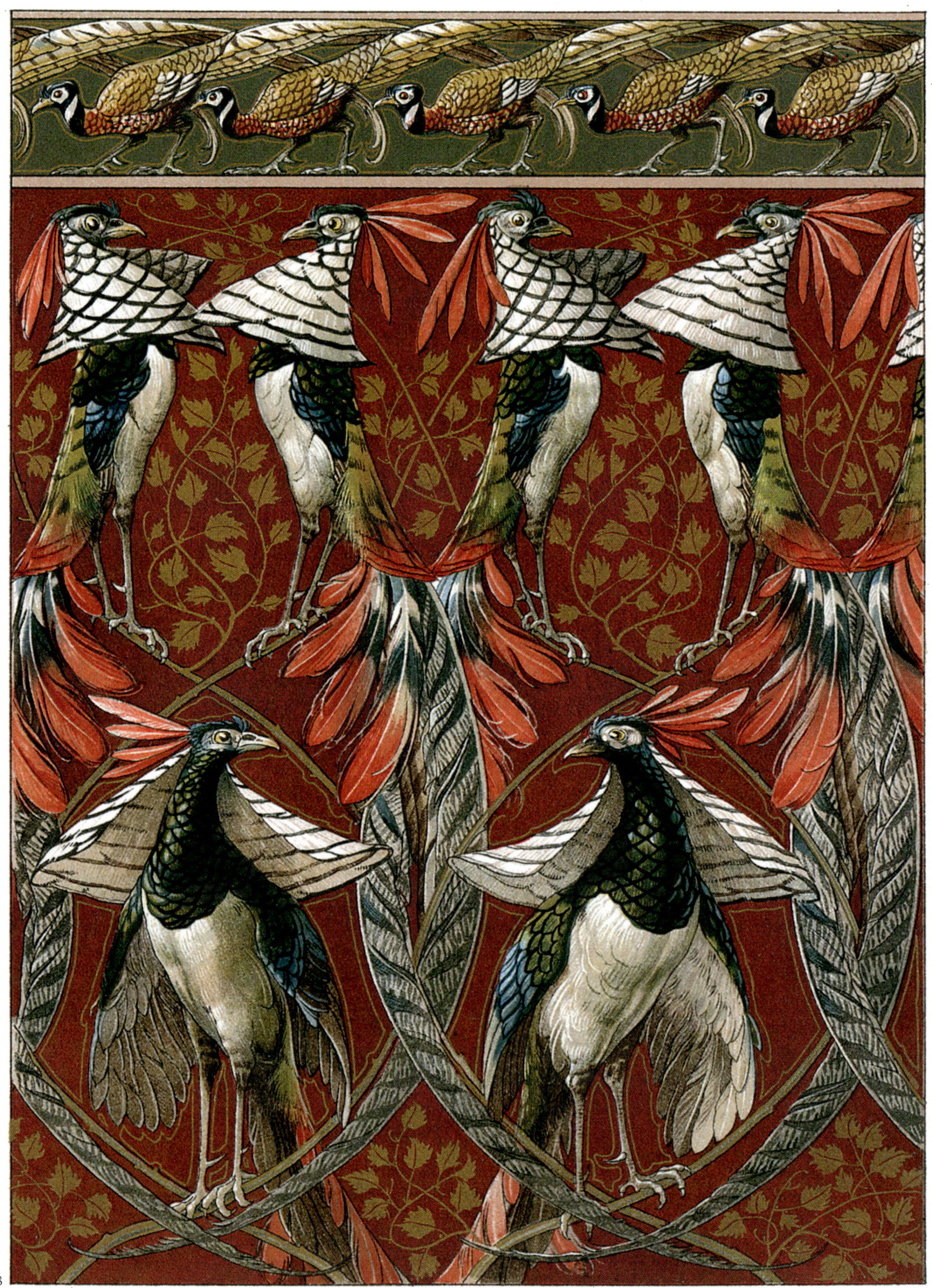

353

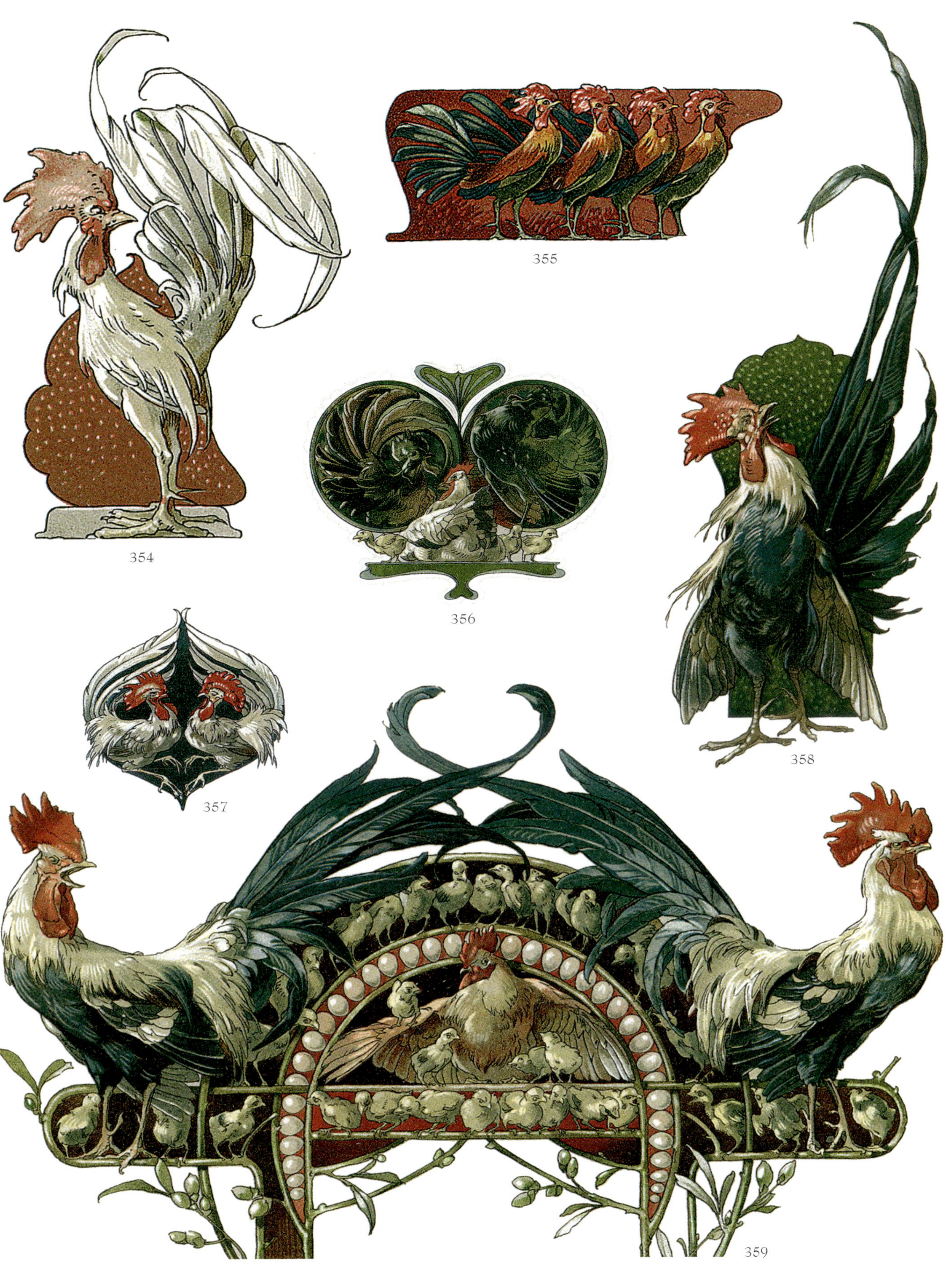
354
355
356
357
358
359

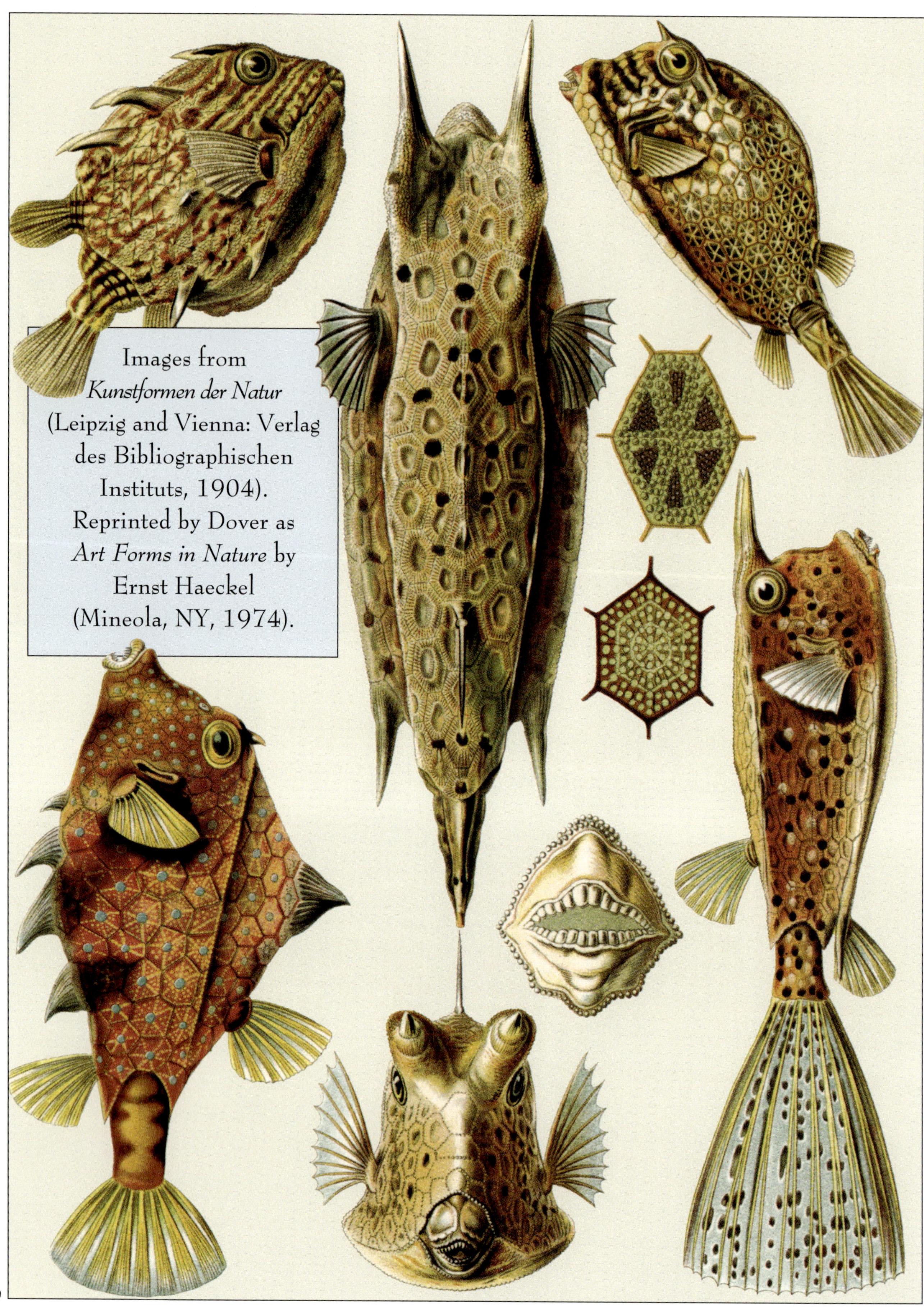
Images from
Kunstformen der Natur
(Leipzig and Vienna: Verlag
des Bibliographischen
Instituts, 1904).
Reprinted by Dover as
Art Forms in Nature by
Ernst Haeckel
(Mineola, NY, 1974).
360

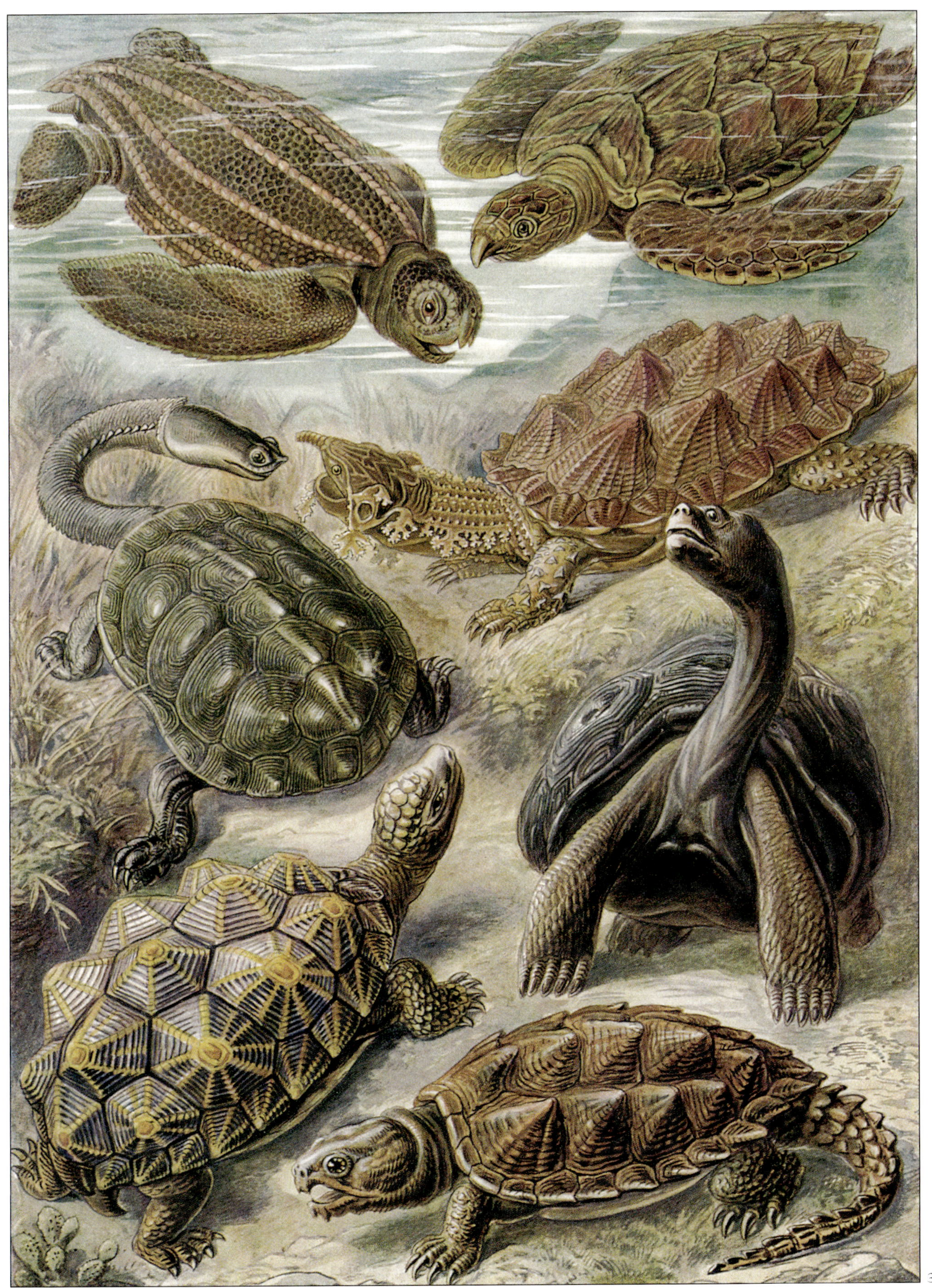

361

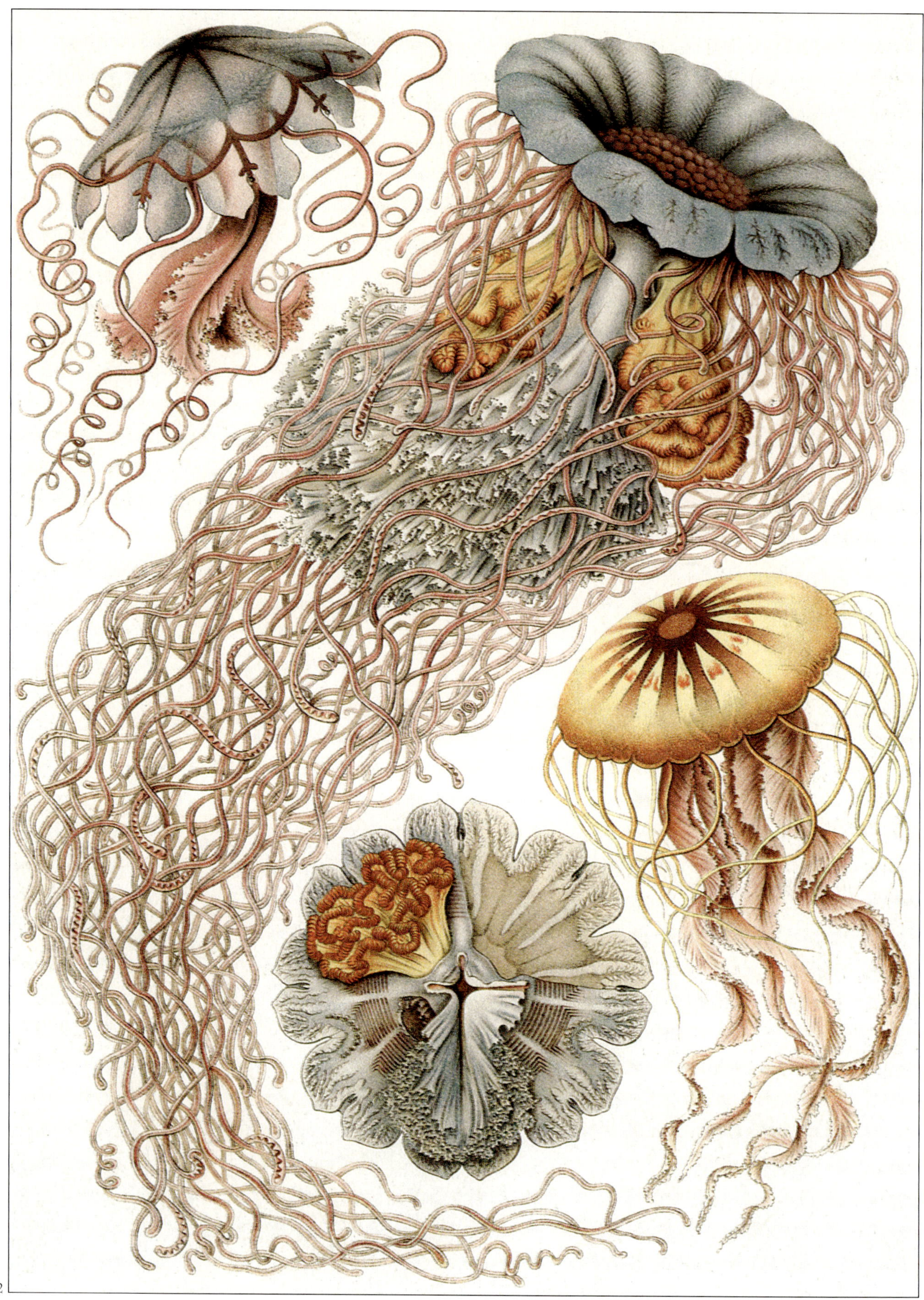

100 ART FORMS IN NATURE

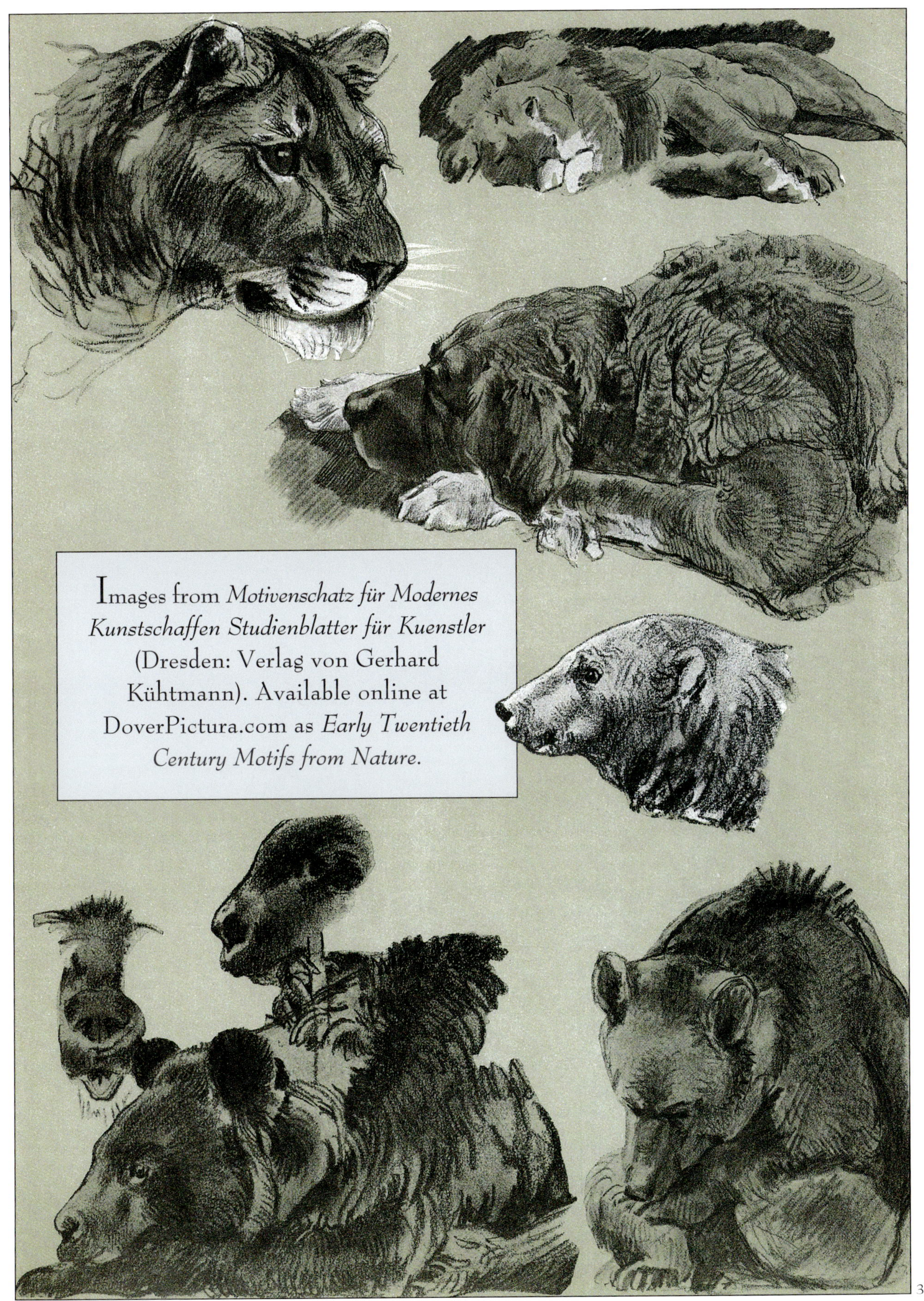

Images from *Motivenschatz für Modernes Kunstschaffen Studienblatter für Kuenstler* (Dresden: Verlag von Gerhard Kühtmann). Available online at DoverPictura.com as *Early Twentieth Century Motifs from Nature.*

363

Images from *The Jungle Book* by Rudyard Kipling, illustrated by Maurice and Edward Detmold (London: Macmillan and Co., Limited, 1908). Reprinted by Dover as a *Calla Edition,* with sixteen color plates reproduced from an extremely scarce, original portfolio from the Cotsen Children's Library in the Dept. of Rare Books and Special Collections of the Princeton University Library (Mineola, NY, 2010).

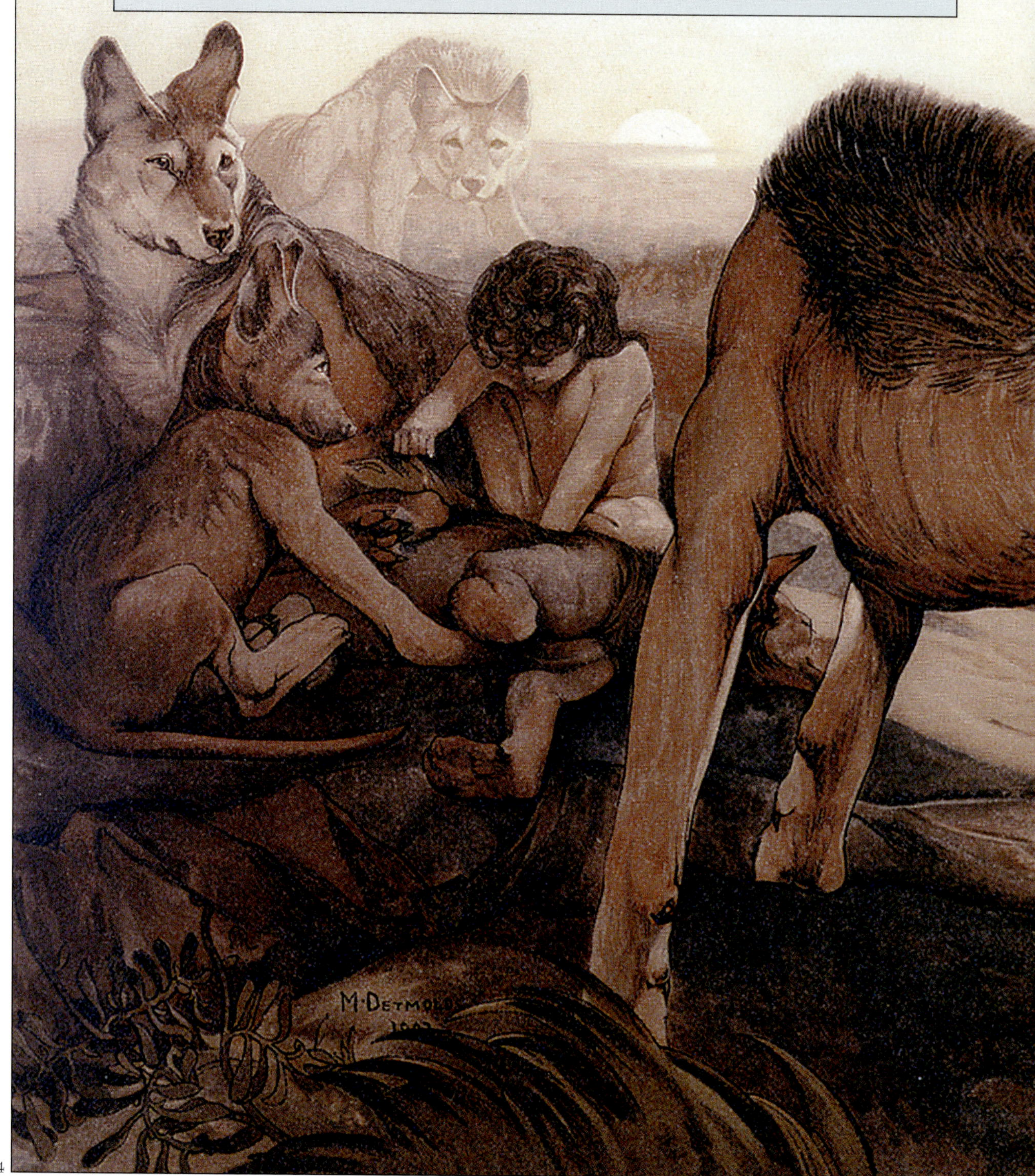

364

The "Council Rock"

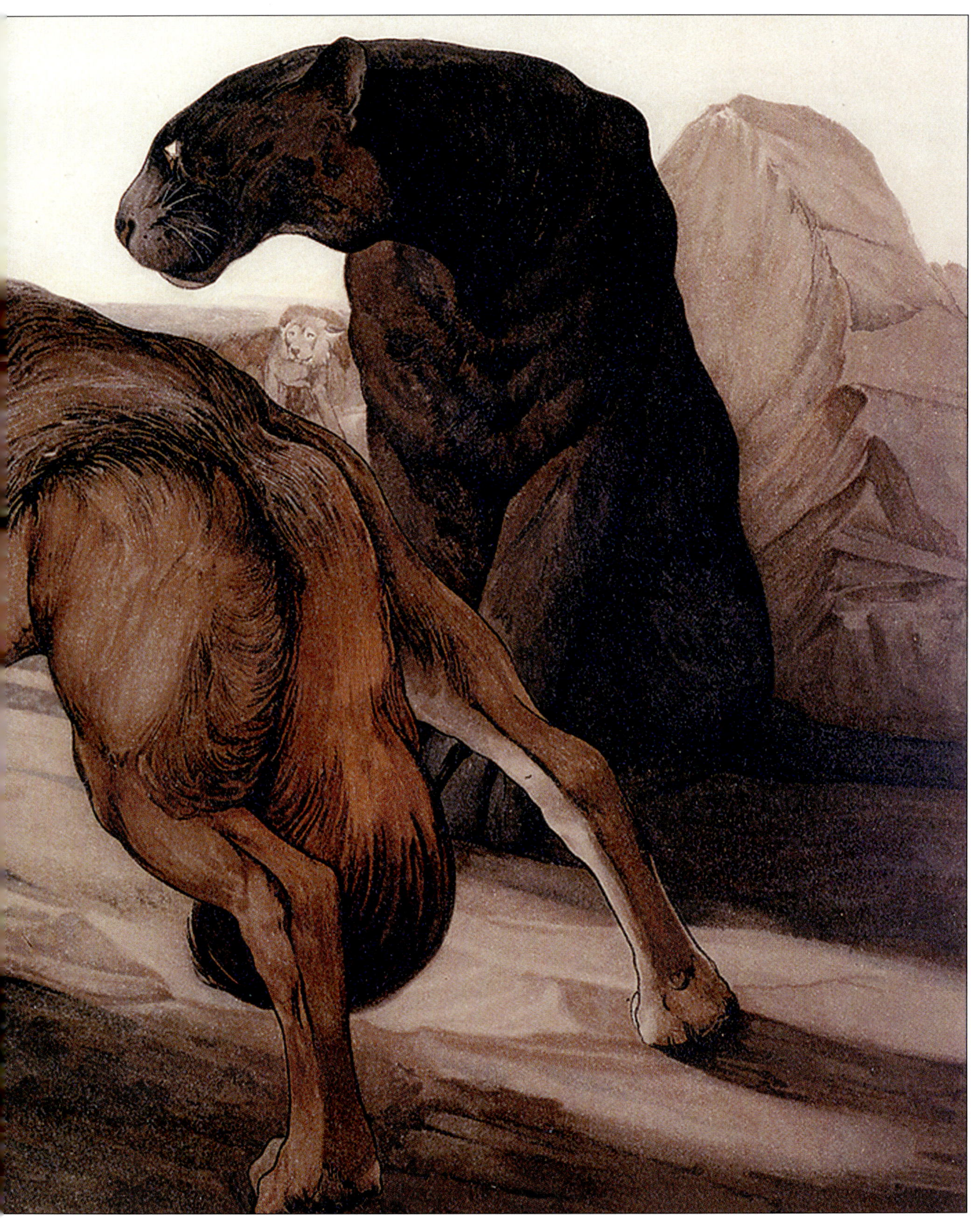

365

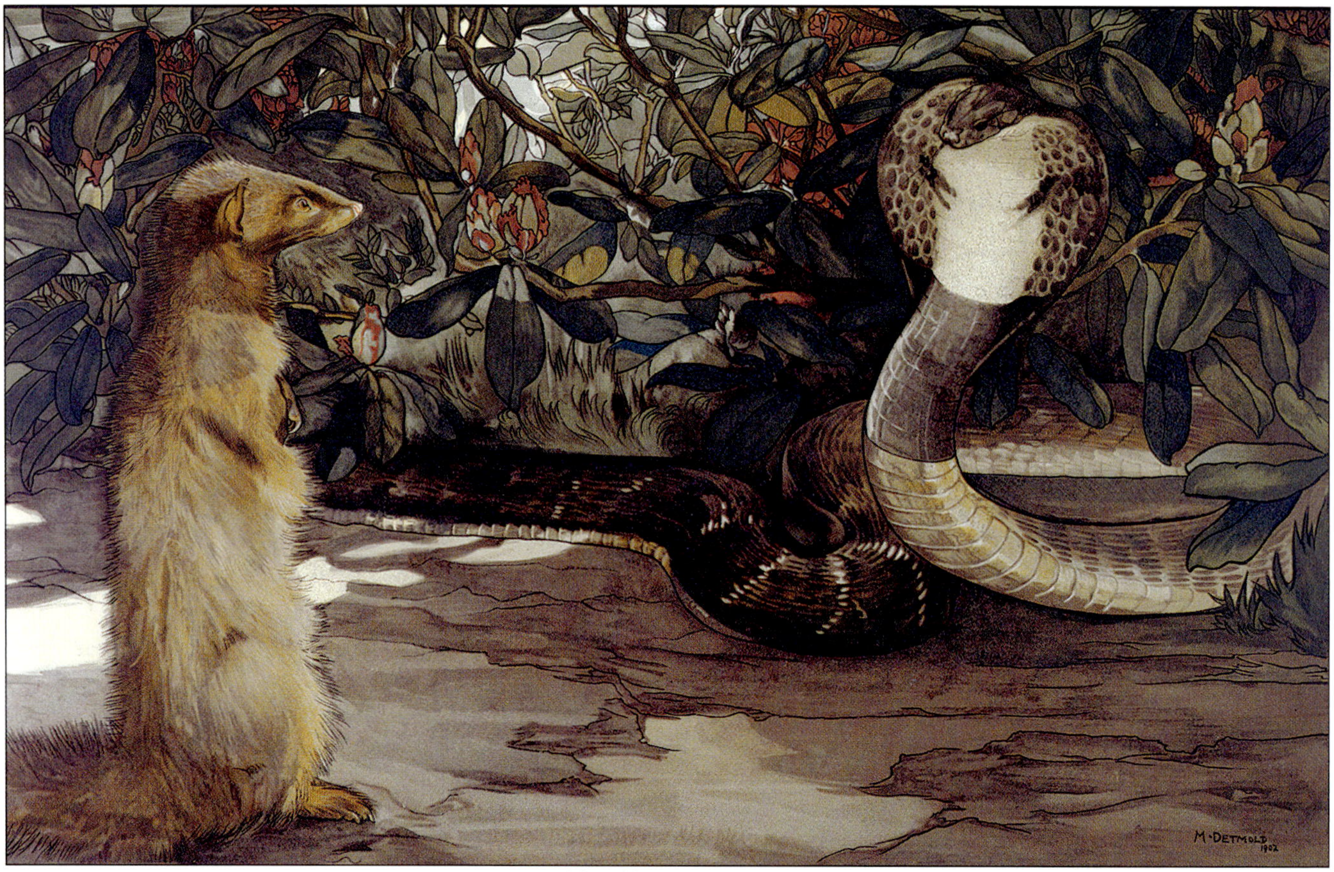

Rikki-tikki-tavi and Nag

366

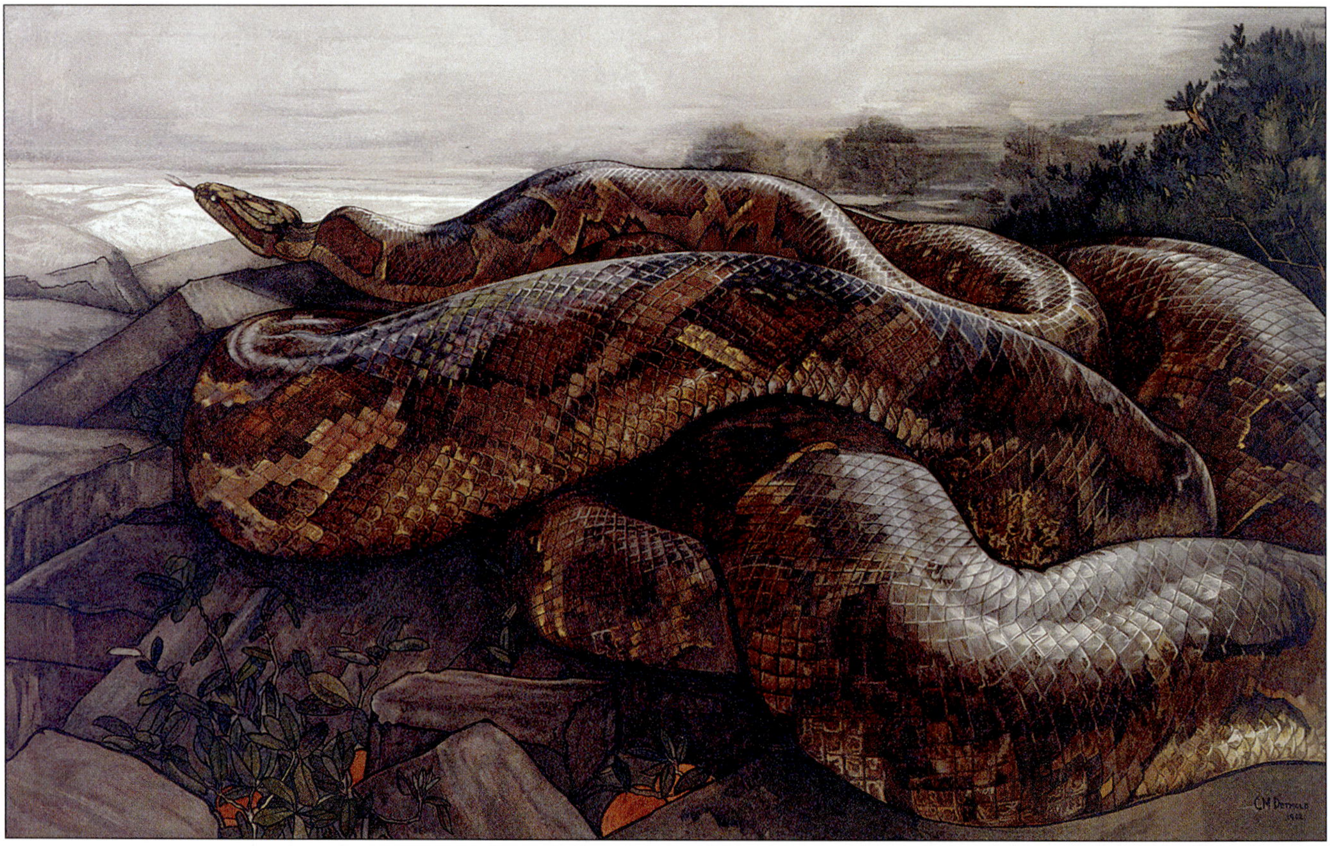

"Kaa," the Python

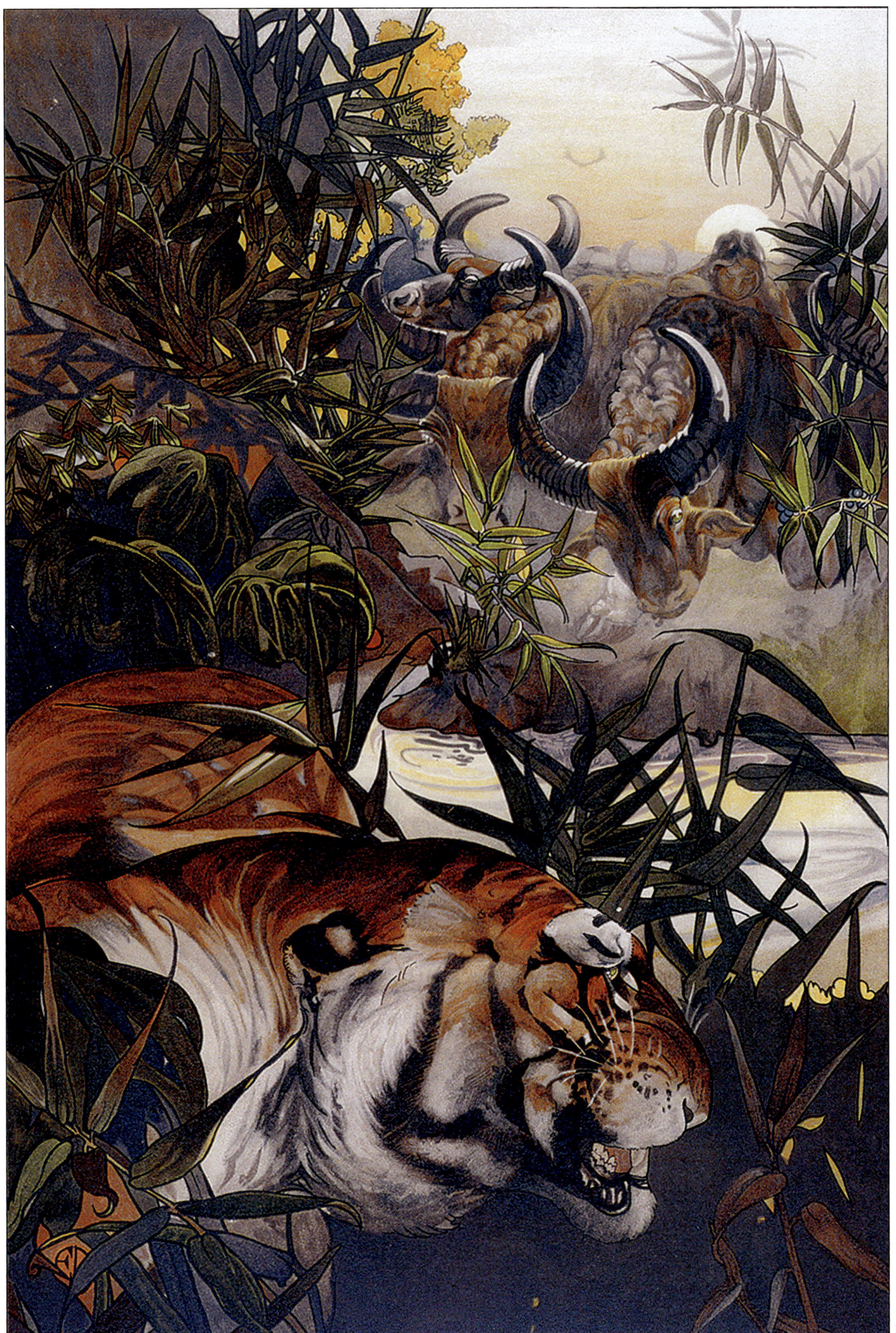

367

Shere Khan in the Jungle

Images from
the Chinese cut-paper
collection of
Florence Temko.
Published by Dover
as *Chinese Cut-Paper
Animal Designs*
(Mineola, NY, 2006).

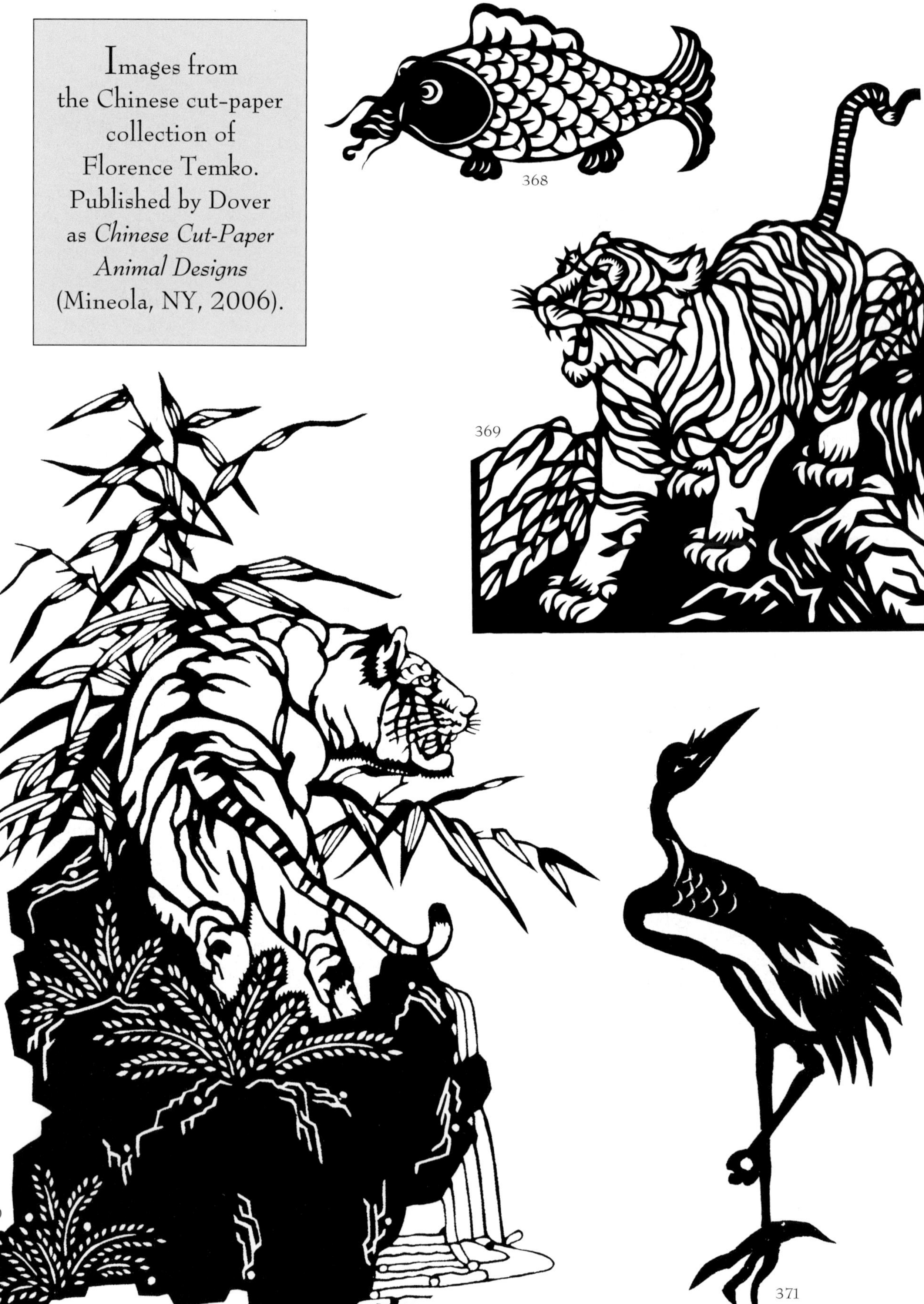

368

369

370

371

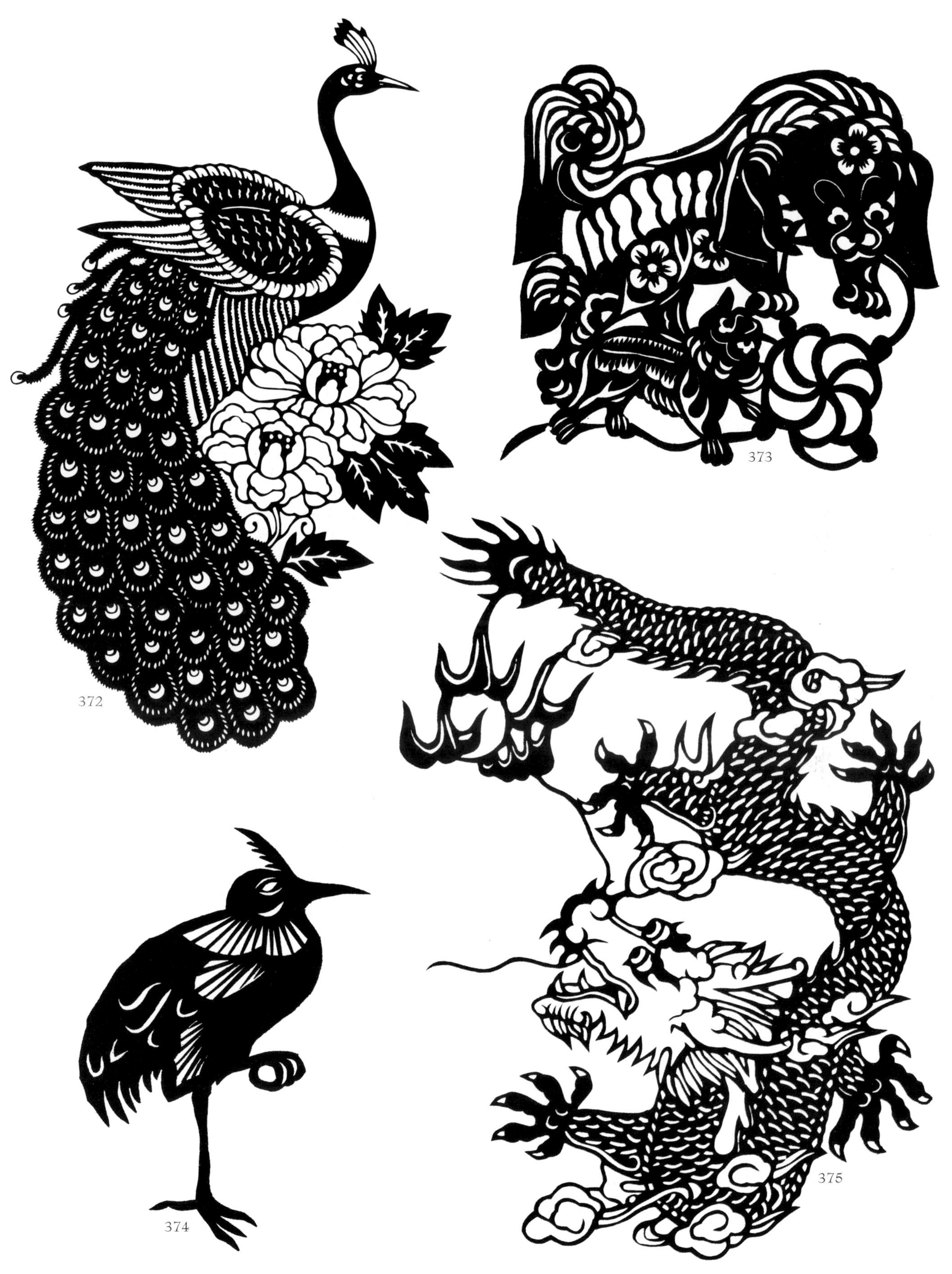

372

373

374

375

376 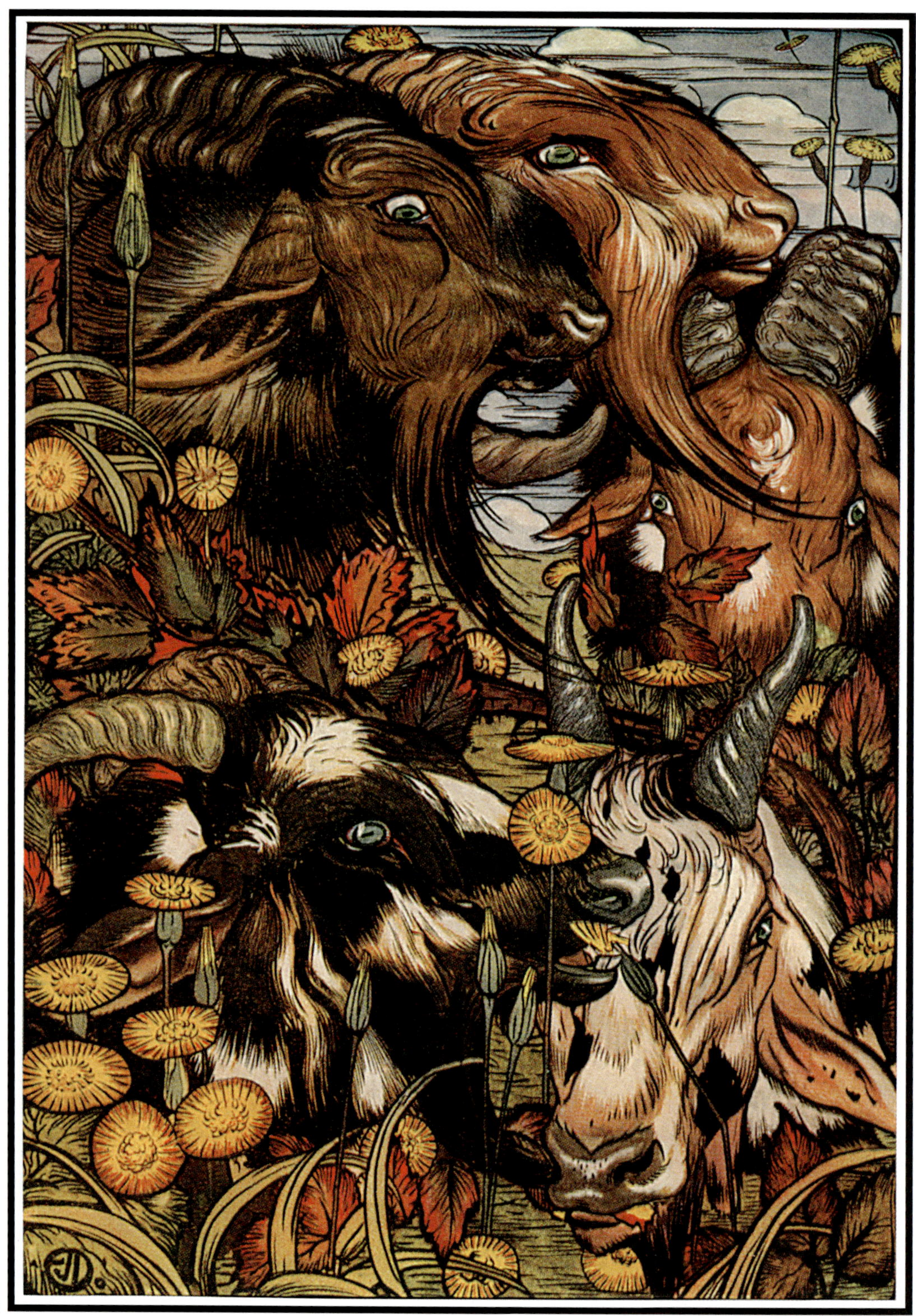

Images from *The Fables of Aesop*, with illustrations by Edward J. Detmold (London: Hodder & Stoughton, 1909). Published by Dover as a *Calla Edition* (Mineola, NY, 2014).

377

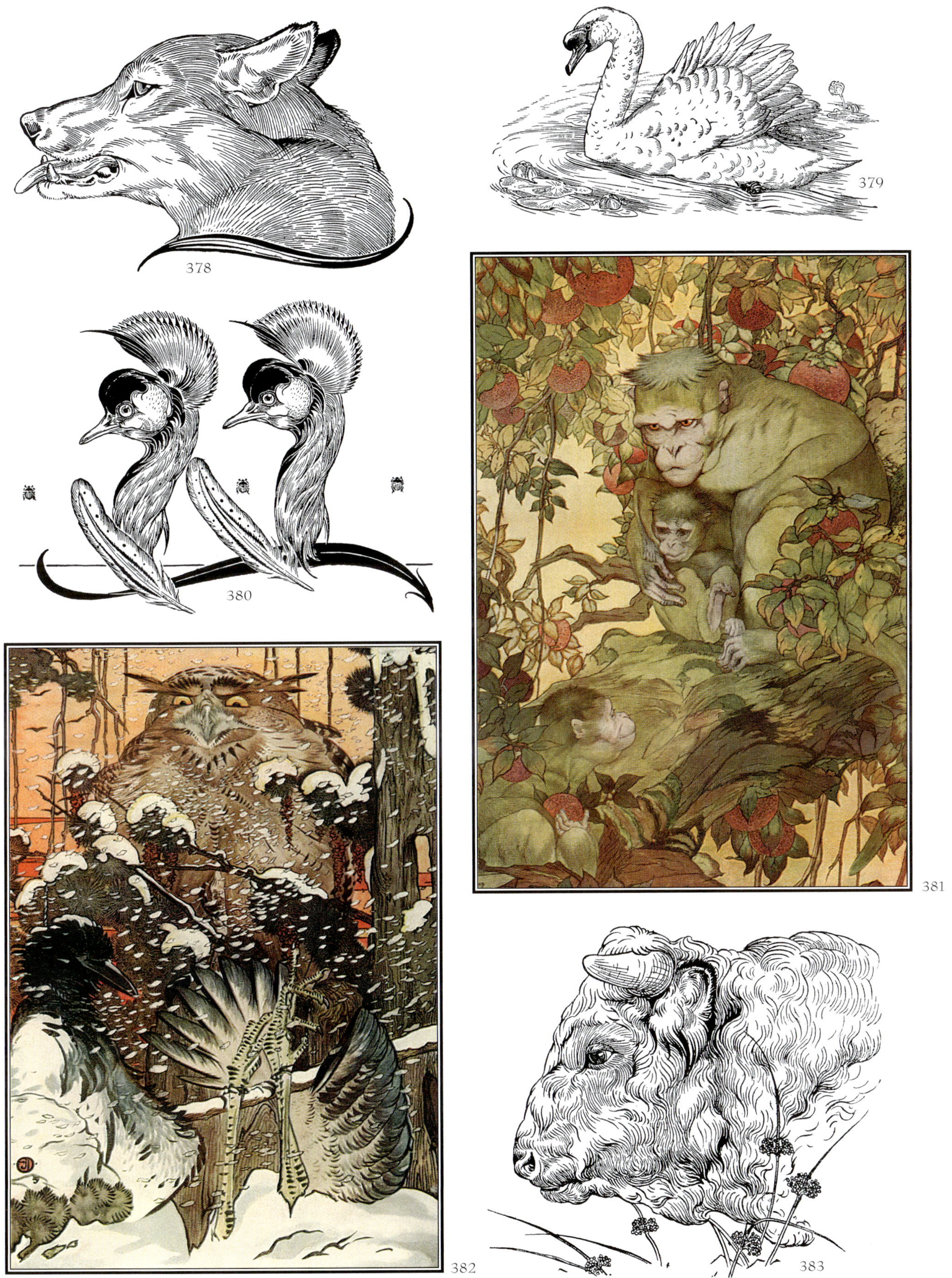

378

379

380

381

382

383

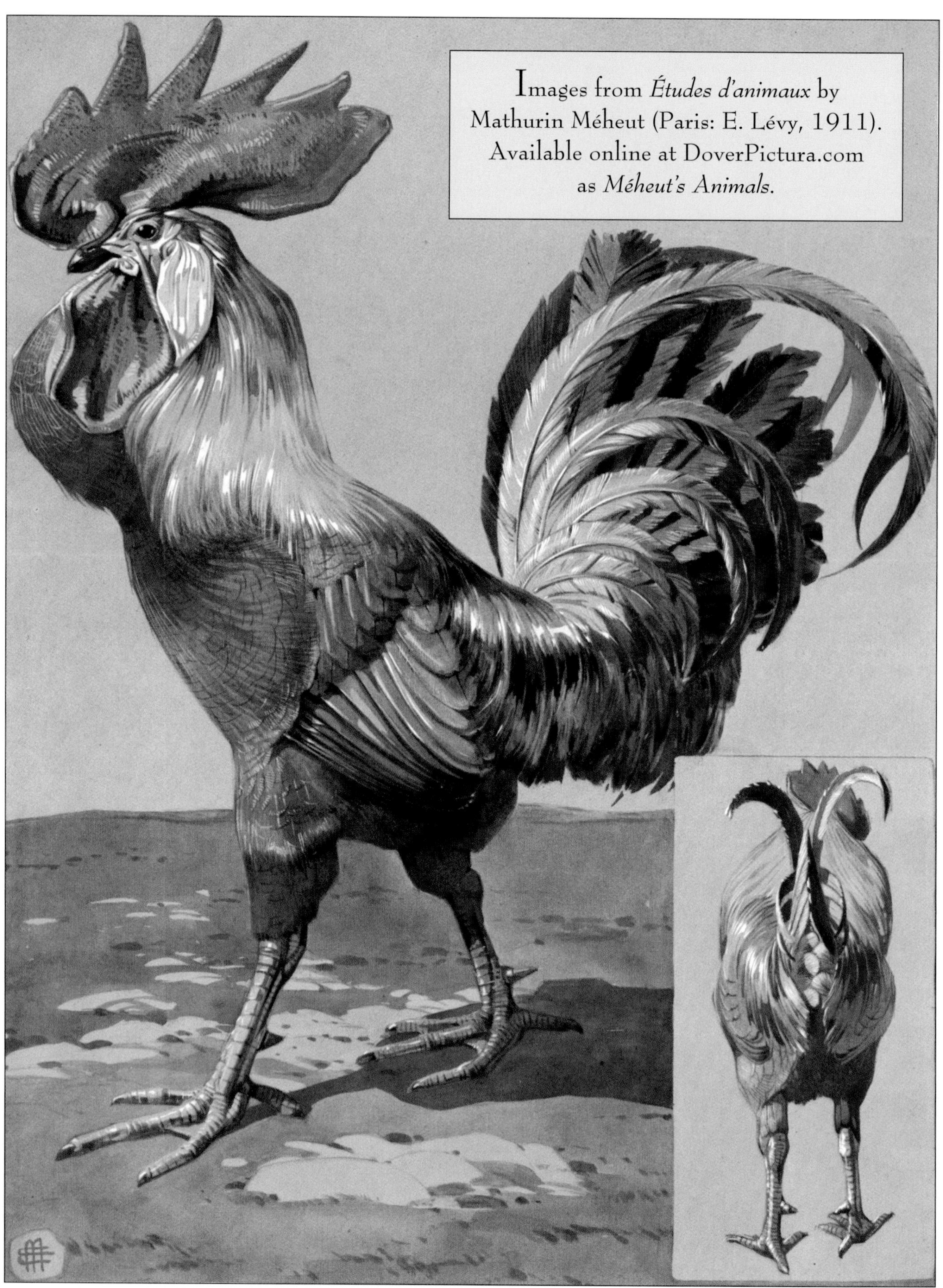
Images from *Études d'animaux* by
Mathurin Méheut (Paris: E. Lévy, 1911).
Available online at DoverPictura.com
as *Méheut's Animals*.

384

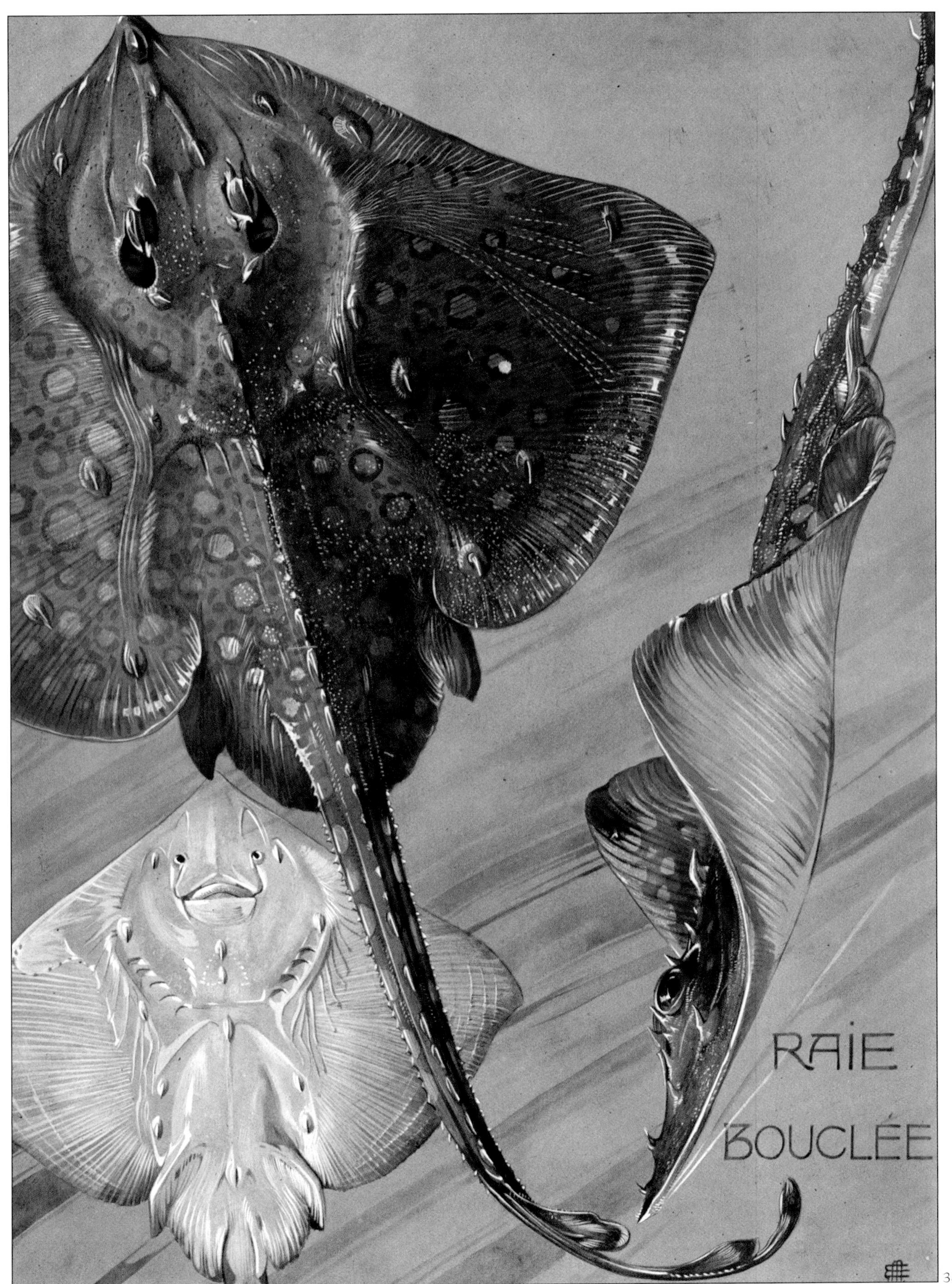

385

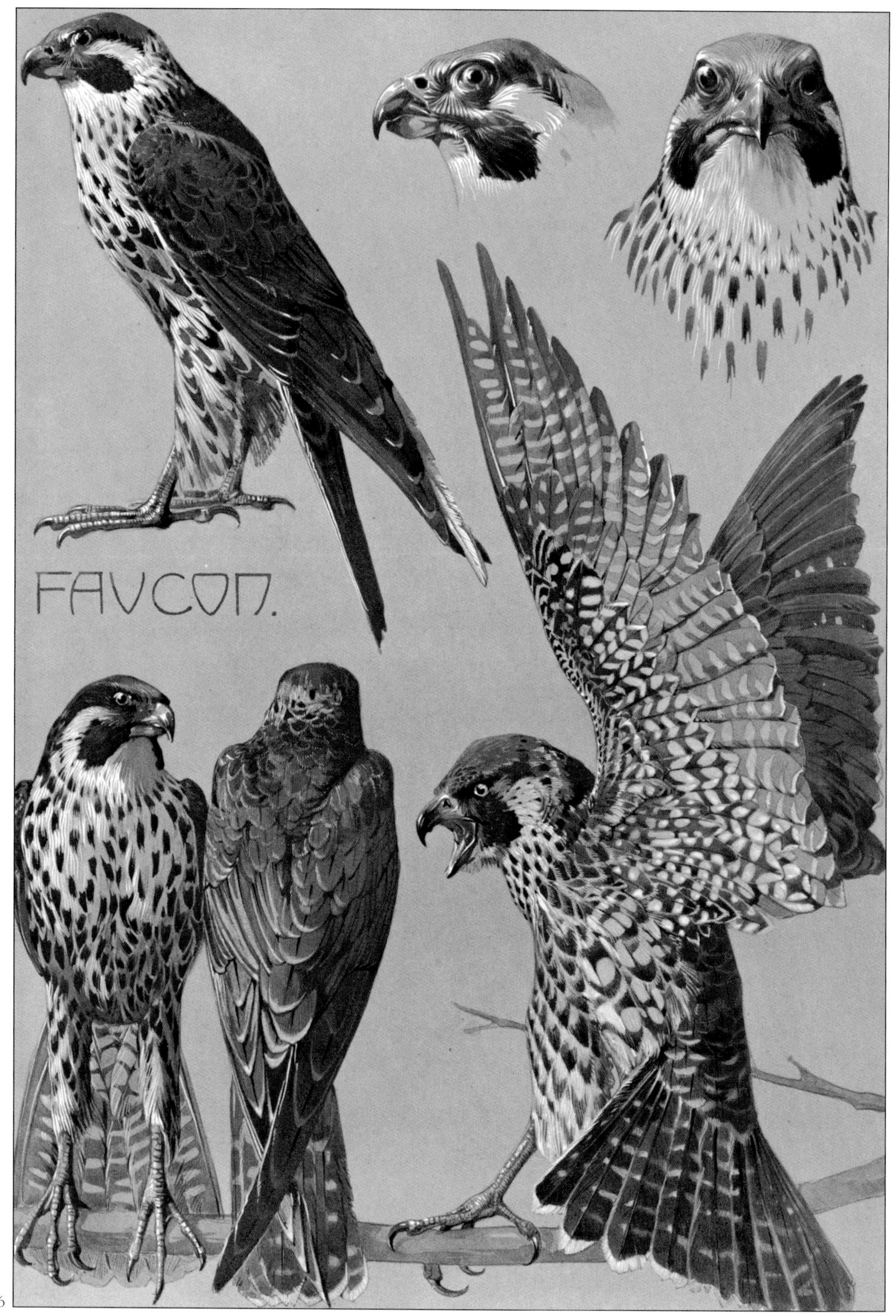

386

Images from the following two portfolios by E. A. Seguy: *Papillons* (Paris: Tolmer Editeur, n.d.) and *Insectes* (Paris: Editions Duchartre et Van Buggenhoudt, n.d.). Reprinted by Dover as *Seguy's Decorative Butterflies and Insects in Full Color* (Mineola, NY, 1977).

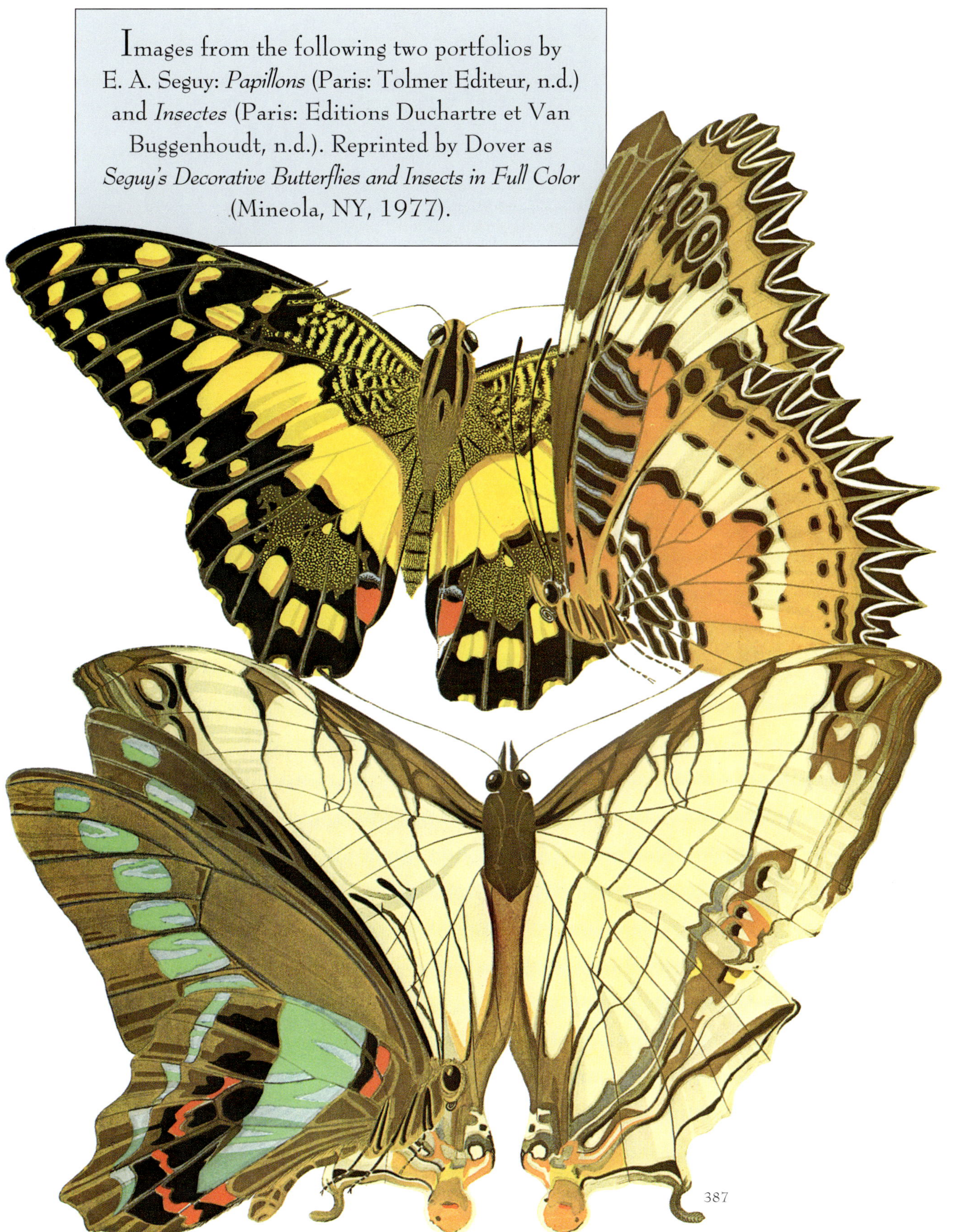

387

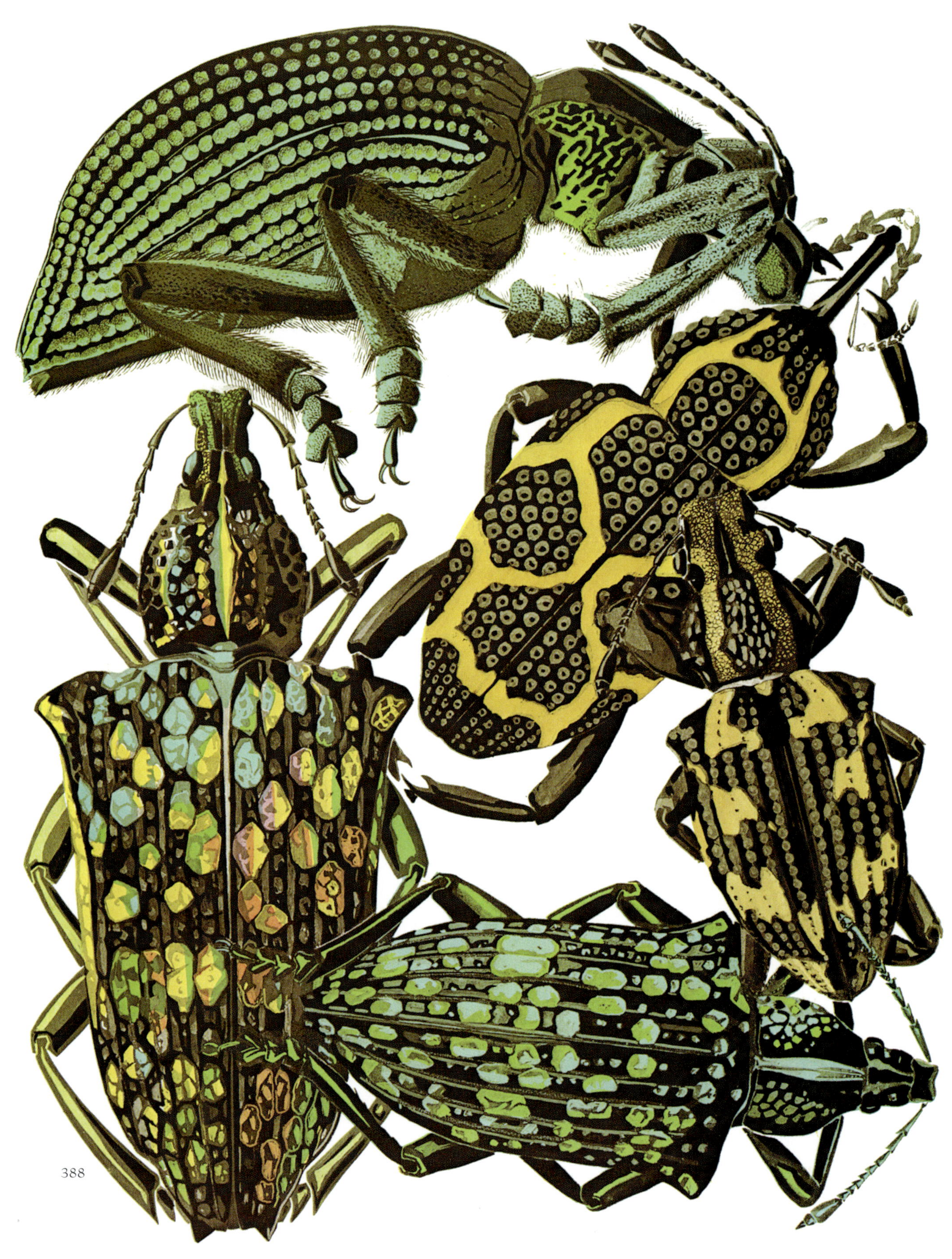

388

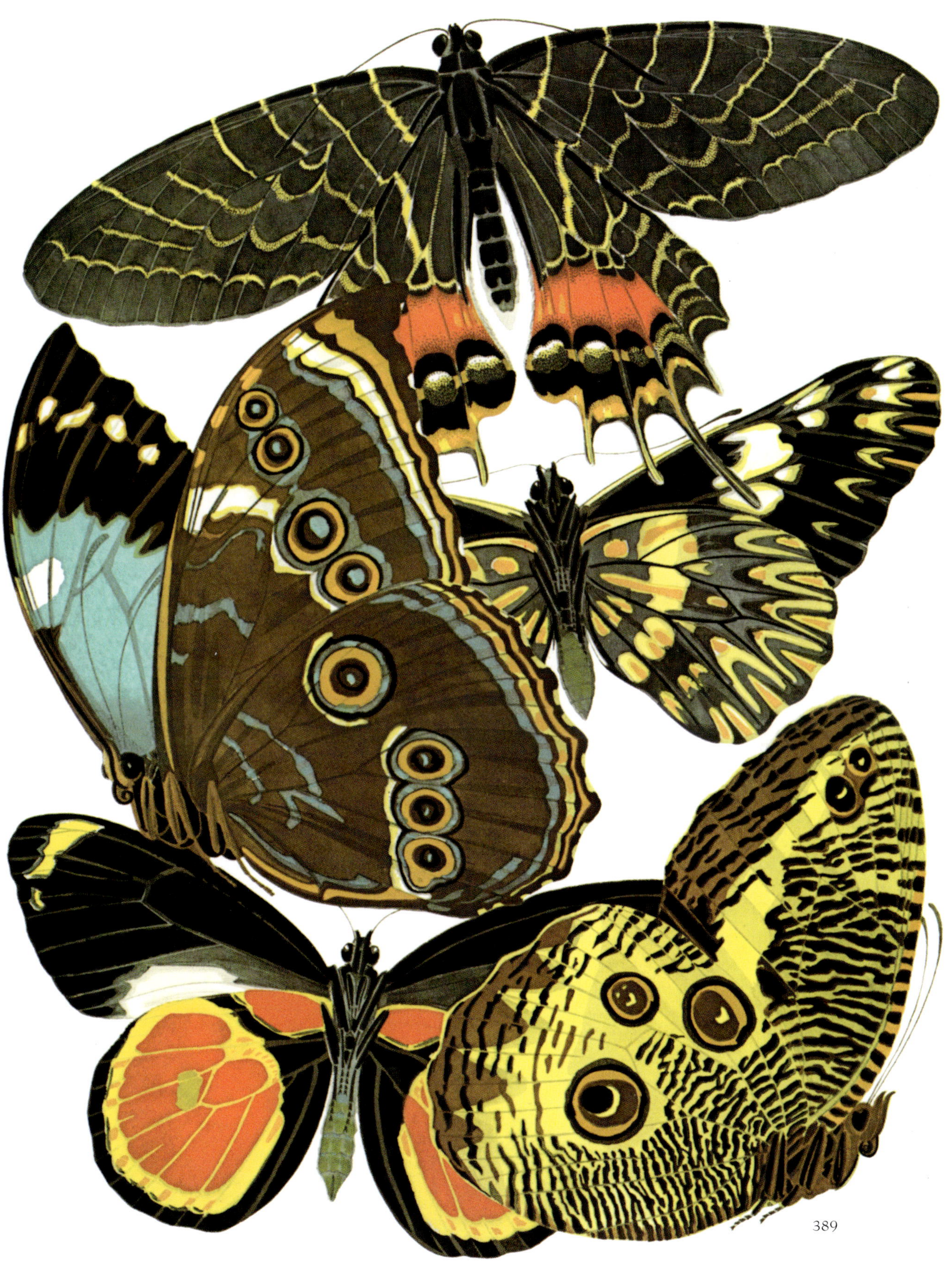

389

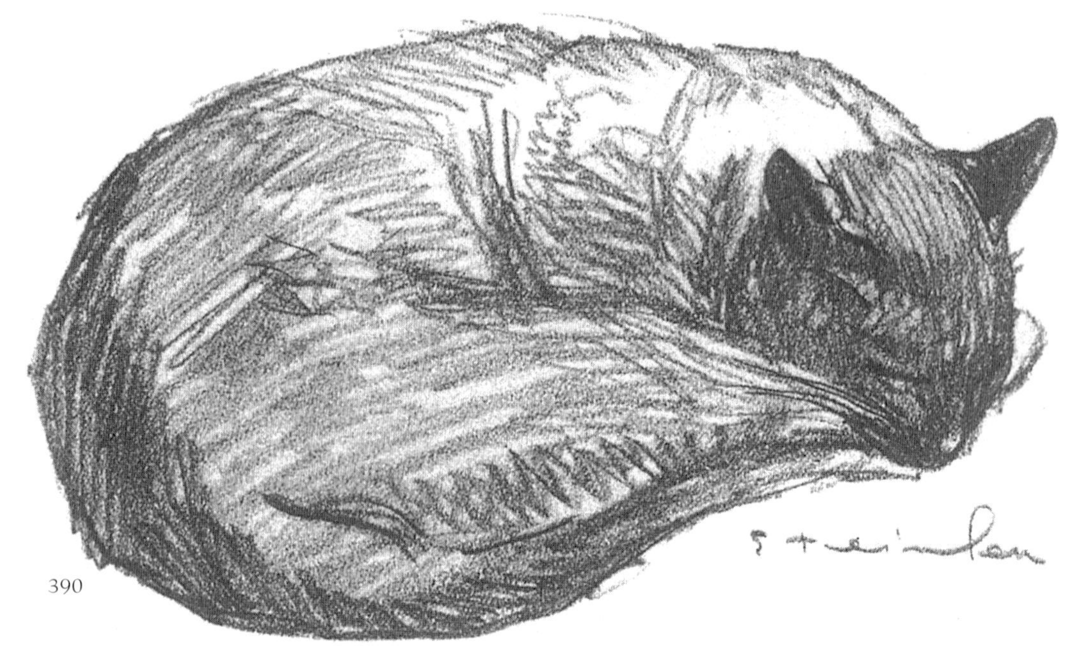

390

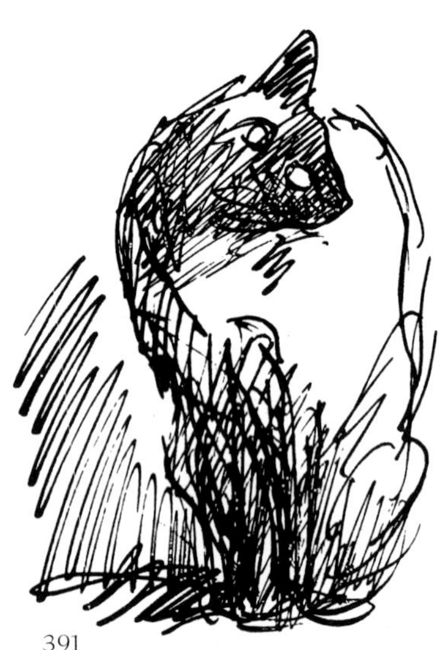

391

Images from *Chats et autres bêtes: dessins inédits* (edition of 545 copies / Paris: Eugène Rey, 1933) and *Des chats: images sans paroles* (Paris: Ernest Flammarion, n.d.). Published by Dover as *Steinlen Cats,* Drawings by Théophile-Alexandre Steinlen (Mineola, NY, 1980).

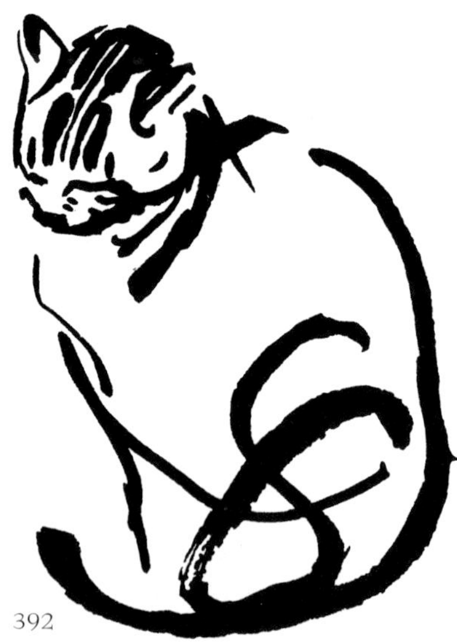

392

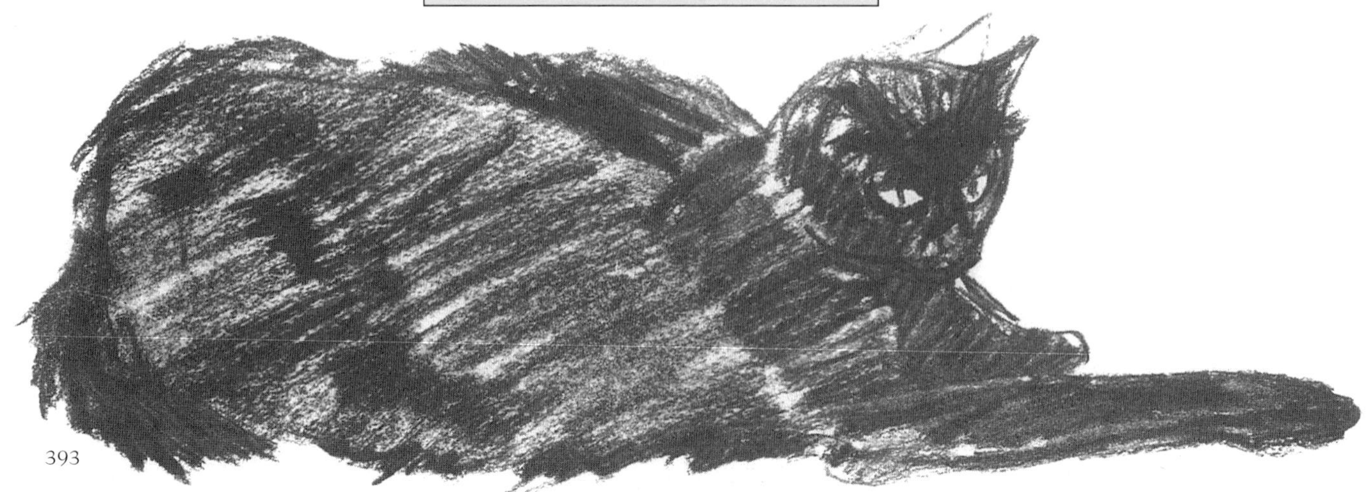

393

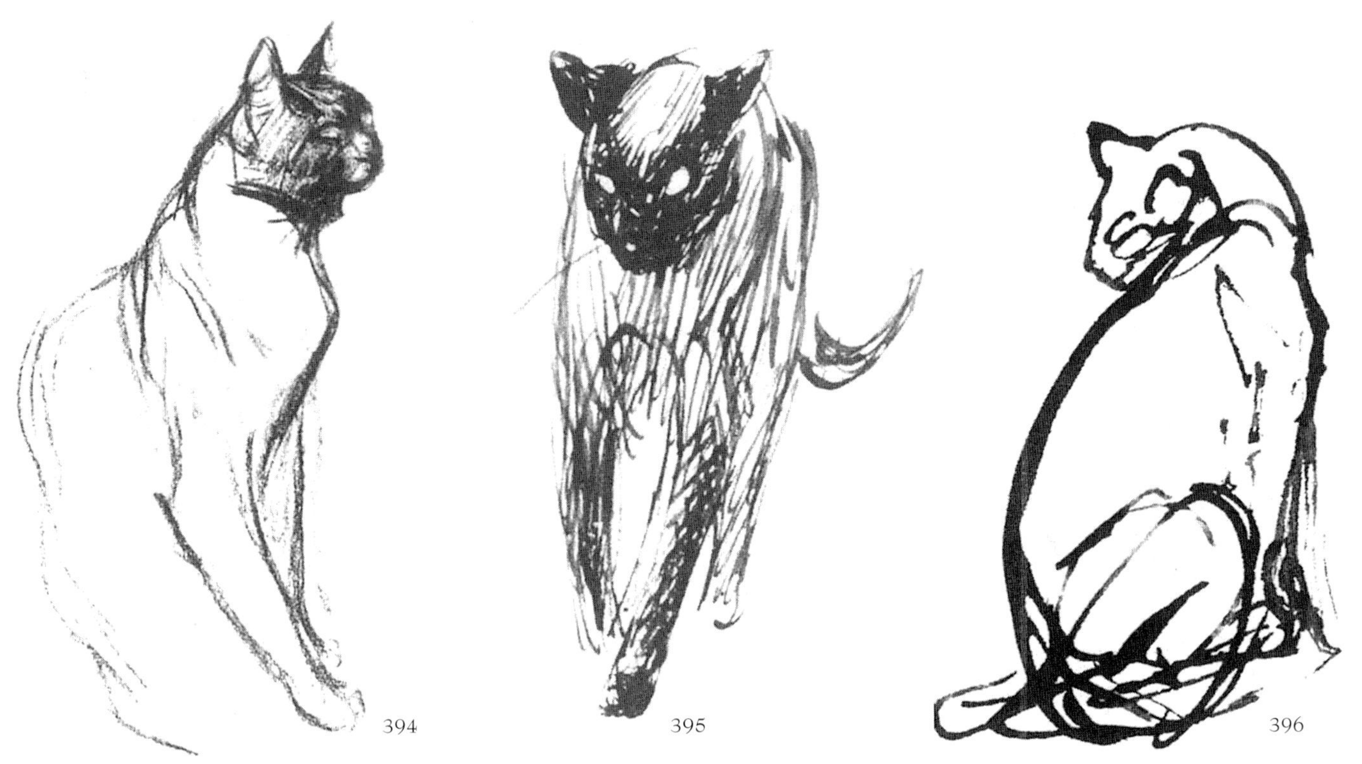

394 395 396

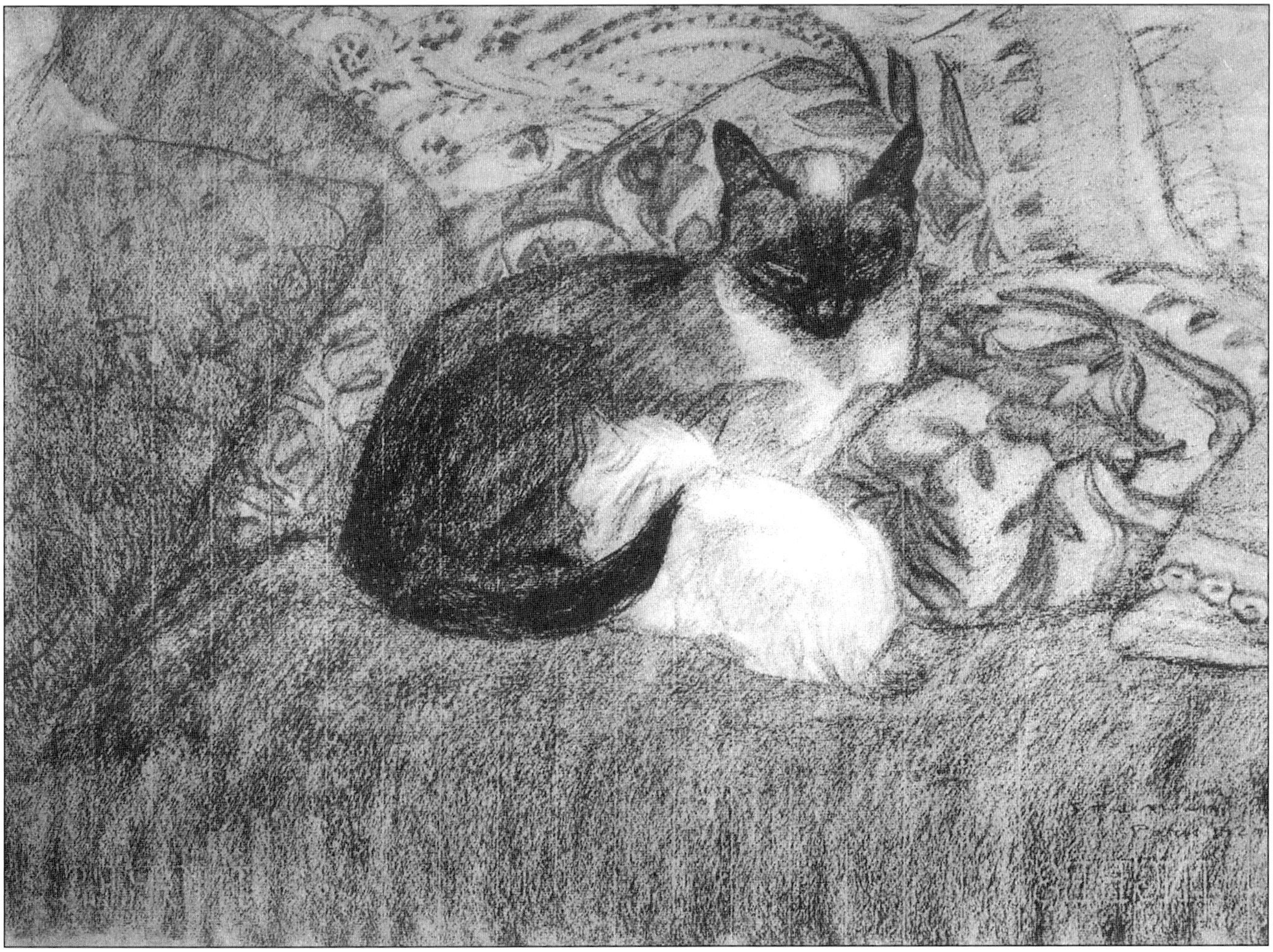

397

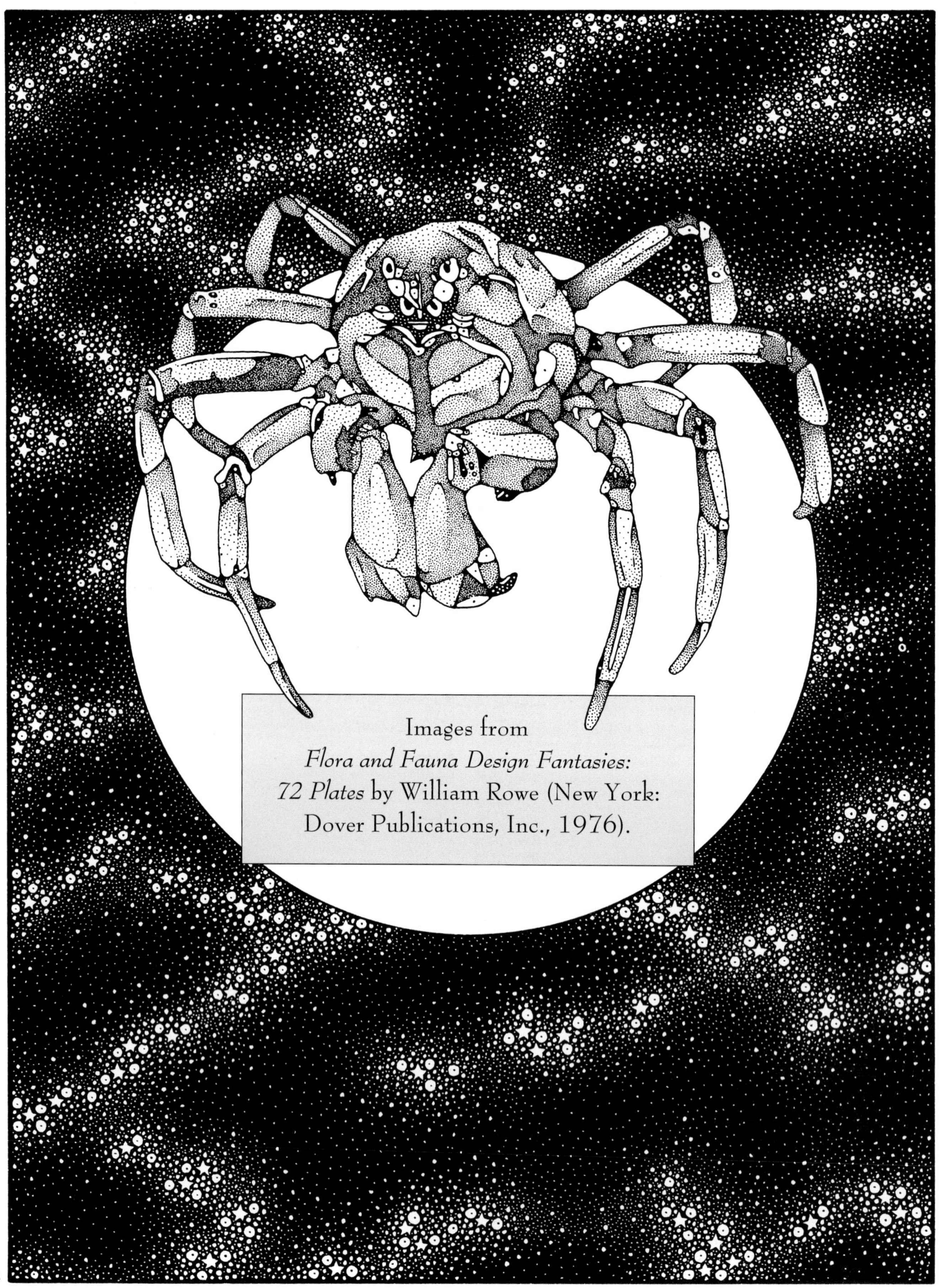

Images from
Flora and Fauna Design Fantasies:
72 Plates by William Rowe (New York:
Dover Publications, Inc., 1976).

398

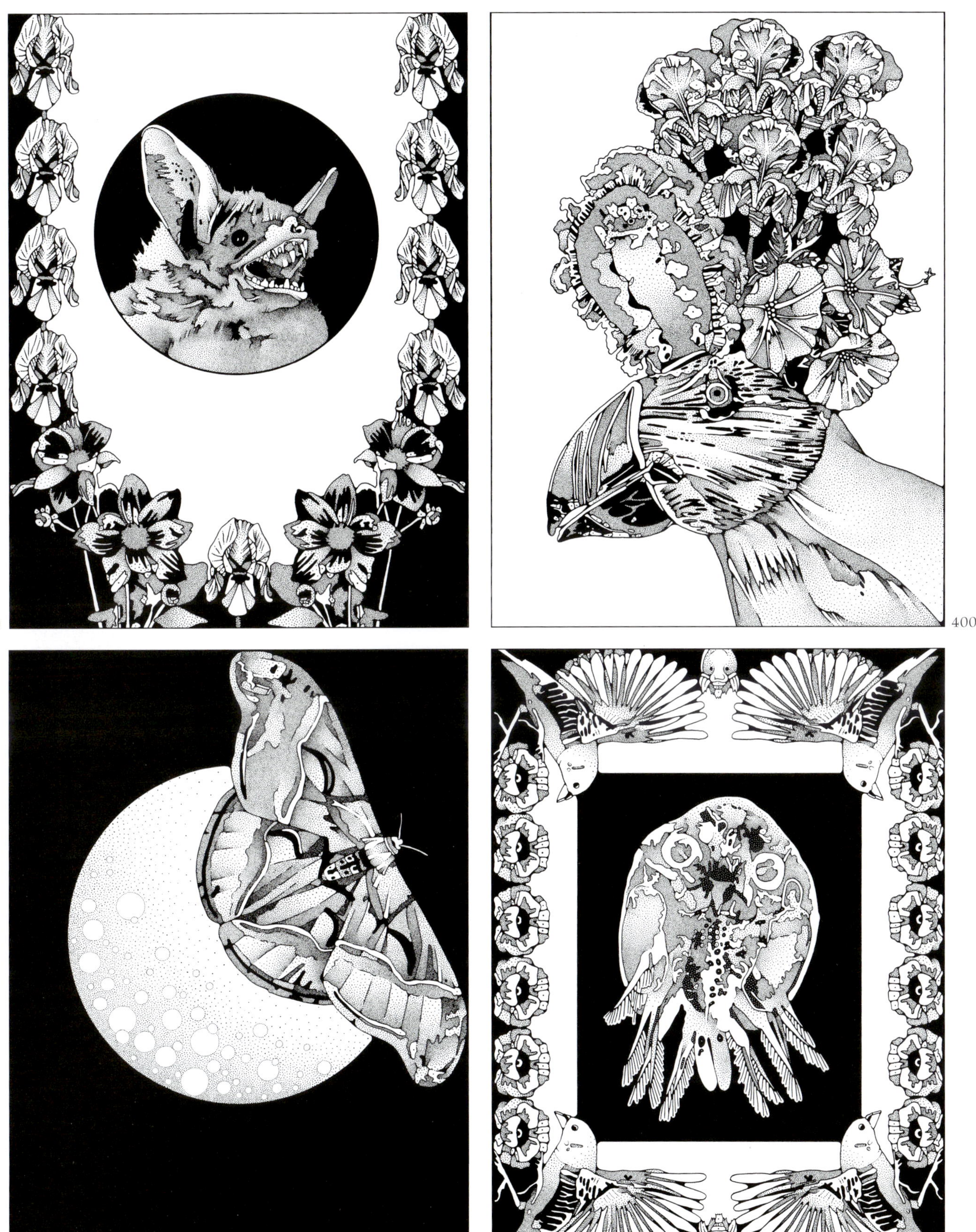

399

400

401

402

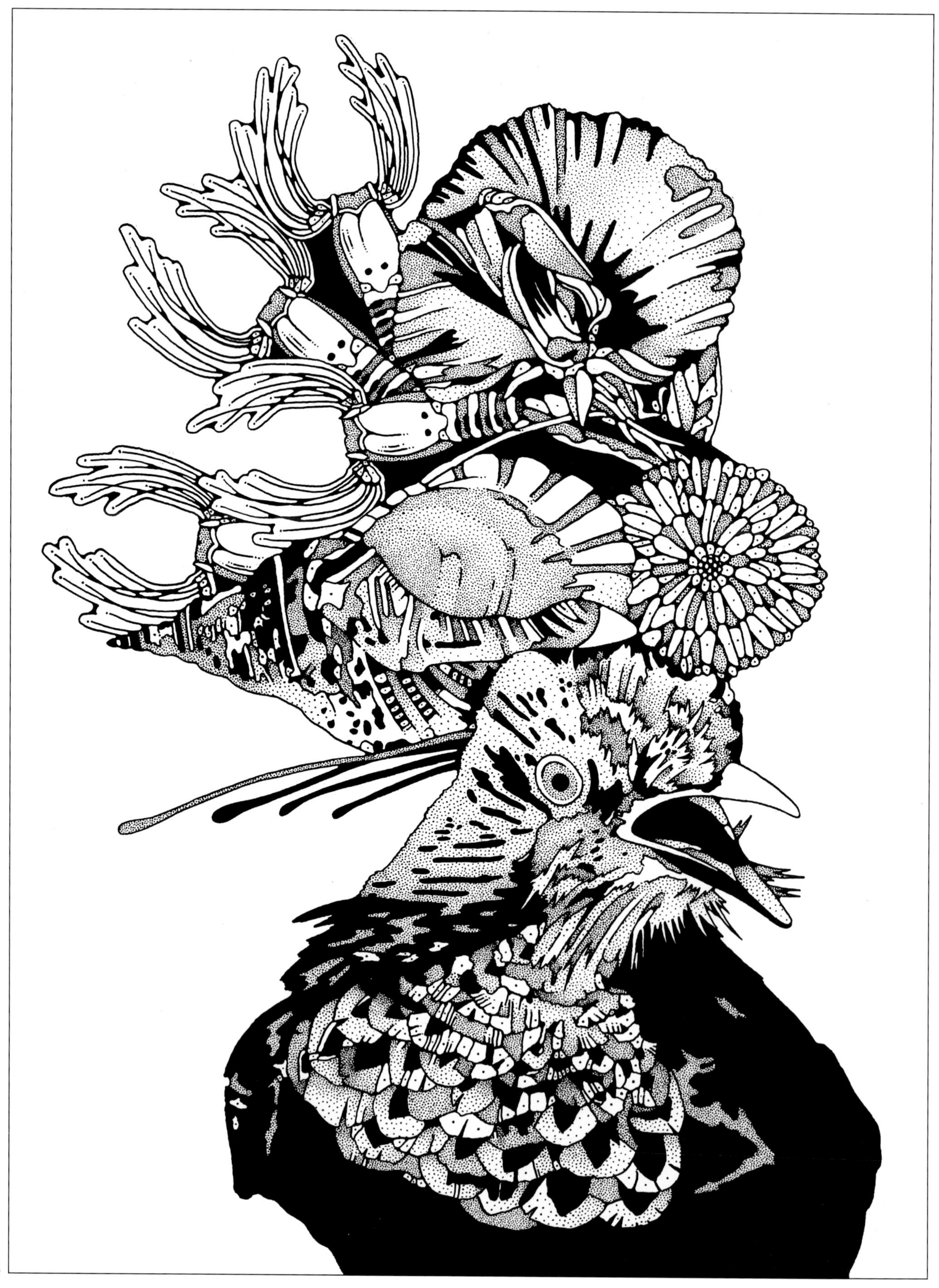

403

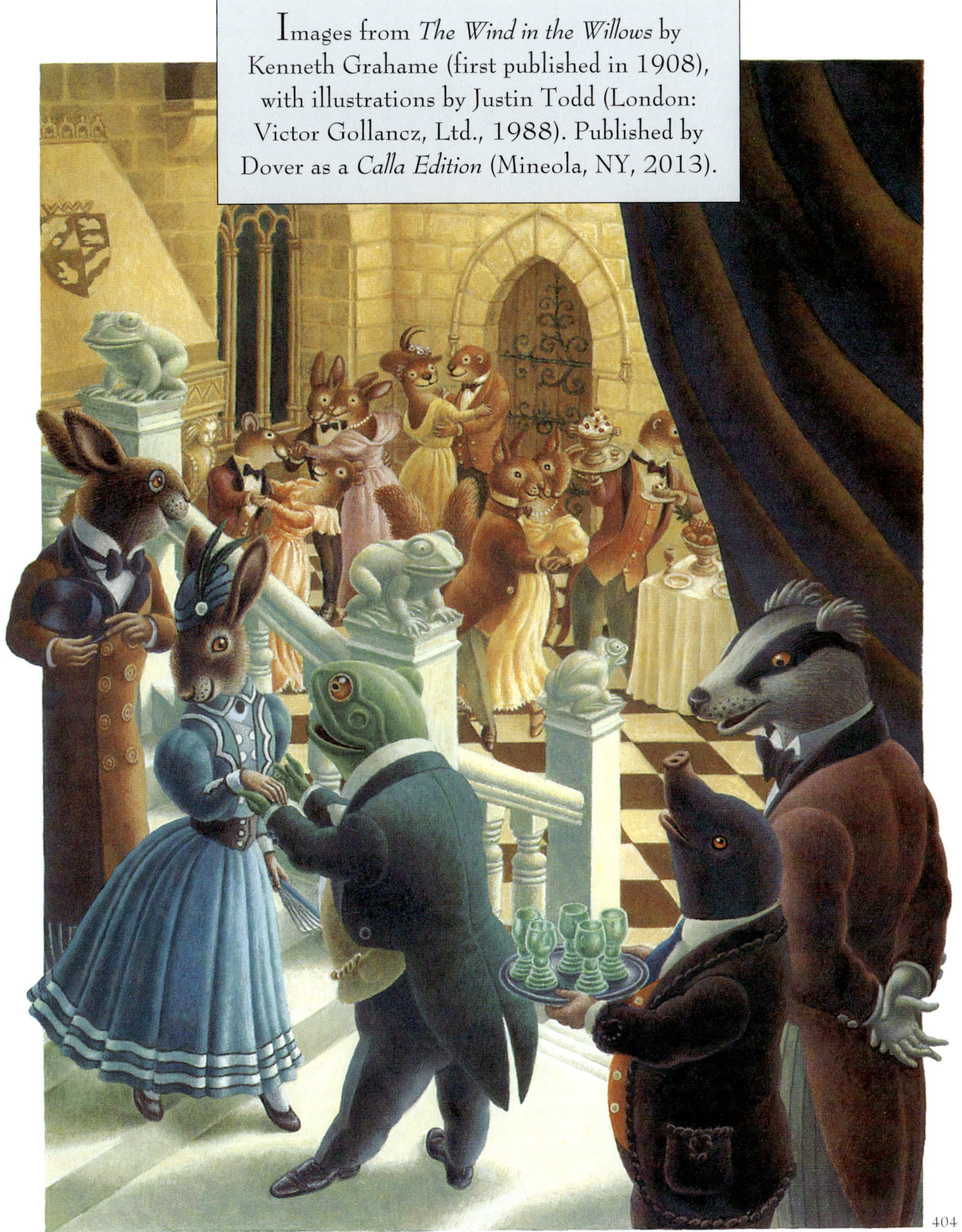

Images from *The Wind in the Willows* by Kenneth Grahame (first published in 1908), with illustrations by Justin Todd (London: Victor Gollancz, Ltd., 1988). Published by Dover as a *Calla Edition* (Mineola, NY, 2013).

404

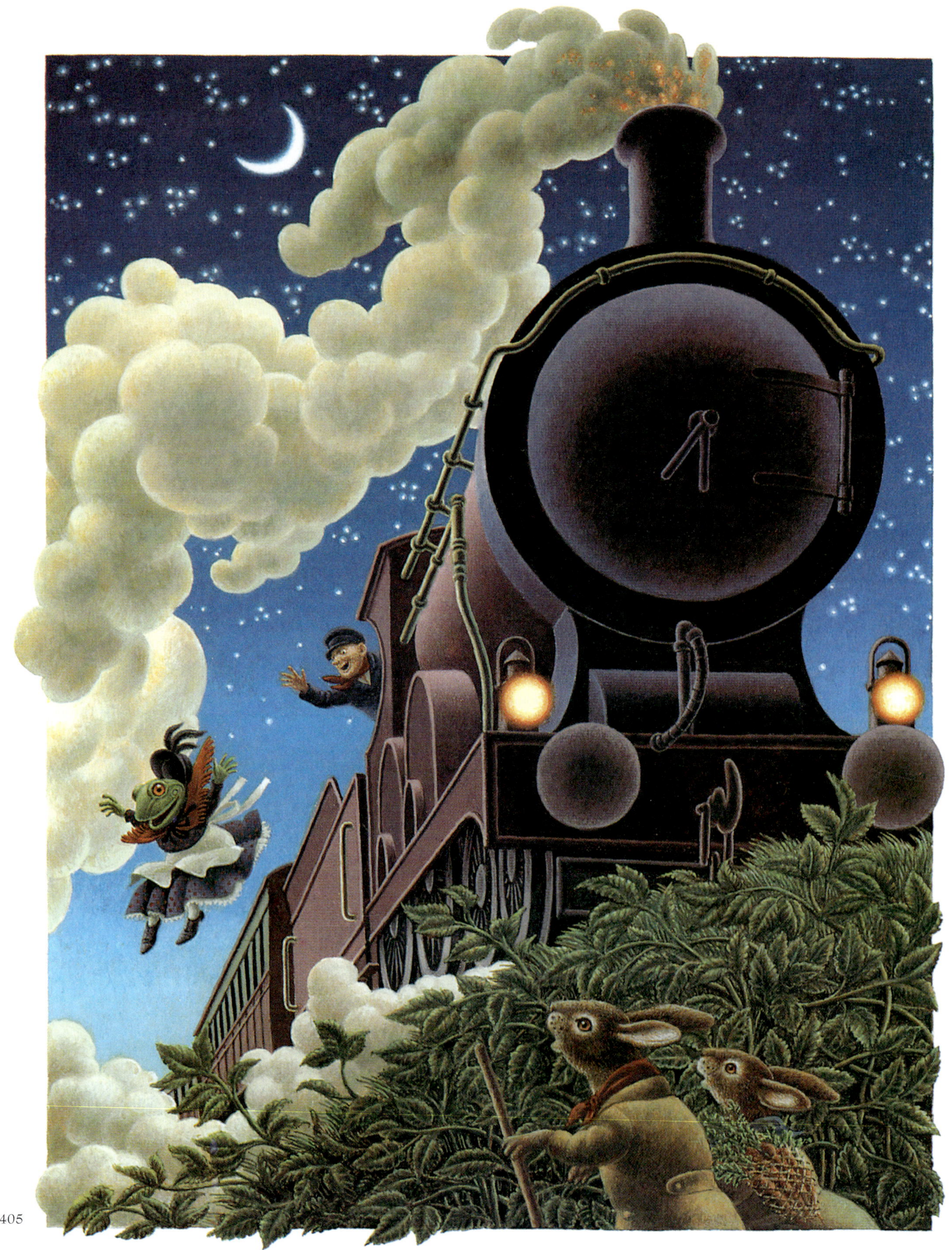

405

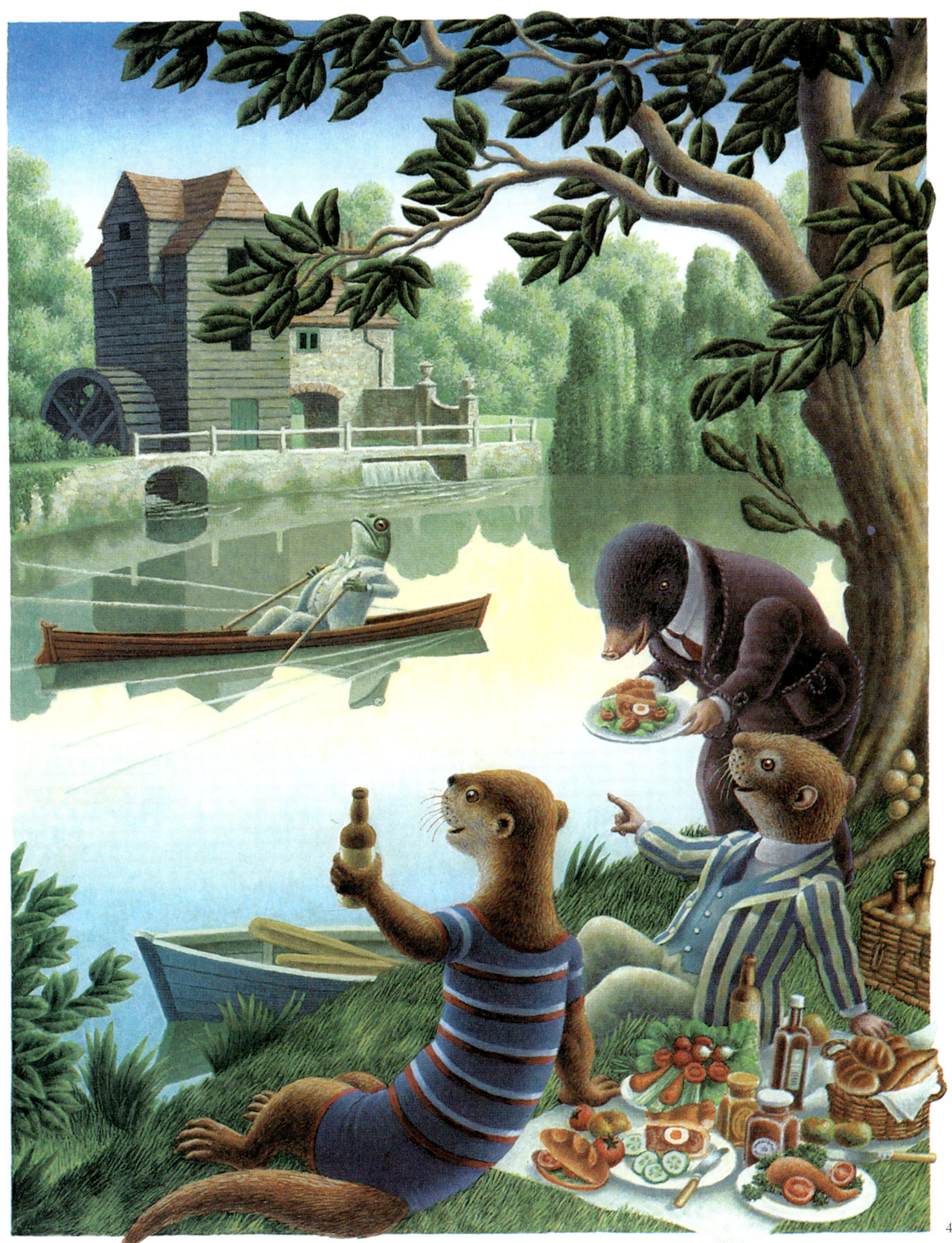

406

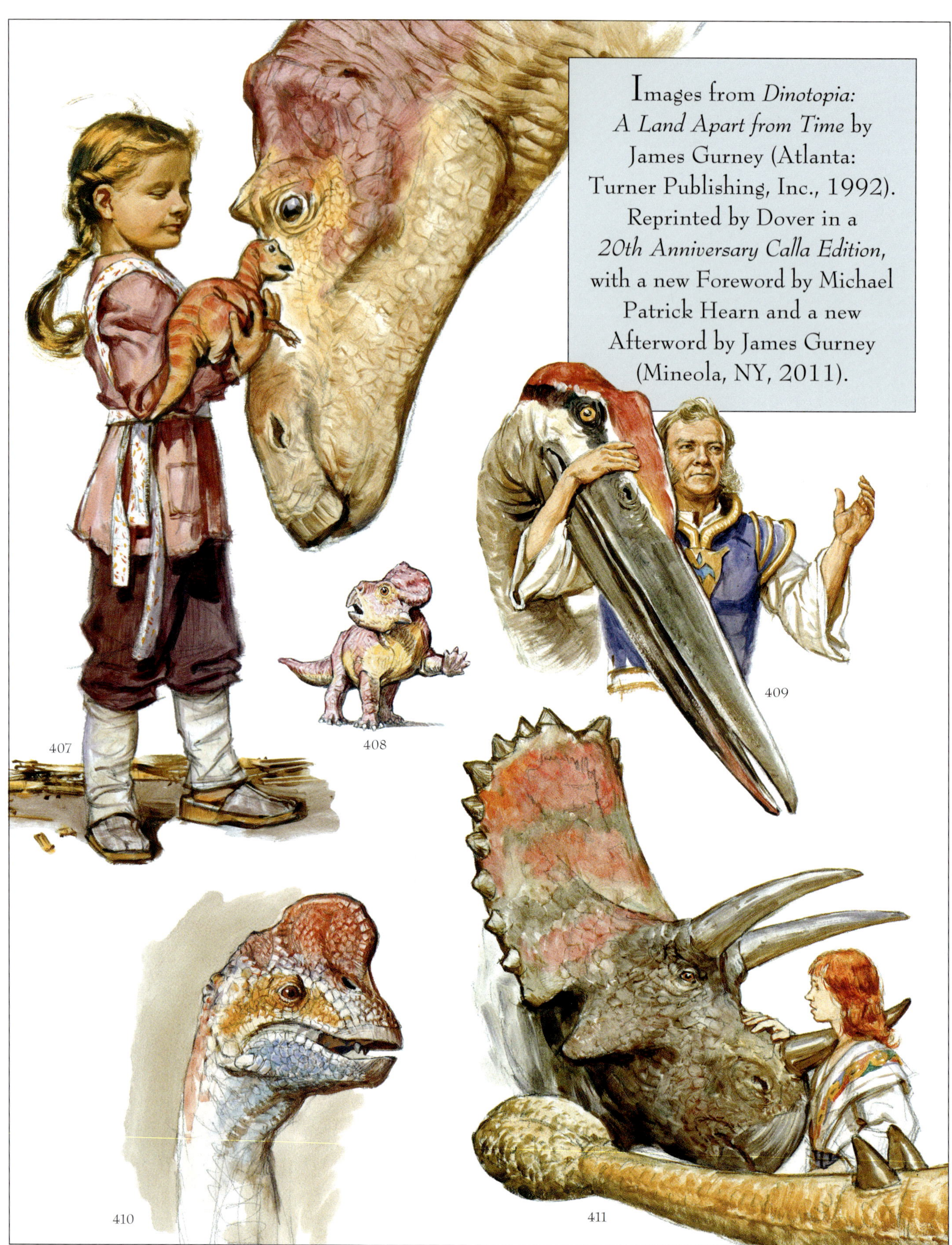

Images from *Dinotopia: A Land Apart from Time* by James Gurney (Atlanta: Turner Publishing, Inc., 1992). Reprinted by Dover in a *20th Anniversary Calla Edition*, with a new Foreword by Michael Patrick Hearn and a new Afterword by James Gurney (Mineola, NY, 2011).

407

408

409

410

411

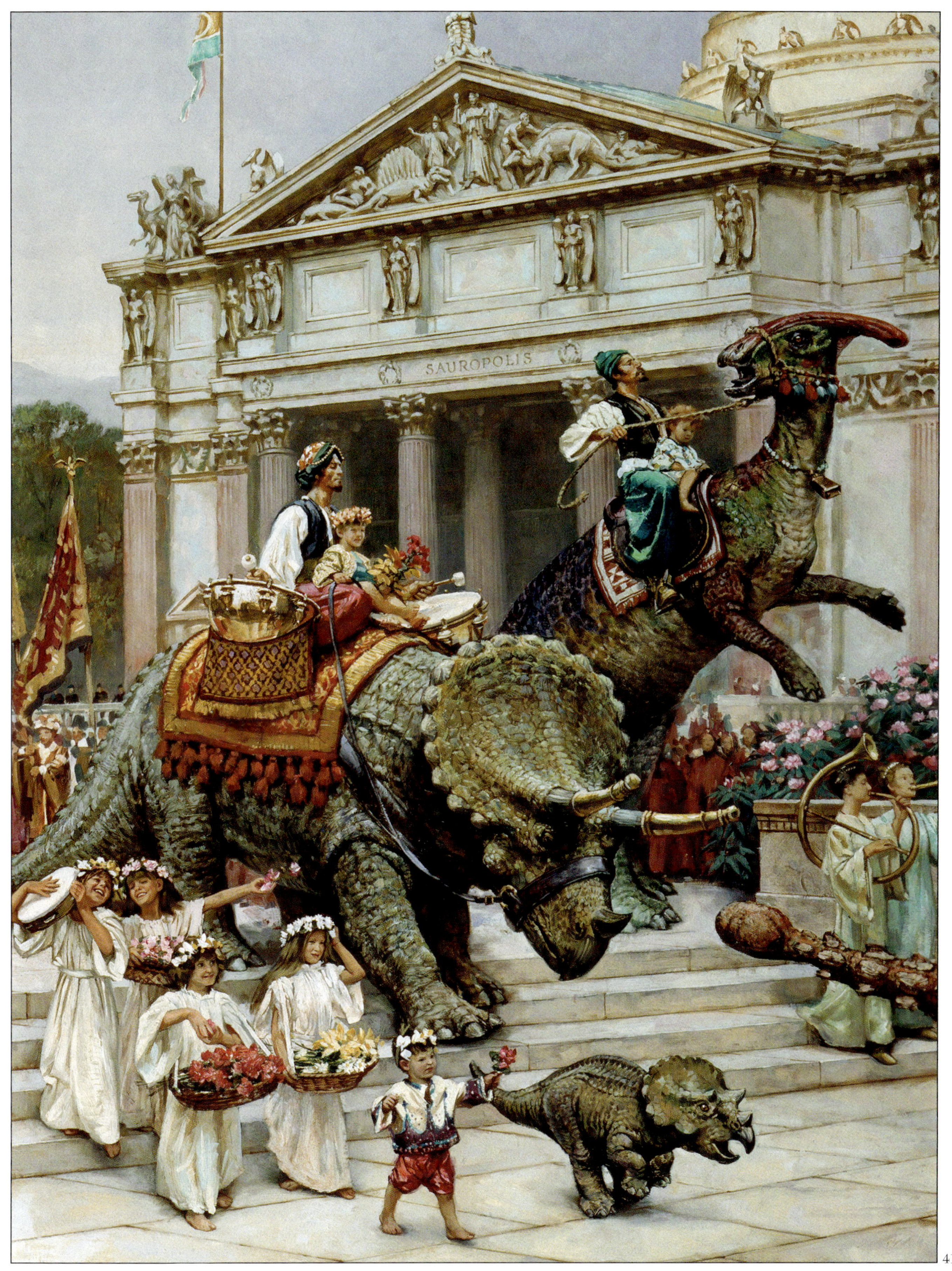

412

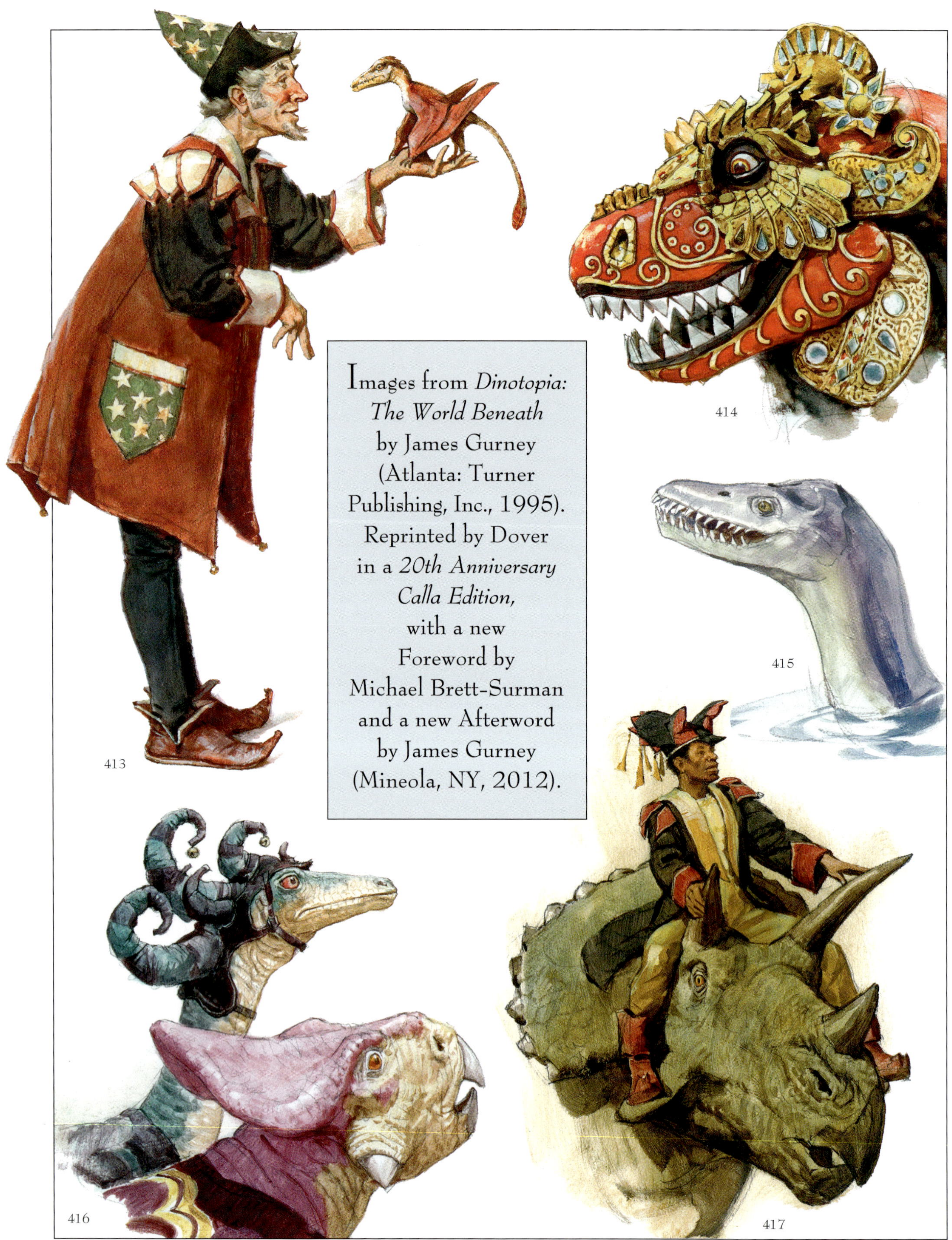

413

414

415

416

417

Images from *Dinotopia: The World Beneath* by James Gurney (Atlanta: Turner Publishing, Inc., 1995). Reprinted by Dover in a *20th Anniversary Calla Edition,* with a new Foreword by Michael Brett-Surman and a new Afterword by James Gurney (Mineola, NY, 2012).

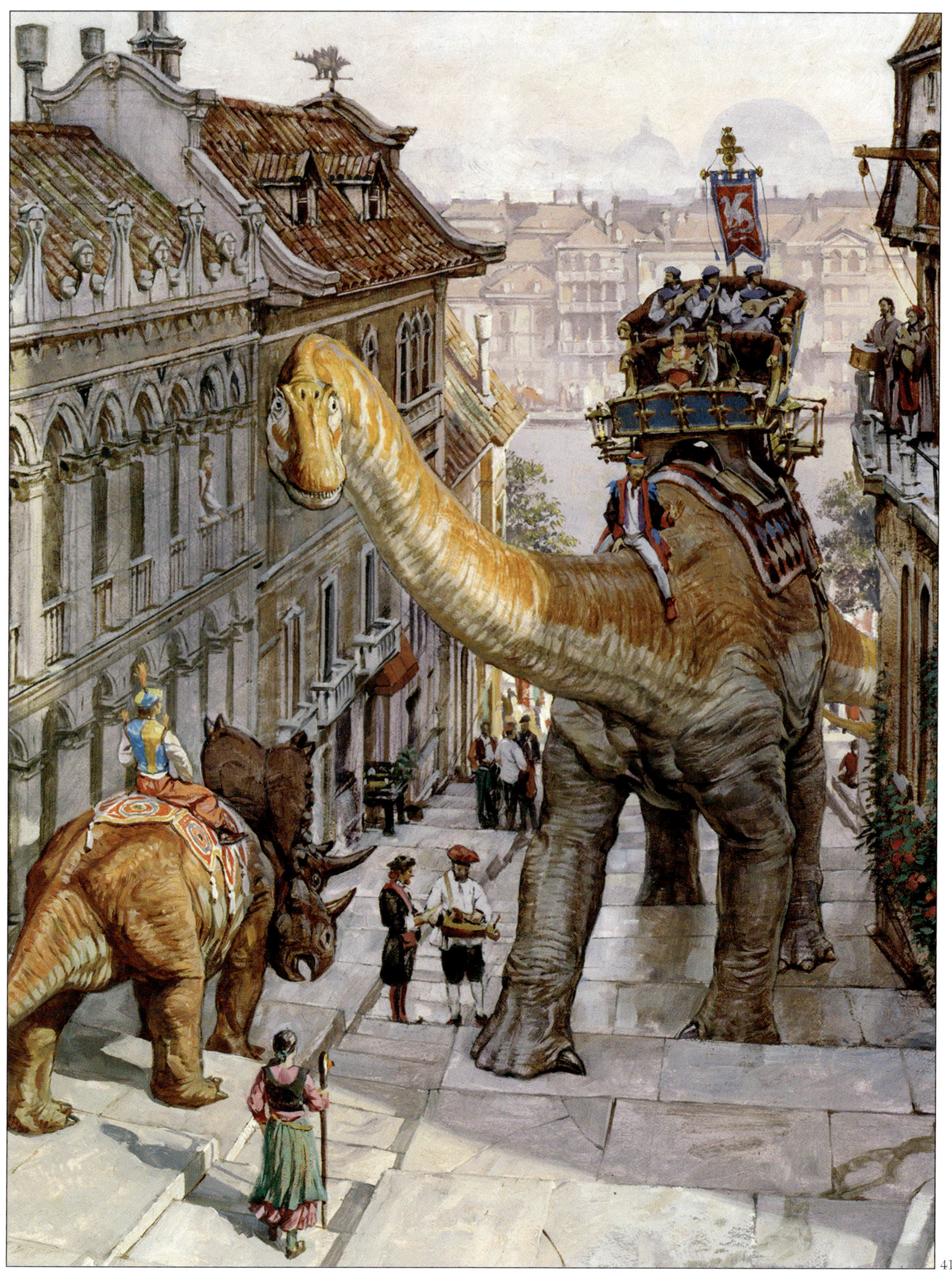

418

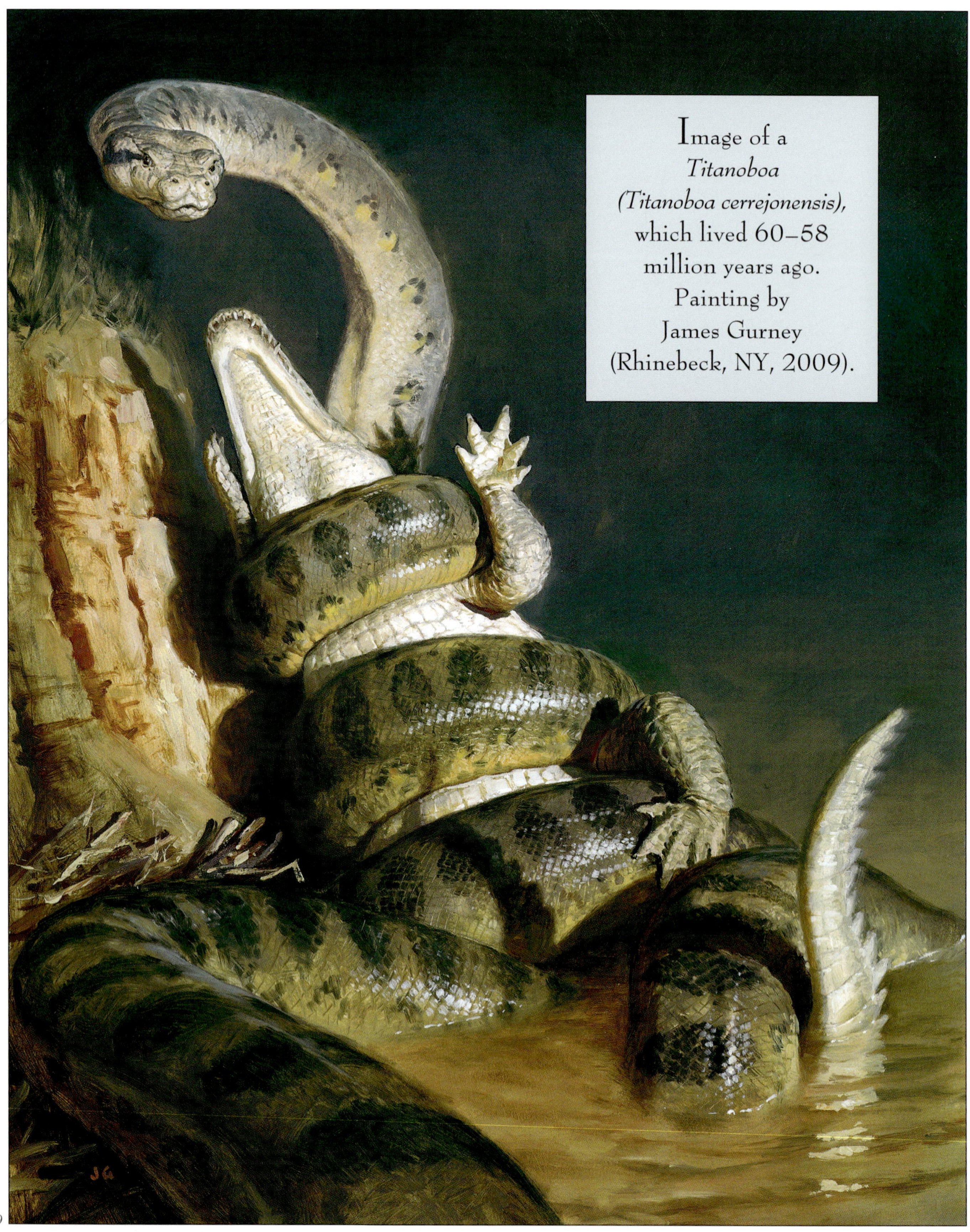

Image of a *Titanoboa* *(Titanoboa cerrejonensis)*, which lived 60–58 million years ago. Painting by James Gurney (Rhinebeck, NY, 2009).

419

INDEX OF ARTISTS

John James Audubon (1785–1851)

Plates 45–47

American ornithologist and artist, worked for 14 years traveling extensively, observing and drawing to create his epoch-making work, *The Birds of America,* each copy of which was comprised of 435 oversize hand-colored prints which depicted over 700 species of American birds. *The Birds of America* is widely considered perhaps the greatest color plate work ever published.

Raymond Bishop [dates unknown]

Plates 50–51

American artist active in the 1930s, created woodcut illustrations for a well-known edition of *Moby-Dick, or, The Whale* by Herman Melville.

Pierre Joseph Bonnaterre (1752–1804)

Plates 26–28

French naturalist, contributed extensively to the eighteenth-century reference work, *Tableau encyclopédique et méthodique des trois règnes de la nature* published in the 1780s and 1790s.

Alfred Edmund Brehm (1829–1884)

Plates 76–79

German zoologist, illustrator, and author, his book *Brehm's Tierleben (Brehm's Life of Animals)* was one of the most popular nineteenth-century zoological books.

Georges-Louis Leclerc, comte de Buffon (1707–1788)

Plates 24–25

French naturalist, mathematician, cosmologist, and major figure in eighteenth-century French intellectual life. His thirty-six volume *Histoire Naturelle,* published between 1749 and 1788 (with a final volume derived from his notes published in 1789, after his death) was read and revered by scholars and naturalists throughout Europe.

Georges, Baron Cuvier (1769–1832)

Plates 32–34

French naturalist and zoologist, he did essential work in establishing the sciences of comparative anatomy and paleontology based on comparing living animals to fossils. Among his most important books is *Le Règne Animal (The Animal Kingdom),* 1817.

Edgar Degas (1834–1917)

Plate 7

French artist, and a founder of Impressionism. His paintings of everyday life in Paris established him as one of the great artists of the nineteenth century. A superb draftsman who sought perfection in his work, he portrayed the fleeting motion of people at Parisian ballets and cafes, and of horses at the racecourse.

Charles Maurice (1883–1908) and Edward Julius Detmold (1883–1957)

Plates 86–87, 102–105, 108–109

British book illustrators. Among other books they jointly illustrated a well-known edition of Kipling's *Jungle Book* published in 1908. After Charles' death in 1908, Edward went on to a long and prolific career as an illustrator of many books on animals, birds, and nature, including *The Fables of Aesop,* 1909.

Edward Donovan (1768–1837)

Plate 30

Anglo-Irish writer and illustrator, amateur naturalist and collector of specimens. Based on specimens collected by explorers, he wrote early books on the insects of China, India, and Australia.

Gustave Doré (1832–1883)

Plates 56–58

French artist, printmaker, and preeminent book illustrator of the nineteenth century. Working primarily in the medium of wood engraving, between an 1854 book on Russia and his 1884 edition of Poe's *The Raven,* Doré illustrated over 50 works of history and literature, leaving a unique legacy of thousands of illustrations.

Albrecht Dürer (1471–1528)

Plates 3, 5

Incomparable German artist of the northern Renaissance, his paintings and drawings often depicted animals and the natural world. Following success as a woodcut artist while still in his twenties, Dürer went on to mastery of oil painting, watercolor, and engraving. His skill and success as a printmaker helped spread his fame very quickly throughout Europe during his lifetime.

Daniel Giraud Elliott (1835–1915)

Plates 59–61

American zoologist, one of the founders of the American Museum of Natural History in New York and Curator of Zoology at Chicago's Field Museum. Elliott wrote the text and commissioned artwork for several magnificent color-plate books, including *A Monograph on Phasianidae (Family of Pheasants)*, 1870–72.

John Gould (1804–1881)

Plate 43

English ornithologist and one of the greatest bird painters in history. In collaboration with other artists he published several magnificent color-plate books depicting birds from many parts of the world, including *The Birds of Great Britain,* in five volumes with 367 plates (1862–73).

Jean-Ignace-Isidore Grandville (1803–1847)

Plates 62–63

One of the most fantastic and intriguing artists of early-nineteenth-century France. His satirical and humorous caricatures of animals and humans continue to be an inspiration to cartoonists and illustrators.

El Greco (1541–1614)

Plate 36

The greatest artist of the Spanish Renaissance, born in Crete, he worked in Rome before settling in Toledo, Spain, where he painted for the rest of his life.

James Gurney (1958–)

Plates 124–128

Artist and author best known for his illustrated book series *Dinotopia*. He specializes in painting realistic images of scenes that can't be photographed, from dinosaurs to ancient civilizations. He is also a dedicated plein air painter and sketcher, believing that making studies directly from observation fuels his imagination.

Ernst Haeckel (1834–1919)

Frontispiece, Plates 1, 11, 29, 93, 98–100

German biologist, philosopher, and artist, supporter of Darwin and the teaching of evolution, and painter of hundreds of life forms.

Johann Georg Heck (1795–1857)

Plates 53–55

German author, editor, cartographer, and draftsman, his *Iconographic Encyclopedia of Science, Literature, and Art* was one of the most famous reference works of the nineteenth century on both sides of the Atlantic, incorporating thousands of illustrations of the natural world and innumerable other topics.

Sir William Jardine (1800–1874)

Plates 40–41

Scottish naturalist, edited the immensely popular forty-volume Victorian work, *The Naturalist's Library,* with color plates by many well-known artists—including Edward Lear—on birds, mammals, insects, and fish.

Numata Kashû (1838–1901)

Plates 66–67

Japanese woodblock artist known especially for his bird and flower prints.

Wilhelm von Kaulbach (1805–1874)

Plates 48–49

Versatile German artist who worked in fresco and was especially noted as a muralist. He was also a prolific and successful book illustrator who took on Shakespeare, Goethe, and the Gospels among his commissions.

John Gerrard Keulemans (1842–1912)

Plate 61

Dutch bird illustrator, began his career in Leyden but had his greatest success after moving to London in 1869, where he contributed to many famous British bird books of the Victorian period, including Legge's *History of the Birds of Ceylon* (1880) and Layard's *Birds of South Africa* (1887).

William Forsell Kirby (1844–1912)

Plates 68–69

English entomologist and folklorist, he was an expert on butterflies and published several books, including *Manual of European Butterflies* (1862) and *The Butterflies and Moths of Europe* (1903).

Pierre André Latreille (1762–1833)

Plates 38–39

French zoologist and expert on arthropods, he wrote several books of his own on entomology and contributed to several works by Cuvier.

Edward Lear (1812–1888)

Plate 52

English artist, illustrator, musician, author, and poet famous for his limericks and humorous poetry, and also one of the major bird artists of the Victorian period. His great book on parrots illustrated with lithographs made from his paintings, *Illustrations of the Family of Psittacidae, or Parrots,* was published in 1832 in a limited edition of about 175 copies and is one of the great rarities in the field.

Leonardo da Vinci (1452–1519)

Plate 6

An apprentice to Verrocchio (a Florentine painter and sculptor) at the age of fifteen, and five years later entered the San Luca's painters' guild in Florence. Known as the founding father of the High Renaissance, Leonardo had a great influence on the world of art.

René Primevère Lesson (1794–1849)

Plate 42

French ornithologist and herpetologist, as a surgeon serving in the French Navy he collected specimens from New Guinea and the Moluccas, where he also became the first European naturalist to see the bird of paradise in the wild. He published several books on ornithology in the 1830s.

Limbourg Brothers, Herman, Paul and Johann (fl. 1385–1416)

Plate 2

Dutch miniature painters active in France in the early fifteenth century, artists who created one of the greatest late medieval illuminated manuscripts, *Les Très Riches Heures du Duc de Berry.*

Joseph Williamson Ludlow (1840–1916)

Plates 64–65

English illustrator who created fifty chromolithographs for Lewis Wright's *The Illustrated Book of Poultry.*

Mathurin Méheut (1882–1958)

Plates 110–112

A native of Brittany, Méheut became an expert in painting marine life and other subjects in nature. After World War I, his interest turned to illustrating books.

Maria Sibylla Merian (1647–1717)

Plates 12–13

A major figure in the history of scientific illustration, Merian was a fabulously gifted artist who in 1699 received a grant from the city of Amsterdam to travel to Surinam, a Dutch colony in South America, for the purpose of studying and painting butterflies and other insects and related flora. The plates Merian painted and published as a result are among the greatest masterpieces of botanical art.

Matthäus Merian (1593–1650)

Plates 9–10

Swiss-born engraver and publisher, father of Maria Sibylla Merian. As an engraver, he worked on many topics and is remembered today especially for his detailed town plans.

Parmigianino (1503–1540)

Plate 35

Italian artist of the late Baroque period, born in Parma and active in Rome after 1524 and later in Bologna. In addition to painting, he was a supremely skilled draftsman and etcher.

John Ray (1627–1705)

Plate 8

English naturalist of the seventeenth century, member of the Royal Society, and author of numerous works in botany and zoology, including *Catalogue of English Plants* (1668), *History of Fishes* (1686), and *Synopsis of Animals and Reptiles* (1693).

Louis Renard (1678–1746)

Plates 22–23

Compiled the book *Poissons,* with 100 fancifully colored engraved plates depicting fish and crustaceans from the Dutch East Indies (now Indonesia).

Pierre-Auguste Renoir (1841–1919)

Plate 37

French artist and leading Impressionist renowned for his brilliant use of color and remarkable treatment of light. Elements of the natural world—trees, gardens, flowers, landscapes, and rivers with all of their moods and colors—often illuminate his work.

William Rowe (1946–)

Plates 118–120

American artist and graphic designer, noted for his mastery of the classic Art Deco style which he applied to the natural world to create unique fantasies and decorative motifs.

Albertus Seba (1665–1736)

Plates 14–21

Dutch pharmacist, zoologist, and collector. His huge and unique treasury of specimens of snakes, lizards, birds, insects, and much else formed the basis for his 1734 thesaurus of engravings of animal samples, *Locupletissimi Rerum Naturalium Thesauri Accurata*

Descriptio, one of the greatest books of natural history publishing.

Anton Seder (1850–1916)

Plates 94–97

Munich-born artist was the first Director of Strasbourg's College of Decorative Arts from 1890 to 1920 and a major figure in the Art Nouveau movement.

E. A. Seguy [dates unknown]

Plates 113–115

Published a series of unique and magnificent design portfolios starting about 1900 and into the 1930s. A master of the pochoir technique, a printing process which yields dense, striking colors through the use of stencils, it is a great mystery that so little is known of Seguy's life apart from his art.

August Specht (1849–1923)

Plates 88–89

German natural history painter and illustrator, contributed to *Brehm's Tierleben.*

Théophile-Alexandre Steinlen (1859–1923)

Plates 116–117

Famous for his trademark cat illustrations, Steinlen, a Swiss-born painter and printmaker, also produced posters of cabaret and music-hall performers.

Justin Todd (1932–)

Plates 121–123

English illustrator who taught at Brighton College of Art and illustrated several works of literature, including *Alice's Adventures in Wonderland* (1984), *Through the Looking Glass and What Alice Found There* (1987), and *The Wind in the Willows* (1988).

Giovanni da Udine (1487–1564)

Plate 4

Italian painter and architect skilled in architectural fresco and stucco decoration, also remembered for his drawings, especially of birds and fruit.

M. P. Verneuil (1869–1942)

Plates 90–92

French artist and designer Maurice Pillard Verneuil studied with Eugène Grasset, and became a major Art Nouveau poster artist in the era of Jules Chéret and Toulouse-Lautrec. His work as a designer and graphic artist continued well into the Art Deco period.

Alexander Wilson (1766–1813)

Plate 31

Scottish-American ornithologist and illustrator, often called the "father of American ornithology." His *American Ornithology; or, the Natural History of the Birds of the United States* (1808–1814) was the greatest American work on ornithology before Audubon.

INDEX OF ANIMALS

(Numbers are figure numbers)

SOURCE INFORMATION

Animal Kingdom, The. London: Geo. B. Whittaker, 1827–35.

Ariosto, Lodovico. *Orlando Furioso*. Milan: Treves, 1881.

Audubon, John James. *The Birds of America, from Drawings Made in the United States and Their Territories*, octavo edition, New York: J. J. Audubon, 1840 and Philadelphia: J. B. Chevalier, 1844.

Autre Monde, Un. Paris: H. Fournier, 1844.

Bonnaterre, Pierre-Joseph. *Tableau encyclopédique et méthodique des trois règnes de la nature*. Paris: Chez Panckoucke, 1788.

Brehm, Alfred Edmund. *Brehm's Tierleben*. Leipzig: Bibliographisches Institut, 1876–79.

Brown, Captain Thomas. *Illustrations of the American Ornithology of Alexander Wilson and Charles Lucian Bonaparte*. Edinburgh: 1831–35.

Buffon, comte de, Georges-Louis Leclerc. *Histoire Naturelle, générale et particulière, avec la description du cabinet du roi*. Amsterdam: J. H. Schneider, 1749–88.

Chats et autres bêtes: dessins inédits. Paris: Eugène Rey, 1933.

Cuvier, Baron Georges. *Le Règne animal distribué d'après son organisation*. Paris: 1817.

Des chats: images sans paroles, Paris: Ernest Flammarion, n.d.

Detmold, Edward J., illustrator. *The Fables of Aesop*. London: Hodder & Stoughton, 1909.

Detmold, Maurice and Edward. *Pictures from Birdland*. London: J. M. Dent & Co., 1899.

Donovan, Edward. *Insects of India*. London: 1800–04.

Elliott, Daniel Giraud. *A Monograph of the Bucerotidae, or Family of the Hornbills*. London: c. 1876–82.

Elliott, Daniel Giraud. *A Monograph of the Paradiseidae, or Birds of Paradise*. London: 1873.

Elliott, Daniel Giraud. *A Monograph of the Phasianidae, or Family of the Pheasants*. New York: 1870–72.

Fontaine, Jean de la. *Fables de la Fontaine*, Paris: Hachette, 1868.

Goethe, Wolfgang von. *Reynard the Fox*. Stuttgart and Tubingen: Cotta, 1846.

Goodrich, Samuel G., editor. *Johnson's Natural History*. New York: A. J. Johnson, 1872.

Gould, John. *The Birds of Australia*, London: 1840–69.

Grahame, Kenneth. *The Wind in the Willows*. London: Victor Gollancz, Ltd., 1988.

Gray, John Edward; Hawkins, Benjamin Waterhouse; and Lear, Edward. *Gleanings from the Menagerie and Aviary at Knowsley Hall*. Knowsley, England: 1846–50.

Gurney, James. *Dinotopia: A Land Apart from Time*. Atlanta: Turner Publishing, Inc., 1992.

Gurney, James. *Dinotopia: The World Beneath*. Atlanta: Turner Publishing, Inc., 1995.

Haeckel, Ernst. *Plant Forms in Nature (Kunstformen der Natur)*. Leipzig and Vienna: Verlag des Bibliographischen Instituts, 1904.

Heck, J. G. *Iconographic Encyclopedia of Science, Literature, and Art (Bilder-Atlas zum Conversations-Lexikon)*. New York: Rudolph Garrigue, 1851.

Jardine, Sir William. *Jardine's "Naturalist's Library,"* 40 volumes. Edinburgh: W. H. Lizars, 1833–45.

Kashû, Numata. *A Picture Book of Birds*. Tokyo: c. 1880.

Kingsley, John Sterling. *The Riverside Natural History*. Boston: Houghton Mifflin Co., 1888.

Kipling, Rudyard. *The Jungle Book*. London: Macmillan and Co., Limited, 1908.

Kirby, W. F. *European Butterflies and Moths*. London: Cassell, Petter, Galpin & Co., 1882.

Knight, Charles, editor. *The Pictorial Museum of Animated Nature*. London: Charles Knight & Co., 1845–.

Kohler, M. *Grand Animal ABC Book*. Konstanz, Germany: Book and Art Publisher Carl Hirsch A.G., c. 1900.

Latreille, P. *Tableau Encyclopédique et Méthodique des Trois Règnes de la Nature: Vingt-Quatrième Partie, Crustaces, Arachnides et Insectes*. Paris: Mme. Veuve Agasse, 1818.

Lesson, René Primevère. *Histoire Naturelle des Oiseaux-Mouches*. Paris: 1829–30.

Limbourg Brothers. *The Book of Hours (Les Très Riches Heures) of the Duke of Berry*. France: c. 1400–16.

Méheut, Mathurin. *Études d'animaux*. Paris: E. Lévy, 1911.

Melville, Herman. *Moby-Dick, or, The Whale*. New York: Harper and Brothers, 1851.

Merian, Maria Sibylla. *De metamorphosis insectorum Surinamensium*. Amsterdam: Gerard Valk, 1705.

Motivenschatz für Modernes Kunstschaffen Studienblatter für Kuenstler. Dresden: Verlag von Gerhard Kühtmann.

Oeuvres de François Rabelais, or Gargantua and Pantagruel. Paris: J. Bry Ainé, 1854.

Poissons, Ecrevisses et Crabes, de diverses couleurs et figures extraordinaires . . . . Amsterdam: Chez Reinier & Josué Ottens, 1754.

Ray, John. *Historia piscium*. Flamburgh, England: 1686.

Rowe, William. *Flora and Fauna Design Fantasies: 72 Plates*. New York: Dover Publications, Inc., 1976.

Scènes de la vie privée et publique des animaux and *Les Animaux*. Paris: J. Hetzel et Paulin, 1842, 1868.

Seba, Albertus. *Cabinet of Natural Curiosities*. Amsterdam: 1734–65.

Seba, Albertus. *Locupletissimi Rerum Naturalium Thesauri Accurata Descriptio*, 4 volumes. Amsterdam: 1734–65.

Seder, Anton. *Das Thier in der Decorativen Kunst, Serie 1–2*. Vienna: Gerlach & Schenk, 1896; Gerlach & Wiedling, 1909.

Seguy, E. A. *Insectes*. Paris: Editions Duchartre et van Buggenhoudt, n.d.

Seguy, E. A. *Papillons*. Paris: Tolmer Editeur, n.d.

Theatrum universale omnium Animalium, 2 volumes. Amsterdam: R. & G. Wetstenios: 1718.

Udine, Giovanni da. *Raccolta di Uccelli*. Italy: c. 1550.

Verneuil, M. P. *L'animal dans la decoration*. Paris: Librairie Centrale des Beaux-Arts, c. 1897.

Wilson, Alexander. *American Ornithology; or the Natural History of the Birds of the United States*. Philadelphia: 1808–14.

Wood, Rev. J. G. *Animate Creation; Popular Edition of "Our Living World," a Natural History*. New York: Selmar Hess, 1885.

Wright, Lewis. *The Illustrated Book of Poultry, with Practical Schedules for Judging*. London: Cassell, Petter, Galpin & Co., 1880.